Startling Figures

Studies in the Catholic Imagination:
The Flannery O'Connor Trust Series

Edited by Angela Alaimo O'Donnell, Ph.D., Associate Director, The Francis and Ann Curran Center for American Catholic Studies

STARTLING FIGURES

Encounters with American Catholic Fiction

MICHAEL O'CONNELL

Fordham University Press

NEW YORK 2023

Fordham University Press has no responsibility for the persistence or accuracy of URLs for external or third-party Internet websites referred to in this publication and does not guarantee that any content on such websites is, or will remain, accurate or appropriate.

Fordham University Press also publishes its books in a variety of electronic formats. Some content that appears in print may not be available in electronic books.

Visit us online at www.fordhampress.com.

Library of Congress Cataloging-in-Publication Data available online at https://catalog.loc.gov.

Printed in the United States of America

25 24 23   5 4 3 2 1

First edition

CONTENTS

When you can assume that your audience holds the same beliefs you do, you can relax a little and use more normal means of talking to it; when you have to assume that it does not, then you have to make your vision apparent by shock—to the hard of hearing you shout, and for the almost-blind you draw large and startling figures.

—FLANNERY O'CONNOR, *MYSTERY AND MANNERS*

The actual experience of the work of art can be called a realized experience of an event of truth. . . . The work of art encounters me with the surprise, impact, even shock of reality itself.

—DAVID TRACY, *THE ANALOGICAL IMAGINATION*

Introduction

"Surprise Me": Going Inside the "Black Box" of Catholic Fiction

This is a book about Catholic fiction in a secular age, and the rhetorical strategies Catholic writers employ to reach an audience that is indifferent, skeptical, perhaps even outright hostile. Although characters in contemporary Catholic fiction frequently struggle with doubt and fear, these works retain a belief in the possibility for transcendent meaning and value beyond the limits of the purely secular. In the chapters that follow, through close readings of some of the best works of contemporary American Catholic fiction, I shed light on the narrative techniques that Catholic writers use to point their characters, and their readers, beyond the horizon of secularity and toward an idea of transcendence.[1]

This project is premised on the belief that literature is meaningful in part because it does something to the reader.[2] When we encounter a work of art, we are altered by this experience; this is something David Tracy draws our attention to in *The Analogical Imagination*: "The actual experience of the work of art can be called a realized experience of an event of truth. . . . The work of art encounters me with the surprise, impact, even shock of reality itself" (111). Tracy's work is a particularly compelling account of the Catholic conception of the limits and capabilities of language to shape and convey experience, but one does not need to be Catholic to accept this premise. As Rita Felski reminds us, in *The Limits of Critique*, "Works of art do not only subvert but also convert, they do not only inform but also transform—a transformation that is not just a matter of intellectual readjustment but one of affective realignment as well (a shift of mood, a sharpened sensation, an unexpected surge of affinity or disorientation)"

(17). The ways in which texts bring about this disorientation and conversion[3] are the focus of this present study.

Most of the authors discussed throughout this book have a favored analogy for how the reading experience functions, and we will touch on many of these in the coming chapters, but my personal favorite comes from George Saunders: "My go-to model for my stories—a model that actually helps me write them—is that a story is a black box, into which the reader goes, and something happens. Something big and breathtaking and non-trivial. I don't have to know what that thing is beforehand—it's going to reveal itself to me at speed and I don't need to be able to pithily reduce it. I just have to micromanage the machinery inside the box so as to maximize the various effects—to sharpen the curves, so to speak" (*Conversations* 158). I find this analogy to be particularly effective because it touches on two themes that I see as central to this book—the aspects of craft that the writer employs to shape the reader's experience of the story, and also the effect the story has on the reader.

Saunders, who was raised Catholic, might not consciously be invoking the sacramental aspect of the confessional in this description of the black box where something momentous takes place—though it is possible the imagery is deliberate (see chapter 6 for more on the significance of confession in Saunders's fiction)—but I do think it is unsurprising that Saunders, as a Catholic writer, uses this type of imagery to discuss how fiction works. In his understanding, fiction is something that can change the reader, which is a very Catholic understanding of the power of story. One reason Saunders's image is such a powerful one is that it foregrounds how the experience of reading is "non-trivial."[4] Catholic writers believe in the power of story to affect the reader, and my intention, over the coming chapters, is to illuminate how this works in the stories of a number of American Catholic writers. We will look at the various narrative techniques and strategies that Catholic writers employ to shape their readers' experience of the work, in the hopes of gaining a deeper understanding of how Catholic literature functions.

No two authors will, to employ Saunders's metaphor, craft the same sort of box, or subject their readers to the same experience, but in Catholic literature we do often encounter similar themes. As any reader of a Saunders story knows, the experience inside the black box he creates is often surprising and violent—these are, I believe, the "sharpen[ed] . . . curves" he mentions—and this is no less true for readers of Flannery O'Connor and Walker Percy, or Tim Gautreaux and Kirstin Valdez Quade. It is as if the reader enters the darkness and is slapped in the face, or a voice whispers from the shadows, "Remember you are dust and to dust you shall return." The black box of Catholic literature can be a dark, violent, disorienting space. In the following chapters, my aim is, in essence, to turn the lights on inside of these black boxes, and to spend time looking at how these writers have "micro-managed" their spaces, so as to better understand what is going on in the exchange between the text and the reader.

Once we have turned these lights on, we will come to see how often Catholic writers employ the strategic use of violence to shape their readers' experience of the text. This is, of course, not the only tool these writers use to affect their readers, but it is remarkable how often characters in Catholic literature suffer, in upsetting, shocking, disorienting ways. These moments can leave the reader shaken and unmoored, and this, I argue, is deliberate—it is a (perhaps necessary) first step toward the recognition, and even possibly the acceptance, of grace. As O'Connor states, "I have found that violence is strangely capable of returning my characters to reality and preparing them to accept their moment of grace" (*Mystery* 112). Violence in these stories is not an end unto itself; instead, it becomes a kairotic moment,[5] in which the individual can make a definitive change in who she is and what she believes. In addition, Catholic authors consistently use violence as a means to unsettle their audience and force their readers to ask questions about what just happened in the story, and why. For the Catholic author, the answers to these questions often point toward a sacramental worldview that includes the possibility of the presence of God.

Three Examples: Wolff, Dubus, Hansen

To show this process at work, let us look briefly at three works from American Catholic writers whom I will not be discussing elsewhere in this book: Tobias Wolff's "Bullet in the Brain," Andre Dubus's "A Father's Story," and Ron Hansen's *Mariette in Ecstasy*. One could write an entire chapter on each of these writers,[6] but my hope is that even a brief examination of these works (two stories and one novel) can help demonstrate both the presence and effectiveness of the strategic use of violence in their work, and that this will serve as an introduction to these trends in the broader field of Catholic literature as a whole.

Both Wolff and Dubus are rightly celebrated as masters of the short story form, but their Catholicism is often overlooked in discussions of their work. They are certainly not celebrated as pillars of American Catholic literature in the way that O'Connor and Percy are, but both were practicing Catholics whose faith played an important role in the themes and structure of their work (Dubus died in 1999; Wolff is still publishing). Both can be described as writers with a moral vision, and their stories demand that the reader grapple with the implications of this vision. And, as with so many Catholic writers, both often employ moments of violence to convey this vision—to change the arcs of their characters and to draw their readers into moments of reflection and contemplation.

Tobias Wolff's short masterpiece, the often-anthologized "Bullet in the Brain," can serve as a perfect encapsulation of this process. In the story, Anders, a jaded book critic, is a bystander in a bank robbery. While everyone else quietly acquiesces to the robbers' demands, Anders cannot accept the seriousness of his predicament. He mocks the robbers' clichéd way of speaking and is unable to cease his critiques even when directly threatened with a gun to his head. Because of this, he is abruptly shot and killed. Despite the foreshadowing of the title, the unexpected quickness of the murder is still a shock to the reader. But the power of the story is not in this relatively straightforward plot arc, but rather in Wolff's depiction of what happens to Anders once the bullet enters his brain. Up to this point, he has been cynical, disengaged, bitter; he seems to find—to use O'Connor's phrasing—"no real pleasure in life." Instead, he has reached a stage where "everything began to remind him of something else" (*Night* 205), and he appears unable to directly appreciate experiences or connect with others. But once the bullet enters his brain, something shifts. As Wolff's sharp prose puts it, "the first appearance of the bullet in the cerebrum set off a crackling chain of ion transports and neuro-transmissions. Because of their peculiar origin these traced a peculiar pattern, flukishly calling to life a summer afternoon some forty years past, and long since lost to memory" (204).

At his moment of death, his last, idyllic thought is of playing on a baseball field in the heat of the summer; the setting is a stark contrast to the cold and bureaucratic bank that serves as the scene of his murder. But Anders is not particularly captivated by actually playing baseball; rather his imagination lingers over the musical rhythm of another child saying he wanted to play shortstop because "'Short's the best position they is'" (205). We can safely assume that for the adult Anders, this kind of grammatical error would have produced scorn, but as a child he loves the rhythm and beauty of the language and what it evokes: "Anders is strangely roused, elated, by those final two words, their pure unexpectedness and their music. He takes the field in a trance, repeating them to himself." And it is this phrase—"*They is, they is, they is*"—that lingers in his mind as his life, and the story, ends (206).

Wolff leaves the reader wondering what it would have taken to get Anders to change, to be reawakened to this kind of innocent joy and pleasure again, if not a bullet to the brain. In O'Connor's classic story "A Good Man Is Hard to Find," the murderous Misfit declares the grandmother, whom he has just murdered, would have been a good woman "'if it had been somebody there to shoot her every minute of her life.'" He is partially right; she did need to be shaken out of her calcified worldview, and the violent encounter with the Misfit does ultimately lead to an experience of grace for her. But unlike Anders, the grandmother actually changes before she is shot; her experience of loss and fear awakens something in her, which allows her to experience a transformation even before she is murdered (I have much more to say about this story in the next chapter). Anders, though, does not have a change in his character; he is literally milliseconds from death as this memory is triggered. But we can still describe this as a moment of grace for him—it is an unlooked-for (and unearned) blessing. Although religion is entirely absent from "Bullet in the Brain," it is possible to understand Anders's final memory as an encounter with beauty that is a form of transcendence, and to see that the story offers this to the reader as well. Wolff indicates that it might not be too late for us—even us book critics!—to remember what brings us joy and captures our imagination. Perhaps, in particular, for us to recall how the rhythms of language can fire our hearts and minds.

So here we have a Catholic writer crafting a story in which a moment of shocking violence leads to an epiphany. But if we didn't know the writer was Catholic, would we think of this epiphanic moment as having religious overtones? Would we immediately see this as an instantiation of, in Paul Contino's words, Wolff's ability to "suggest . . . [how] the stories we tell, the narratives of our lives, are upended to make room for what we call God's story" ("This Writer's Life"). I don't think it is terribly likely. But I also don't think this means the story fails some sort of qualification test for "Catholic literature." The Catholic elements are there if we look for them, and even if we do not, the story still points the reader toward a new recognition of beauty and wonder, which is also a form of sacramentality. It is a Catholic work, regardless of whether the reader is aware of it, because it is informed by a Catholic sensibility and points the reader beyond the self, toward a horizon of greater meaning.

When we turn to "A Father's Story" and *Mariette in Ecstasy*, though, we are dealing with something slightly different, because both Dubus and Hansen do incorporate overtly Catholic elements into these texts. Their characters are practicing Catholics. They discuss the sacraments, sin, miracles, and atonement. Indeed, both are overtly theological works, where the characters are grappling with questions of faith and belief and religious identity. Readers cannot ignore these elements and still hope to make sense of the works. Like Wolff, though, both use moments of violence as a central part of their Catholic vision.

In his introduction to Dubus's essay collection, *Broken Vessels*, Wolff explains: "[For Dubus], the quotidian and the spiritual don't exist on different planes, but infuse each other. His is an unapologetically sacramental vision of life in which ordinary things participate in the miraculous, the miraculous in ordinary things. He believes in God, and talks to Him, and doesn't mince words" (xv).[7] We see this quite clearly in "A Father's Story," where the narrator, Luke Ripley, spends the first half of his narrative describing the basic facts of his life, and it quickly becomes clear to the reader that what matters to him, what he calls "my real life . . . the one nobody talks about anymore," is his faith life (*Selected Stories*, 455). He says that as a child, "I expected to be tortured and killed for my faith," but what the story eventually reveals is a different form of testing of faith (456). He details his active prayer life, his daily Mass going and his regular confessions, and it is clear that these things are not just rote activities that provide him with structure and daily rhythms (although they do do this), but they also give his existence a depth and significance it would otherwise lack. This is what gives the second half of the story, where the nature of Ripley's faith is tested, so much emotional weight, since we understand what his faith means to him.

Much like "Bullet," this is a story where the first half feels like one kind of a story, and then, abruptly, everything changes and the entire focus and significance of the story shift. In both cases, a moment of violence initiates the change. In "A Father's Story," Luke's college-age daughter Jennifer comes to him in the middle of the night and tells him she has hit a person while driving home, perhaps intoxicated, after a night out with friends. But the way Dubus alters the focus and tone of the story is nearly as jarring for the reader as it is for the character; for the first half of the story he does not tell us that anything traumatic is coming, and even when the shift happens, he does not immediately tell us that there was an accident. Rather, he aligns us with Luke's disorientation:

> She told me all of it, waking me that night I had gone to sleep
> listening to the wind in the trees and against the house, a wind so
> strong that I had to shut all but the lee windows, and still the house
> cooled; told it to me in such detail and so clearly that now, when she
> has driven the car to Florida, I remember it all as though I had been
> a passenger in the front seat, or even at the wheel. (465–66)

Here, we know something significant has happened, and we're jolted out of the somewhat meandering thoughts of our narrator (my students often complain that the first half of the story is boring, both because "nothing happens" and because Luke's exposition-heavy narrative—in the words of one creative writing major—"does too much telling, not enough showing"), but we do not yet know what has happened, which puts us a bit on edge.

Dubus leads us through Jennifer's account of the accident, and then, in almost agonizing detail, we follow Ripley as he drives out to look for the body. He tells us that as he drove to the scene, he "prayed that he [the victim] was alive, while beneath that prayer, a reserve deeper in my heart, another one stirred: that if he were dead, they would not get Jennifer" (468). He has no control over the first part of the prayer, but he does everything in his power to ensure that the latter half comes to pass. He does eventually locate the body, and he recounts for us the step-by-step process of trying to find a pulse, a heartbeat, a breath, which he cannot do with any certainty amid the sounds of the heavy wind. Eventually he realizes the young man is dead, and he decides he needs to protect Jennifer from any consequences. He leaves the body where he found it, and the next day he stages an accident with her truck, to provide cover for her dented fender. He does not report Jennifer's accident to the police, and does not confess what he has done to his priest. He realizes that he has sinned, that he is guilty of "failure to do all that one can to save an anonymous life, of injustice to a family in their grief, of deepening their pain at the chance and mystery of death by giving them nothing—no one—to hate" (475). This experience leaves him shaken: "I do not feel the peace I once did: not with God, nor the earth, or anyone on it" (475). But he also claims that he does not feel guilt or shame; he feels he has done the right thing, and that his actions demonstrate a form of parental love that even God the Father must understand. The story closes with Ripley's conversation with God:

He [God] says, you love her more than you love Me.
I love her more than I love truth.
Then you love in weakness, He says.
As You love me, I say. . . . (476)

Here, too, we have a main character who is transformed by an experience of violence. He is neither the victim nor the perpetrator of it, but he is nevertheless still changed by it. As he says, "when she knocked on my door, then called me, she woke what had flowed dormant in my blood since her birth, so that what rose from the bed was not a stable owner or a Catholic or any other Luke Ripley I had lived with for a long time, but the father of a girl" (475). The structure of the story, particularly the final exchange between Ripley and God, asks the reader to reflect on whether

Ripley's actions are justified, and to question if this kind of love is a form of strength or weakness. Is he acting virtuously, or damning himself?

This is one of my favorite stories to teach, even though many students actively dislike it, because even these disgruntled students are stirred up and want to dive into the moral and ethical questions raised by the conclusion. Dubus structures the story in such a way as to get us thinking about the connections between our faith and our actions, and to question what we would be willing to do for those we love. Ripley makes a decision to protect his daughter, and we have his explanation of why he does what he does, but as he says about his own sons, "Their reasons were never as good or as bad as their actions, but they needed to find them, to believe they were living by them, instead of the awful solitude of the heart" (475). Ripley claims his love for his daughter is like God's love for his Son, and all of His children, but we do not have to accept that this is true simply because he claims that it is. Some readers will leave the story believing that Ripley demonstrates virtuous love, others will feel he acts selfishly and is deluding himself about the true nature of his actions. The story reads its readers, demanding contemplative engagement, and the rhetorical strategy Dubus employs to get his readers thinking about virtue and morality is, once again, a shocking moment of violence.

Ron Hansen's *Mariette in Ecstasy*, like "A Father's Story," is a work that demands contemplation and thoughtful engagement from the reader. It is not violent like "Bullet in the Brain" or "A Father's Story," in the sense that there are no murders, deliberate or accidental, and the central action of the novel does not hinge on violence carried out by one character toward another (or toward oneself).[8] But the novel does center a bleeding body in pain, in the form of the protagonist Mariette's experience of the stigmata.

Mariette in Ecstasy repeatedly draws attention to the physicality of Christ's suffering, and to the centrality of this suffering in the Christian faith. The religious order that Mariette joins is called the Sisters of the Crucifixion; their church is Our Lady of Sorrows. One of the few objects in Mariette's room is a crucifix, and Hansen's language foregrounds the corporeality of the image: "just a few feet above Mariette's pillow is a hideous Spanish cross and a painted Christ that is all red meat and agony" (23). This is fitting, since the foundation of her faith is a vision of the suffering Christ. When describing her own faith journey, she recounts a mystical vision she had with her sister: "With Annie I first found myself before Jesus crucified. . . . Such blood flowed from his hand and his head! And he was having such trouble breathing! We watched in tears, Annie and I, and she told me, 'Look, Mariette, and learn how one loves'" (74).

In a novel that is riddled with intertextual sources, many of the passages that Hansen includes are meditations on Jesus's suffering, which reflect their authors' own desire to share in this pain. During one of her first dinners in the convent, the sisters read from Julian of Norwich's *Revelations of Divine Love*, where Julian "'asked three gifts from God: one, to understand his passion; two, to suffer physically while still a young woman of thirty; and, finally, to have as God's gift three wounds'" (25). Later in the novel we get a similar passage from St. John of the Cross, who asks God for "'naught but suffering and to be despised for your sake'" (69), to which Mariette responds "'I, too, have prayed for that.'" She also tells her confessor, echoing Julian's language, "'Ever since I was thirteen, I have been praying to understand his passion. Everything about it. To have a horrible illness so I could feel the horrors and terrors of death just as Christ did'" (40).

And, it seems, God grants her prayer. Shortly after her sister dies, she receives the full stigmata: "She holds out her blood-painted hands like a present and she smiles crazily as she says, 'Oh, look at what Jesus has done to me!'" (112). The moment is destabilizing, for Mariette and the reader; although the repeated invocations of Christ's passion have prepared us for something like this, the crazy smile and blood-splattered hands read more as horrific than beatific. She becomes, literally, a "startling figure" in their midst, and she does shock and confound those who encounter her, and the reader as well.

Indeed, one of the strengths of the novel is that Mariette's experience of the five wounds of Christ is wrapped in layers of ambiguity—neither the reader nor the characters are entirely sure why she has it, if it is real, or what it signifies. While Mariette's suffering leads some who encounter it closer to God—one sister licks the blood from her palm and declares, "'You have been a sacrament to me'" (121)—for others it is a scandal and a stumbling block to belief, and a hindrance to their relationship to God. A faction of the sisters resents her and claims she is faking the wounds. Even Mariette's confessor, one of her great supporters, admits, "We are bored and dull and tired of each other, and we have such a yearning for some sign from God that this matters, that our prayers and good works are important to Him. Is she preying upon that? Is she trying to entertain?" (148). The prioress, Mother Saint-Raphael, declares, "'I have no idea why God would be doing this to us'" (160). Although she initially doubts the veracity of the miracle, and is resentful of Mariette, by the end she does come to believe it is real. But she still sends Mariette away from the convent, telling her, "'I personally believe that what you say happened did indeed happen. We could never prove it, of course. Skeptics will always prevail. God gives us just enough to seek Him, and never enough to fully find him. To do more would inhibit our freedom, and our freedom is very dear to God'" (174). Throughout the novel, Hansen's narrative style keeps the reader at a distance, inviting us to question what is really going on, and asking us to spend time reflecting on why this might be happening. This kind of distancing allows for, even demands, the kind of freedom Mother Saint-Raphael is talking about.

The last intertextual passage in the book is from St. Paul (2 Corinthians 4:8–10): "'We are afflicted in every way possible, but we are not crushed; full of doubts, we never despair. We are persecuted but never abandoned; we are struck down but never destroyed. Continually we carry about in our bodies the dying of Jesus, so that in our bodies the life of Jesus may also be revealed'" (178). The book ends less than a page later, without providing clarity or resolution to its central mysteries, so this passage lingers for the reader. Do we believe it? And if we do, what are the implications of such belief? Hansen asks the reader to contemplate the mystery of Christ's suffering, and how it relates to our contemporary world. This is the lasting message of the novel—faith and doubt go hand in hand, and it is possible that our sufferings do unite us with Christ's, and perhaps Christ is present in our own suffering as well.

This is a recurring theme in Catholic fiction. In the coming chapters we see authors continually using forms of violence to impact characters and readers, but the central theme of many of these stories is actually suffering, in its various forms. Jesuit writer James Martin, in a reflection on Christ's crucifixion, notes, "Physical pain is not the only kind of suffering we endure—or that Jesus suffered. And so this is not the only kind of pain he understands" (385). Martin explains that "for those who think of Jesus as far removed from the suffering we face, the Gospels show us not simply physical sufferings, but emotional ones as well. We do not, as St. Paul said, have a God who does not understand our suffering, but who participated in it. This is an entry for us into Jesus's life and an entry for him into ours" (392). Whether through depictions of physical or emotional trauma, Catholic writers posit a potential link between suffering and coming to a new awareness of one's participation in the life of Christ. This is, of course, not always easy, and it is not always embraced by the characters within a work. There are times when such connections can only be made off the page, beyond the text.

"Elusive. Other. Upsetting."—The Nature of Catholic Fiction

By looking at these three works by Wolff, Dubus, and Hansen, I am not attempting to provide a complete taxonomy of how violence functions in Catholic literature, but these stories do serve as examples of both the centrality of violence in many Catholic works and of the different ways violence can function in these stories. Sometimes, as in "Bullet in the Brain," a direct experience of violence, or suffering, leads a character to new insights or an experience of grace; this is a common pattern in O'Connor's work, but as we will see it is also present in Percy's novels and Saunders's stories as well. In "A Father's Story," the moment of violence leads characters (and readers) to grapple with moral and ethical questions; this is something we will look at in the fiction of Percy, Gautreaux, Saunders, and Phil Klay. Finally, in *Mariette in Ecstasy*, the "startling figure" is tied directly to reflections on Christ's suffering and the nature of religious belief; we will examine this connection between suffering and belief in the work of both J. F. Powers and Alice McDermott, and in Phil Klay and Kirstin Valdez Quade's stories as well.

Of course, one could look at all of these examples and reasonably claim that I have stacked the deck, and point out that one could just as easily choose any number of Catholic stories that feature no bleeding and broken bodies, no corpses whatsoever. This is surely true (though I would counter that a disproportionate number of Catholic works, particularly ones that are held up as classics of the genre, do foreground moments of violence). It is important to acknowledge that not all of the works we look at in the coming chapters feature violence as a central aesthetic strategy employed by their authors to affect the reader, and even for writers who do use this kind of violence, my focus is not exclusively on the violent moments in their work. Rather, my primary interest is in the specific narrative choices these writers make to shape their reader's experience of the text—the ways they, to return to Saunders's black box imagery, shape "the machinery inside the box so as to maximize the various effects" of their fiction. What we will discover is that even the stories that are not inherently violent still find ways to surprise and disorient us. When we seek to understand how Catholic stories affect their readers, we do come back, again and again, to (often violent) moments of disorientation that open a space for the movement of grace. In short, reading Catholic fiction can—perhaps should!—be a confounding experience.

In *Mariette in Ecstasy*, Mariette's sister, trying to make sense of Mariette's essential nature, declares, "'Saints are like that, I think. Elusive. Other.

Upsetting'" (92). The same can be said for the best Catholic stories. They cannot be easily pinned down or dismissed. These are stories meant to be experienced, and the true meaning of the work is revealed in the interplay of our own expectations and the ways in which the text is structured to subvert them. The shock and disorientation of Catholic literature often occur when we are presented with a story we do not understand, which we cannot totally make sense of, where our sense of what is right and wrong gets flipped over and we are left confused, and lost, and searching. We approach the text expecting one thing and are given another. In this sense, the very last words of Hansen's novel, which the adult Mariette claims are God's words to her, serve as a fitting entry point to this study: "Surprise me" (179). This command is at the heart of Catholic storytelling. When we step into Saunders's black box, we are going to experience something momentous, disorienting, surprising, which can push us in unanticipated directions and open us up to new revelations.

Chapter Summaries

I begin the process of exploring the surprising and disorienting nature of Catholic literature by looking at the use of violence in Flannery O'Connor's fiction. In the first section of this chapter I look to her letters and essays to illuminate her own explanations and justifications for the violence in her work. I then turn to a close reading of her early masterpiece "A Good Man Is Hard to Find" to demonstrate how the violence functions in a typical O'Connor short story, both on the characters of the grandmother and the Misfit, and also on the reader. I close the chapter with a discussion of *Wise Blood*, arguing that in the character of Mrs. Flood, O'Connor has provided us with a reader surrogate, whose experience of witnessing violence acts as a catalyst to reevaluation of her mundane worldview.

In chapter 2 I turn to the fiction of J. F. Powers, whose work is now often overlooked in discussions of American Catholic literature. Although his stories are less violent than those of O'Connor and Percy, he, too, employs strategies of disruption to unsettle and upend the expectations of characters and readers alike, leading to moments where new insight and grace are present—though often overlooked. I examine this process first in his short story "Prince of Darkness," in which the powerful closing lines make clear that his work offers both the main character and the reader "not peace but a sword." In Powers's work, the "sword" of disappointment helps prune the soul, and the violence and cruelty of the world can lead to contemplation, if not always to clarity. I then demonstrate how this process plays out in more detail in Powers's masterpiece, *Morte d'Urban*, where Fr. Urban Roche, the worldly and successful missionary priest, is brought low by a golf ball to the head. I look at how this moment is usually read as a necessary step on his road toward embracing actual holiness, and question whether this is truly the case.

Chapter 3 deals with the work of Walker Percy, the last of the mid- to late-twentieth-century masters of American Catholic fiction. I argue that his work serves as a connecting thread between that of O'Connor and Powers and the more contemporary writers I discuss in the latter half of the book. Using Percy's concept of the diagnostic novel, I examine the connection between the pervasive violence of his fiction and his diagnosis of the ills of modern society. The violence in Percy's novels comes in two broad categories: the largely impersonal violence that is a product of widespread social and cultural ills, which in turn can be attributed to the ascendancy of the metanarratives of science and dehumanized "progress," and the intensely personal, self-directed suicidal violence that is a product of an individual's feelings of meaninglessness. I trace out these elements in both *The Moviegoer* and *Lancelot*, noting how the rhetorical strategies Percy employs in both texts draw in the reader and invite us to come to the same insights that his characters gain.

Chapters 4 to 6 and the Epilogue all deal with writers who are actively publishing today and, taken together, provide a snapshot of the still vital discourse taking place within American Catholic fiction. I begin this pivot in chapter 4 by looking at the work of Tim Gautreaux, a former student of Percy's, whose fiction is heavily influenced by Percy and O'Connor. His stories use violence to change characters and readers as well, but in a way that emphasizes postconciliar Catholic thinking, particularly in their emphasis on the significance of community and in his prioritization of the importance of social action. I assume that most readers are relatively unfamiliar with Gautreaux's work, so I spend a little more time unpacking particular pieces. I begin by tracing out the familiar pattern of violence leading to transformation in his first novel, *The Next Step in the Dance*, and then show how an early short story, "Same Place, Same Things," undermines this pattern. I then move to his two most recent novels, *The Clearing* and *The Missing*, showing how in these works he is focused on exposing the myth of redemptive violence and moving characters and readers toward an appreciation for the path of nonviolence.

Chapter 5 focuses on Alice McDermott, perhaps the most celebrated contemporary American Catholic writer. I connect the themes in her work back to J. F. Powers, noting how they both are primarily interested in the routines of domestic life, and the ways in which Catholic faith and culture help give shape and structure to these routines. As in Powers's fiction, McDermott's work is not overly violent, but it is concerned with suffering and the reality of death, and her stories foreground the ways in which people try to make sense of their own mortality. I begin by positioning her work in the broader narratives surrounding postsecular fiction and the state of contemporary Catholic literature, and then look closely at a number of novels, particularly *Charming Billy, Someone*, and *The Ninth Hour*. In these novels, she shines her fictional lens on the pain and suffering of the world and looks at how we attempt to make sense of these traumas. She poses hard questions about the adequacy of faith in the modern, skeptical age, while still making space for the presence of mystery and the transformative reality of grace.

Chapter 6 examines the work of George Saunders. Saunders is not often discussed as a Catholic writer, but through a close examination of his interviews I demonstrate why this is a mistake. He is an intensely moral writer, and he repeatedly invokes the significance of his Catholic upbringing on his thematic concerns. Throughout the chapter I show how Catholicism permeates his work, beginning with the confessional urge that is central to *Lincoln in the Bardo*. From there, I move to drawing connections between his work and that of O'Connor, Percy, and Powers; in each case, I show how he uses moments of violence and trauma as a way to disorient both characters and the reader. I do this through close readings of three stories: "The Falls," "CommComm," and "Tenth of December." Like O'Connor, Saunders makes broad and persuasive claims for the power of fiction to affect the reader, and perhaps no writer since O'Connor has been able to use humor and violence in such perfect balance to achieve these ends.

I close the book with an epilogue that touches on the work of Phil Klay and Kirstin Valdez Quade, two representatives of a younger generation of Catholic writers that is continuing to develop and expand the dimensions of Catholic literature. In Klay's fiction, violence is tied directly to the experiences of war and its aftermath. I focus primarily on "Prayers in the Furnace," one of the stories in his National Book Award–winning collection, *Redeployment*, which is about how individuals respond to violence, both that they themselves have perpetuated and that they have experienced. Klay emphasizes the ways in which war breaks individuals and communities while maintaining the possibility that faith in Christ's own experience of suffering really does mean that no one needs to suffer alone. Quade's fiction connects pervasive violence to systemic breakdowns in the social fabric, but also to the experience of faith itself, and she explores whether moments of violence really lead to the kinds of transformation we have come to expect from other Catholic stories. I look first at her story "Christina the Astonishing (1150–1224)," a retelling of a Catholic saint's life, which encapsulates the idea that saints are, in Hansen's language, "Elusive. Other. Upsetting." Then I turn to her short story "The Five Wounds," alongside the novel of the same name, which is a revision and expansion of the story. The story explicitly connects the protagonist's experience of physical suffering to Christ's own, leading to a moment of insight; the novel goes on to explore how the kinds of dramatic transformation brought about through such an epiphany might not last. Both Klay and Quade explore the nature of suffering and use their work to provoke their readers into a reflection on what it takes to actually change.

1 / The "Blasting Annihilating Light" of Flannery O'Connor's Art

Any discussion of the rhetorical strategies that American Catholic writers employ in their fiction needs to begin with the work of Flannery O'Connor, both because O'Connor is the most prominent American Catholic writer, and because her use of violence as an aesthetic strategy to affect both characters and readers is incredibly influential. As any reader of O'Connor knows, her work is positively saturated with violence, and attempts to understand her thematic concerns and technical precision will necessarily involve some analysis of her use of violence. Fortunately, there are many excellent studies on violence in O'Connor's fiction,[1] so I need not start this discussion from first principles. Indeed, the true challenge for the critic writing about O'Connor and violence is really a problem of selection. Where does one begin, when there is so much material to cover? When looking at her short stories, the ones that do *not* feature a moment of shocking violence are the exception; both of her novels are marked by violence perpetrated by, and upon, the protagonists (in *Wise Blood*, Hazel Motes kills a man and then blinds himself; in *The Violent Bear It Away*, Francis Marion Tarwater drowns his cousin and then is raped by a stranger). This is well-trodden ground for critics, and many arguments have been put forth to explain the origin and function of the violence in her work.

All of this presents a challenge for a scholar interested in violence in American Catholic fiction. One must discuss O'Connor, because her work casts such a long shadow over the entire field, but much of what there is to say about O'Connor and violence has already been (very well) said. One does not want to simply summarize what has become critical commonplace. At the same time, O'Connor's influence can be found in nearly every Catholic writer who has come after her, and if we are to make sense of the various rhetorical strategies employed by American Catholic fiction writers, particularly the pervasive use of violence, then we need to begin by looking at O'Connor's work. To this end, I spend some time addressing three central questions: where does the violence in O'Connor's fiction come from, what does it do to her characters, and what does it do to the reader? I admit that readers well versed in O'Connor scholarship may find some of this discussion to cover familiar ground, but I think it necessary and important to trace out these elements, since they play such an influential role in shaping the entire field of American Catholic fiction.

O'Connor's Aesthetic of Violence

Although O'Connor's fiction can be unsettling and destabilizing for a modern reader, her explanations of her own work are much more straightforward. She describes why she uses violence, how she intends it to function within the story itself, and how she envisions it affecting her readers' sensibilities. O'Connor repeatedly states that she does not want to be overly didactic in her writing, since the end result of such fiction is "another addition to that large body of pious trash for which [Catholic writers] have so long been famous" (*Mystery* 180), but she has no problem declaring that she intends to make her particular, Catholic Christian worldview evident to her readers, and that violence is one of her primary strategies for doing so: "the Catholic writer often finds himself writing in and for a world that is unprepared and unwilling to see the meaning of life as he sees it. This means frequently that he may resort to violent literary means to get his vision across to a hostile audience" (*Mystery* 185).

O'Connor had a clear conception of the audience for which she was writing, and this in turn shaped the form of her fiction.[2] O'Connor conceived of her readers as either largely atheistic—"my audience are the people who think God is dead" (*Habit* 92)—or at least unconcerned with the spiritual realities that she saw as the foundational principle of existence: "I have found that what I write is read by an audience which puts little stock either in grace or the devil" (*Mystery* 118), and "Today's audience is one in which religious feeling has become, if not atrophied, at least vaporous and sentimental" (*Mystery* 161). In perhaps her most descriptive statement on her imagined audience, she explains,

> When I sit down to write, a monstrous reader looms up who sits down beside me and continually mutters, "I don't get it, I don't see it,

I don't want it." Some writers can ignore this presence, but I have never learned how. I know that I must never let him affect my vision, must never let him gain control over my thinking, must never listen to his demands unless they accord with my conscience; yet I feel I must make him see what I have to show, even if my means of making him see have to be extreme.[3]

Through her fiction, O'Connor wanted to force her readers to see reality as she saw it, so that they might reassess their assumptions about the nature of existence. She described this as her "prophetic function of recalling people to known but ignored truths" (*Conversations* 89). This movement toward some process of reflection and reassessment is also the thematic focus of most of her fiction, and for her readers and her characters she often initiates this awakening through some moment of violence. Her stories and novels repeatedly focus on individuals who either feel themselves superior to religious belief, or who profess a Christian worldview but take no account of the meaning, and cost, of such belief. She then places these individuals into a moment of conflict, which is almost always violent, with the end result being that the individuals are led to reconsider what they believe about ultimate meaning and value. The violence undermines, or obliterates, characters' sense of self, and this process can lead to a reorientation of these characters' entire understanding of existence.

O'Connor's claim, "I have found that violence is strangely capable of returning my characters to reality and preparing them to accept their moment of grace" (*Mystery* 112), is perhaps the most straightforward explanation she provides for the pervasiveness of violence in her fiction, though it does not exactly address the central question of *why* she believes violence achieves this function. Two elements here require further illumination: first, O'Connor's conception of reality, and second, her understanding of free will, vis-à-vis this acceptance of grace. For O'Connor, who subscribed fully to the Catholic Church's conception of reality, humanity is sinful and fallen, and therefore finally imperfectible without God's grace. In O'Connor's view, modern man believes exactly the opposite; he believes in self-sufficiency, progress, and the eventual eradication of all pain and suffering. Because of this, "the modern secular world does not believe in . . . sin, or in the value that suffering can have, or in eternal responsibility" (185). This radical disconnect between her understanding of reality and her conception of her audience's understanding shaped every aspect of her fiction. She believed that for the Catholic writer to "write about a man's encounter with God" in a way that is "understandable, and credible" for a secular audience, the writer must "bend the whole novel—its language, its structure, its action" (161–62).

In O'Connor's stories, the encounter with violence forces her characters to relinquish their reliance on their own self-sufficiency and acknowledge that they are not in complete control of their lives, and she ties this loss of control to humanity's need for redemption. O'Connor believed that "Redemption is meaningless unless there is cause for it in the actual life we live, and for the last few centuries there has been operating in our culture the secular belief that there is no such cause" (*Mystery* 33). No one (in fiction or reality) will seek out help without first recognizing their own need, and O'Connor uses her fiction to demonstrate just such a metaphysical need. For O'Connor, the process of conversion, of leaving behind one's false ideas of reality in pursuit of the truth, relies upon self-knowledge and insight, and this insight comes about as a result of grace.

Grace, though, as O'Connor envisions it, is often a violent affair. She wrote, "I don't know if anybody can be converted without seeing themselves in a blasting annihilating light"[4] (*Habit* 427); this light is the light of grace, and it is no accident that the adjectives she uses to describe it are violent. As her letters and essays make clear, she believed violence was one of the sources of this annihilating light for her characters. The moments of violence force her characters to see themselves as they truly are, which opens them to the realization that they are not in fact totally self-sufficient, and that they do need "to be redeemed." This insight can be the precursor to radical change.

But O'Connor's fictional project does not end with her characters; she clearly wanted her fiction to shine this blasting annihilating light on her readers as well. In "The Fiction Writer and His Country," O'Connor laid out her aesthetic strategy:

> The novelist with Christian concerns will find in modern life distortions which are repugnant to him, and his problem will be to make these appear as distortions to an audience which is used to seeing them as natural; and he may well be forced to take ever more violent means to get his vision across to this hostile audience. When you can assume that your audience holds the same beliefs you do, you can relax a little and use more normal means of talking to it; when you have to assume that it does not, then you have to make your vision apparent by shock—to the hard of hearing you shout, and for the almost-blind you draw large and startling figures. (*Mystery* 33–34)

The violence in O'Connor's work is her attempt to shock her audience into seeing reality anew. Christina Bieber Lake describes this artistic strategy as "O'Connor's 'shock and awe' campaign . . . against her readers, whereby violence occurs in the effort to get people to pay attention" (27). I would go one step further and argue that O'Connor does not simply want to capture her reader's attention, she wants to lead them toward the same kind of radical conversion her characters undergo. O'Connor uses violence to bring her readers up short, to lead them to ask fundamental questions about what happened and why, in the hope that the result of this questioning will be an acknowledgment of the fundamental mystery at the heart of reality, which (for O'Connor) is the presence and providence of God. This double movement, of disrupting the self-enclosed worldview of her characters and revealing mystery to her readers, is of central importance in understanding why O'Connor's fiction is built on and around violence. She wanted her fiction both to illuminate how modern individuals can come to rely once again on God and to serve as a source of possible transformation for her readers as well; she believed that fictional violence could accomplish both goals.

As a close reading of almost any canonical O'Connor story will demonstrate, within the world of her fiction violence accomplishes exactly what O'Connor intends: it breaks through the façades that her characters create around themselves, and it allows (or perhaps forces) them to see life in a new way. They are transformed, or they resist this transformation and are left bereft. I explore this process in greater detail in my discussion of "A Good Man Is Hard to Find." But what is much less clear is whether her fiction has the impact on her readers that she desires. Any given reader's reaction to a text is a subjective experience, and it is impossible for an author to entirely control a reader's response to his or her work, but through stylistic and technical decisions an author can at least attempt to define the parameters of this response. I focus on the ways O'Connor attempts to shape readerly perception within the fiction itself, and how a contemporary reader might respond to these techniques.

"A Good Man Is Hard to Find": The Template of Violence

"A Good Man Is Hard to Find," an early O'Connor masterpiece, contains all of the elements we should expect in her best work: dark humor, violence, grace, and the possibility for change. The story begins as a domestic snapshot, focusing on the tensions between the grandmother and her son and grandchildren as they set out on a road trip; in the latter half, though, the tone and tenor shift dramatically as the family suffers a car crash and the escaped convict known as the Misfit appears on the scene, ushering in the murder of the entire family. On one level, it is a story of seemingly senseless violence, but, as in most of O'Connor's work, the violence does have an underlying meaning: in this case it plays a key role in the transformation of the grandmother, and possibly the Misfit as well. Like all of O'Connor's most successful works, though, this story resists such simplification. Among other things, it is also about the changing nature of the South, the violence of the modern world, the mistaken beliefs of the older generation, and the callousness of the younger one.

It is worth noting up front that since this is one of O'Connor's most-discussed stories, most readers who are reasonably well versed in O'Connor studies know what this story means and how it works, and a quick internet search can help those who are unfamiliar with her work make sense of the shocking ending. This is not to say that new, important interpretations are not being offered, but in terms of how the violence functions in "A Good Man Is Hard to Find," I do think we have arrived at a critical consensus, which can lead to a sort of domestication of the work. The violence of the story has lost some of its ability to shock and disorient because we understand her intentions and her methods. In order to fully grasp how the story works, it is important to recover just how unsettling the story can initially be.

Two things define the grandmother throughout the first part of the story: her desire to get her own way, which is aligned with her commitment to a false past, and her preoccupation with dignity and class, which is tied to her xenophobic outlook. She tries to manipulate her son Bailey into going to Tennessee instead of Florida because she wants to visit "some of her connections" (*Works* 137). O'Connor doesn't say why Bailey wants to go to Florida, but historian Dewey Grantham describes Florida as a symbol of "modernization and progress" for the South in the first half of the twentieth century (113). The grandmother's reluctance to go there points toward her resistance to embracing the modern world, and her insistence on visiting family aligns her with traditional southern values. Her obsession with her own past is best exemplified in the plantation house that she remembers from her youth. Like the character of General Sash in "A Late Encounter with the Enemy," this house is representative of a romanticized and fictionalized past. The house did exist, but in order to make it sound more appealing, especially to the younger generation, the grandmother mythologizes it. She manipulates history, inventing a story about it having "a secret panel" filled with treasure, in order to make it sound more attractive (*Works* 143). Her commitment to this idealized and fictive past is what leads to the family's accident and their subsequent destruction.

The grandmother's other defining characteristic, her concern with class, is evident in the way she dresses for their car trip. She has on one of her finest outfits so that "in case of an accident, anyone seeing her dead on the highway would know at once that she was a lady" (138). She is more concerned with how she will appear when dead than she is with the actual reality of death. Because this is an O'Connor story, there is an accident and a moment of judgment on the grandmother, but not one based on her appearance. In the final judgment, it is her indecorous smile, not her proper clothes, that marks her salvation. O'Connor sets up this dichotomy between appearances and reality in order to emphasize the emptiness of the grandmother's worldview. Her notions of class create boundaries that separate and isolate her. As her family drives past a poor Black child on the side of the road she comments, "look at that cute little pickaninny," and although she is aware "little niggers in the country don't have things like we do," she feels no empathy; her only thought is to paint a picture of the child (139). It takes a physical encounter with the excluded other for the grandmother to transcend the false ideologies that isolate her.

The most significant example of her obsession with class comes after the accident, when she encounters the Misfit. The accident has shaken up the family, and for the first time we see a crack in the grandmother's façade of propriety. Her driving hat is no longer crisp and proper; it now has a "broken front brim standing up at a jaunty angle" (145). (When Bailey is taken into the woods to be killed the hat brim comes completely off.) The grandmother's violent encounter with the Misfit forces her to discard the constructed version of reality that she prefers; it is one of many instances where violence is the primary agent in "returning [a] character to reality" (*Mystery* 112). The destruction of the grandmother's hat symbolizes the breakdown of her outward barriers, but it is the dialogue with the Misfit that reveals her inner transformation.

As soon as the Misfit's hearselike car tops the hill we know that death has come upon the family; the only question is how they will face it. The grandmother initially tries to protect herself through ideas of class: "You wouldn't shoot a lady, would you?" and again: "I know you're a good man. You don't look a bit like you have common blood" (*Works* 147). In her mistaken worldview, the concept of class rights will protect her. She cannot die because she is a lady; the Misfit cannot kill them because he is not common.[5] Through her dialogue, O'Connor succeeds in making both the Misfit and the grandmother believable as actual people and not just archetypes, but both characters' lack of proper names reveals their larger-than-life status. The grandmother, like Julian's mother in "Everything That Rises Must Converge," derives her identity solely in relation to her family. Without her family connections it seems she would cease to be. The Misfit, on the other hand, derives his identity from his position as a marginal figure in society. When he describes his life experiences, it reads like a laundry list of things completely foreign to someone like the grandmother: he has been "in the arm service . . . been an undertaker, been with the railroads," and he has been in prison (149 [sic]). He has also been abroad, and she blames foreign influence for the deterioration of society: "in her opinion Europe was entirely to blame for the way things were now" (142). This is one of the few moments in the story that directly references World War II and its aftereffects, and one can infer that the Misfit's experiences in the "arm service, both land and sea" contributed to his present condition in life. He is a living example of the effect of the war and its repercussions on the southern order. O'Connor brings these two people together to show what happens when these worlds collide.

Initially, the grandmother cannot identify the Misfit: "The grandmother had the peculiar feeling that the bespectacled man was someone she knew. His face was as familiar to her as if she had known him all her life but she could not recall who he was" (146). Once she does recognize him, she tries to contain him by referring to his good blood. Her attempts to classify, and thus dismiss, him prevent her from really seeing him at all. It is only when she identifies him as another suffering person, confused and in need of love, that she recognizes him not as the Misfit, a man without a place in society, but as "one of my own children" (152). By naming him as one of her children, the grandmother finally recognizes her connection to the Misfit. The woman who wanted to travel to Tennessee to visit her relations, and to avoid meeting the Misfit, realizes that he is in fact also her kinsman. She is able to break through her isolationist, exclusionary belief system in order to embrace someone whom she has formerly marginalized. In the moment when her "head cleared for an instant," she intuits, perhaps not fully consciously, her own role in the creation of someone like the Misfit. The class-based prejudices that she has subscribed to and perpetuated throughout her life result in the marginalization of certain members of society. The Misfit is a societal outcast because people who have the same worldview as the grandmother have made him so, and imprisoned him as a way of attempting to control him.[6]

The Misfit, the prisoner who has escaped his imprisonment, is representative of a segment of society that was more or less created by the exclusionary practices of the White elite, and has now turned violent. In this story, we see that the patriarchal system, built on the violence and oppression of slavery, leads to the production of violent figures like the Misfit, who in turn contribute to the further disruption of order in the modern world. By naming him "one of my babies," the grandmother recognizes that her own actions have had an influence upon him, albeit an indirect one, and that she has in some way contributed to his exclusion from society. The man imprisoned for killing his family is adopted into a new one. This moment of recognition and acceptance cannot undo the violence set in motion by a long system of oppression, but it does, perhaps, provide a view of how systemic violence can change.

The grandmother's recognition of the authentic identity of the Misfit, not simply as a killer or as a societal outcast but as one who needs to be loved, marks her transformation from the self-interested woman who wants only to get her own way, the woman worried about what people will think of how she looks when she is dead, to the kind of person capable of leaving behind her old prejudices. Only when she is faced with the reality of the world that exists outside of her sphere of experience is she able to change; and, in O'Connor's vision, this encounter is necessarily violent. If it were not for the extreme violence, the shock of the moment, the grandmother would not have spent any time considering her prejudices. It is only after the violence forces her to rethink what she believes, and why she believes it, that she is able to identify with the Other; this identification moves her beyond the constraints of her stale ideology.

We can see the grandmother leave her prejudices behind, but the religious significance of this movement is less clear. What happens in the grandmother's soul to bring about her transformation? While I have thus far been focusing primarily on the social aspects of the story, there is a clear, overt Christian dimension here as well, because for O'Connor the two are inseparable. Although O'Connor famously advised her readers to "be on the lookout for such things as the action of grace in the Grandmother's soul, and not for the dead bodies" (*Mystery* 113), one does not need to turn to such extratextual commentary in order to see the metaphysical dimension to the text. O'Connor has the Misfit introduce this aspect himself. In a story filled with abrupt and jarring shifts in tone and plot, the Misfit's metaphysical and existential musings still stand out as particularly out of place. The grandmother, in the midst of the slaughter of the rest of her family, cries, "'Jesus. Jesus,' . . . as if she might be cursing," to which the Misfit replies, "'Yes'm . . . Jesus thown everything off balance'" (*Works* 151 [*sic*]). After more gunshots in the woods, the Misfit once again picks up this train of thought, "'If He did what He said, then it's nothing for you to do but thow away everything and follow Him, and if He didn't, then it's nothing for you to do but enjoy the few minutes you got left the best way you can—by killing somebody or burning down his house or doing some other meanness to him. No pleasure but meanness'" (152 [*sic*]). It is only when the Misfit reveals how incredibly lost he is, not only socially but spiritually as well, that the grandmother's "head clear[s] for an instant" and she reaches out to him. The grandmother's touch is a manifestation of a maternal love, and while we cannot know with any certainty what has changed inside of her to lead to this action, the context of the moment, with its discussion of Jesus's presence, leads us toward interpretations that include some aspect of the Christian mysteries. O'Connor provides the reader with enough information to induce thoughtful reflection, but not enough to provide total closure or certainty.

The grandmother's flash of recognition is a conversion moment, and it not only redeems the grandmother, it also leads to the potential change in the Misfit as well. Two places in the text mark his possible transformation. The first is immediately after he shoots the grandmother, when he removes his glasses to clean the blood off them. In a story where the grandmother's conversion was predicated on her ability to see things as they actually are, his move to clean his glasses is a symbol for his taking on new eyes to see the world. Without his glasses, his eyes appear "defenseless-looking"; he has let down his guard and is receptive to a new outlook on life (153). This new perspective is encapsulated in the last line, when he tells his accomplice, "It's no real pleasure in life" (153). If one pairs this line with what he said to the grandmother about there being two choices in life, following Christ completely or else living a violent life because life offers "no pleasure but meanness," then we see a transformation taking place. By rejecting all pleasures, he rejects the pleasure of meanness/violence as well; it is possible that he will then turn to the other choice he offered, and will then "thow away everything and follow [Christ]."[7] This line signals the possibility for personal and even social change. The violence of the modern world may be tempered by an encounter with the "manners" and values the grandmother represents, once they have been cleansed of their prejudices; and the violent nature of the individual might be redirected toward the good, if met with love rather than disdain.

But here, too, the story only hints at these outcomes. As readers, we are invited to reflect and question, because the story does not offer any clarity. Most readers who finish the story, without knowing anything about O'Connor or the general critical conversation around her work, will feel shocked by what has just happened. The radical change in tone, and the surprising murders that end the story, lead the reader to reassess what they've just read—to go back and look for clues earlier in the story that would point toward the eventual outcome.

When I first encountered this story as a college freshman in 1998, I was totally baffled by it, and my desire to figure out what was going on and what it at all meant led me to the upper floors of Hesburgh Library at Notre Dame, and eventually to writing my undergraduate Honors Thesis on O'Connor's fiction. I couldn't make sense of what I had read, and I spent more than a few hours puzzling over her stories, her letters, her essays, trying to put it all together. My experience was in line with the one discussed in *The Habit of Being*, where an English professor writes on behalf of him/herself, two colleagues, and their "some ninety university students" who cannot make sense of the story; their best interpretation is that the latter part of the story, from the Misfit's appearance onward, is "Bailey's dream" (436). It is easy for the contemporary reader, with the aid of existing scholarship, to chuckle at this response, but if we encounter O'Connor's work with no guidance at all, it can still be this confusing. Anyone who has ever taught "A Good Man Is Hard to Find" to undergraduates knows that not all readers (really, very few readers, in my experience) immediately recognize that the final moment of violence leads to transformation for either character. Often, those who do note it in class discussion admit that the reason they can see this change is because they went online to try to make sense of the ending. They were left confused and desiring answers, just as I was twenty-five years ago, but in the age of the internet these answers are right at hand.

In this sense, it is possible that O'Connor's fiction has lost some of its power to impact the reader. The stories still unsettle, still confuse. The violence in the stories still leaves the attentive reader asking questions, but whereas in the past answering these questions required a great deal of thought and personal reflection, today there is less need for this. Formerly, a reader would need to work hard at analyzing all elements of the carefully constructed plot in order to understand how O'Connor both sets up the grandmother's character and prepares her for the radical transformation that comes about when she discovers her kinship with the Misfit. Now, a brief internet search saves the reader from doing this work; O'Connor's "blasting annihilating light" is replaced by the dim lights of the search bar—which leaves one to wonder: if we don't have to work to arrive at conclusions or interpretations on our own, if we are never left truly shocked and disoriented for any length of time, will we still be affected in the same way? If O'Connor wanted to use violence to cause a form of disorientation that would then lead to reflection, the contemporary reader who is engaged enough to care about what has happened can skip past the personal reflection, where the true work of the story would take place.

This is not to say that O'Connor's stories are no longer powerful or effective. Clearly, new readers continue to discover her work and to be moved by it. The stories are not simply puzzle boxes to be solved, and even once we do understand what she is up to, and the violence is no longer quite as shocking or disruptive to our own sensibilities, there is much in the stories for the reader to reflect on, and engage with.

Wise Blood: "What's he getting out of doing it?"

If I am correct, readers finish "A Good Man" feeling confused, befuddled, and bewildered, and this is part of the deliberate strategy worked out by O'Connor. She wants the reader to feel this way because, as she explains in a number of places, she views confusion and disorientation as a, if not necessary then at least sufficient, precursor to seeing things anew. It is a central tool she uses to shape the reader's process of constructing meaning from the text. But it is worth asking whether this kind of disorientation is enough to actually change the reader's perception. Unlike the grandmother or Mrs. Turpin (or any number of other O'Connor protagonists), the reader is not directly experiencing the violence. Is being a befuddled witness enough to lead to change?

Interestingly enough, in *Wise Blood*, O'Connor's first novel, she addresses this directly in the character of Mrs. Flood, who—more than any other O'Connor character—functions as a reader surrogate. She stands in for O'Connor's imagined audience, the one who says, "I don't get it, I don't see it, I don't want it." Except here, Mrs. Turpin is forced to see "it," where the "it" is the violence of O'Connor's vision. And Mrs. Flood, like most contemporary, secular Americans, initially has no understanding of, or interest in, what she sees. It is horrifying and off-putting, and yet it still gets under her skin. Hazel's actions ultimately point Mrs. Flood toward the horizon beyond herself, and this is transformative. This is the same role that O'Connor's fiction can, potentially, play for the reader. It will not, in and of itself, save anyone, or bestow grace. But it might cause us to ask the questions that Mrs. Flood asks, leading us to ultimately question ourselves and our worldview.

The pattern of transformation found in *Wise Blood* is similar to the one in "A Good Man Is Hard to Find," except that the main character, Hazel, occupies the role of the Misfit rather than the grandmother (which is fitting since Hazel is far more like the crazed and violent Misfit than the somewhat benighted grandmother). Like the Misfit, Hazel is a man without a family or a permanent home; he is also a veteran who has suffered violence and lost his faith because of his difficult experiences in the world.[8] The Misfit was torn between a self-centered, nihilistic worldview and a radical embrace of Christianity; Hazel's novel-long struggle is between what he wants to believe—that nothing matters—and what his nature, his "wise blood," leads him to believe, which is that Christianity is real, and that nothing else truly matters. And, like the Misfit, Hazel murders a relatively innocent individual, only to hear an act of penance at the moment of the victim's death. Although we get no definitive insight into the state of Solace Layfield's soul, his deathbed confession indicates that he is attempting to atone for his sinful past and prepare himself for the afterlife; perhaps he, too, would have been a good person "if it had been somebody there to shoot [him] every minute of [his] life."

Of course, there are significant differences between Hazel's definitive transformation and the Misfit's possible one. If the Misfit does come to embrace Christianity, this conversion would take place because he was ultimately receptive to the grandmother's act of reaching out and positioning him as part of her own family. Hazel callously refuses to hear Solace's confession and is seemingly unaffected by his own murderous actions. He is not shocked out of his nihilistic worldview by his own violent actions.[9] He, like the grandmother, needs to suffer an assault from an outside force in order to recognize that he needs to relinquish his sense of total autonomy. The grandmother's moment of transformation is initiated by the destruction of her family car; Hazel's conversion is also directly linked to the loss of his automobile.[10]

While Hazel's murder of his double was his symbolic assault on the inauthenticity that he perceives in himself and his world, the destruction of his car is an external assault on Hazel's faith in his own unlimited freedom. Once his car is destroyed, he realizes that it could not take him where he needed to go. It leaves him in a moment of true existential dread, where he needs to face the reality of what he has been preaching all along: "'Where is there a place for you to be? No place'" (93). There is no other place for him to flee, and he is totally alone. As he tells Mrs. Flood, "'There's no other house nor no other city'" (129). Either he is alone and all is meaningless, or his inner compulsion, which has been telling him all along that he does need to be redeemed, is correct. Like the grandmother when she was faced with her death, Hazel has been brought to a place where he will either cling to his own understanding of the world or he will surrender it and be transformed.

It appears that he makes the latter decision; he ends up blinding himself, filling his shoes with glass and wrapping barbed wire around his chest, penitential acts that he performs "'To pay,'" although he refuses to offer any further explanation of what he is paying for (125). And it is this refusal of explanation that makes Hazel's story so fascinating. Because of the structure of the novel, we cannot know what has transpired inside of Hazel to bring about his conversion, or even what sort of belief he has converted to. The narrator denies us any insight into Hazel's consciousness, because after the moment in which he contemplates the wasteland that holds the wreckage of his automobile, the narrative voice is no longer focalized through Hazel. For a few paragraphs, as it details Hazel's refusal of the policeman's ride and his walk back into town and the purchase of the quicklime that he will use to blind himself, it maintains an objective tone. And then, as Hazel tells Mrs. Flood that he plans to blind himself, the point of view shifts to her consciousness. Everything else that happens to Hazel is mediated through Mrs. Flood's understanding of it.

This deliberate shift to the consciousness of a marginal figure, just as the main character is undergoing the conversion moment to which the entire novel has been building, serves as another example of O'Connor's ability to disorient even the most careful reader. The reader, even if he or she despises Hazel (as most do), is compelled to wonder why he has done what he has done, and although there are clues in the fiction, there is no definitive answer.[11] O'Connor refuses to give us the objective evidence we would need to make a definitive claim. In many of O'Connor's other stories we know the eventual fate of her characters, either because she explicitly tells it to us or she provides enough details to lead us to a point where the question becomes either a simple yes or no—was the character transformed by grace (usually presented via a moment of violence) or were they not? But in *Wise Blood*, while we know that Hazel has been transformed by the violence he experiences and perpetrates, it is unclear if this transformation is a positive one. It certainly does not look like we would expect such a transformation to look; Hazel's violence against his own body seems crazed, and his hostility to his landlady does not seem like the behavior of a grace-filled man. Hazel, after his transformation, appears, if possible, even more miserable than he was before, and he dies alone. If this is grace, it is unattractive at best—and yet the form of the novel indicates that something transcendent is at work here.

By shifting the narrative consciousness to Mrs. Flood, O'Connor preempts our inherent dismissal of Hazel's conversion; O'Connor provides us with a figure who asks the questions, and voices the objections, that we would like to make. And since Mrs. Flood is our proxy, her fascination with Hazel, and what his radical behavior represents, becomes our fascination as well. Mrs. Flood, like the grandmother (and really all of

O'Connor's heroines), is the object of O'Connor's irony, but she nevertheless offers a sane and rational critique of Hazel's actions. When she finds him throwing his money in the trash, she is incensed that he is wasting what could profitably be used to help "'the poor and needy'" (124); when she sees that he has wrapped himself in barbed wire, she says, "'What do you do these things for? It's not natural'" and then she clarifies that, if nothing else, "'it's not normal'" (126–27). She goes on to claim, "'It's like one of them gory stories, it's something that people have quit doing—like boiling in oil or being a saint or walling up cats. . . . There's no reason for it'" (127). While it is easy to make fun of this list of irrational acts (and it is supposed to be funny), she is not wrong; normal people do not become self-flagellating saints. Hazel's extreme ascetical practices are not normal, or rational, but to offer a rational explanation for them is to miss the point. While they do serve some crucial function in Hazel's own life, and the reader wonders, along with Mrs. Flood, just what this function is, in the novel itself the function of this violence is to shock—to arrest—Mrs. Flood, and the reader along with her. What does the encounter with Hazel's self-violence do to this normal, rational, generally unreflective woman, this character who voices our own concerns about the presence of such grotesque violence?

Every time Mrs. Flood learns of a new violent act that Hazel is committing against his own body, she becomes more disturbed, but also more interested. She spends her time contemplating him; he becomes a living sacrament[12]—a visible sign of an invisible reality. He is a concrete representation of an understanding of existence that has nothing to do with monetary gain, the pursuit of pleasure, or normalcy, and his witness changes Mrs. Flood. But if it were not for the violence of his actions, she would not have paid any attention to him; with each fresh act of mortification she discovers, her fascination grows. His declaration that he is blinding himself leads her to wonder, "What possible reason could a sane person have for wanting to not enjoy himself any more? She certainly couldn't say" (119). And although the chapter ends with that line, causing the question to linger in the reader's mind, the final chapter of the novel picks up with the exact same thought, "But she kept it in mind because after he had done it, he continued to live in her house and every day the sight of him presented her with the question" (120). This is the fundamental question that Hazel poses to Mrs. Flood, and that O'Connor poses to her readers: what in life is more valuable than enjoyment, and does this thing, whatever it may be, require suffering, or at least a type of surrender?

This double movement, of Hazel's violent act and Mrs. Flood's reflective questioning, provides a crucial interpretive model for O'Connor's work. The violence spurs the questions, but the questions are the things that truly matter. Reflection needs to follow on the heels of violence, if true transformation is to take place. Hazel is, for the most part, unwilling to fully engage Mrs. Flood's questions, which is a problem for some readers, since it reinforces the contention that Hazel is entirely isolated and shut off from community, which is a necessary part of the Christian faith. But I agree with Hank Edmondson, who claims that Hazel's brusque responses to Mrs. Flood are a form of "true charity" (71); rather than attempting to "make Mrs. Flood feel better . . . Haze, by his manner and disposition, unsettles his landlady, causing her to question the premise of her life, and ultimately, provoking her to examine her eternal future" (71). Hazel's harsh and often dismissive responses to Mrs. Flood's questions lead her to ask more penetrating questions, just as the continuing revelations of his self-mortification deepen her fascination. After discovering that he spends his days walking in shoes "lined with gravel and broken glass and pieces of small stone," Mrs. Flood "began to fasten all her attention on him, to the neglect of other things" (*Works* 125–26). She asks him why he does it, but his rude reply, "'Mind your business . . . You can't see,'" prompts her to ask a more reflective question: "'Do you think, Mr. Motes . . . that when you're dead, you're blind?'" (126). For a novel fixated on sight, Mrs. Flood's sudden interest in the afterlife, and the possibility for vision there, is an indication of transformation at work. Her interest only deepens after she finds out about the barbed wire; this leads to her questions about what is normal, or natural, and her assertion that Hazel only acts as he does because he "'must believe in Jesus'" (127). After this exchange, "Watching his face had become a habit[13] with her; she wanted to penetrate the darkness behind it and see for herself what was there" (127).

When his broken, dead body is returned to her, she can no longer ask him any questions. All she can do is contemplate his "stern and tranquil" face, and tell him, "'If you want to go on somewhere, we'll both go'" (131). Only he has already moved on, and because of his presence in her life, it seems that she will go on after him. The final paragraph of the novel indicates that she has finally consciously come to a moment of transformation. The violence inherent in Hazel's actions, and ultimately in his death, has brought her to a place where she will exchange one set of values, based on her own pleasure as the highest good, for something radically different, something that she cannot even accomplish on her own: "She shut her eyes and saw the pin point of light but so far away that she could not hold it steady in her mind. She felt as if she were blocked at the entrance of something. She sat staring with her eyes shut, into his eyes, and felt as if she had finally got to the beginning of something she couldn't begin, and she saw him moving farther and farther away, farther and farther into the darkness until he was the pin point of light" (131). Although she feels blocked, the entire structure of the chapter, which emphasizes her progressive vision, indicates that in this moment her ability to see Hazel until he becomes the light in the darkness indicates that he will serve as a guiding light for her. In O'Connor's Catholic theology, Mrs. Flood cannot begin this journey on her own. She needs grace to bring her along, and Hazel's witness will serve as that grace for her.

But even this final moment in the novel is ambiguous, since there is no absolute clarity about whether Mrs. Flood will try, or be able, to follow this "pin point of light." The reader is left to make the final evaluation of whether she will, or even if she should. And this freedom, of interpretation and choice, mirrors the reader's own position as they close the novel. If Mrs. Flood truly is our proxy character, if she raises our objections and is drawn past them, into the contemplation of mystery, then perhaps O'Connor is indicating that this is our position as well. Before she is pulled into the mystery of Hazel's final days, Mrs. Flood firmly believes she is in charge of her life and her actions—"she thought of her own head as a switch-box where she controlled from"—but Hazel's witness causes her to reflect on an entirely different orientation of understanding existence: "but with him, she could only imagine from the outside in" (*Works* 123). Once she begins to contemplate the possibility that there is an outside, beyond one's own sphere of influence and control, Mrs. Flood begins to wonder about her own limitations. Within the sphere of the novel, there is no absolute surety that Hazel is right, or that Mrs. Flood's intimations about the reality of a transcendent worldview are true. The reader is free to dismiss Hazel's actions as crazed and bizarre and still make rational sense of the novel, but the reader, like Mrs. Flood, is also left with a lingering question: "Who's he doing this for? she asked herself. What's he getting out of doing it?" (125). By not providing a definitive answer, O'Connor leaves us wondering. By denying the reader closure, O'Connor, in the words of her friend and official biographer, William Sessions, guides her audience in "an act of reading that was expected to lead to the most important act of all: contemplation" (241). Both for the characters within her fiction, and the readers of it, it is this contemplation, this reflection—more than the violence that precipitates it—that will bring about transformation.

2 / Disorientation and Reorientation in J. F. Powers's Fiction

While Flannery O'Connor is the most influential and acclaimed American Catholic novelist, her contemporary J. F. Powers is now the most overlooked; his work, though, can serve as an important counterweight to O'Connor's more extreme approach. Whereas O'Connor often utilizes shocking violence to affect her audience, Powers employs a subtler hand. To return to George Saunders's metaphor for the reading experience, when we enter the "black box" of an O'Connor story, what we often experience is a surprising slap in the face; with Powers, the experience is more like someone telling you a joke while simultaneously picking your pocket in the darkness. It is still unexpected and disorienting, but often we do not even notice what is actually happening until after the experience is over. In the end, though, it can be just as impactful. Both writers are equally critical of aspects of their secular society, but whereas O'Connor's stories are primarily oriented toward leading her audience to recognize the presence of grace at work in the world, Powers is more interested in alerting his audience to the persuasive power of false narratives, both that the culture at large is telling, but also the ones we tell ourselves.

Like O'Connor (and Percy), Powers received critical acclaim during his lifetime, having won the 1963 National Book Award over such literary luminaries as Vladimir Nabokov, Katherine Ann Porter, and John Updike, but by the time he died in 1999 his books were out of print.[1] Since then, the New York Review of Books has reissued them, but as Denis Donoghue writes in his introduction to *The Stories of J. F. Powers*, the audience for his work remains small, though devoted: "news of the [works'] quality is passed from one adept to another, like word of an idyllic village in an unfashionable part of France" (vii–viii). In his lifetime Powers, though never a terribly popular writer, was widely acknowledged as a masterful storyteller with an important message. Shortly after meeting Powers, Thomas Merton described him as "a man with the hand of God on him" (*Solitude* 58), and O'Connor called Powers "one of the country's finest short story writers" and "the best [comic novelist] we have" (*Presence* 14, 168). But in the twenty-first century, even among readers and critics of Catholic literature, his work is overlooked.[2] He has, in Donna Tartt's words, fallen into "obscurity and neglect" (69).

The most common explanation for why this is the case is the simplest: because, as his *New York Times* obituary headline read, he "Wrote about Priests," and contemporary readers and critics, Catholic and secular alike, are uninterested in reading about the trials and tribulations of pre–Vatican II Catholic clergymen. Critics claim these stories are about a world that no longer exists, so there is little reason to revisit them, except out of a sense of duty or nostalgia. As Joseph Bottum, writing in *First Things*, claimed, "The major reason for the fading of J. F. Powers is the decline of his topic once the reforms of Vatican II took hold—or rather, once what was perceived in America to be the 'spirit' of Vatican II had destroyed the setting of his fiction." Paul Elie, himself a noted scholar of midcentury American Catholic writers, identifies a similar "narrow and dated" quality to Powers's work: "Powers sought to portray the priest as a perennial figure, an everyman skirting the lures and snares of prosperous postwar America; but the very vividness and specificity of his portraiture made it clear that his priests—local potentates chafing under ecclesiastic authority but never challenging it openly—were figures from the era before the Second Vatican Council and its reforms" ("Bartleby" 84).

While it is certainly true that he writes primarily (though not exclusively) about the daily lives of priests operating in a Catholic milieu largely unlike our own, this does not mean that these stories can no longer speak to our contemporary moment. On the contrary, in his depictions of the Church struggling with how to engage with the modern world, and his exploration of how power and popularity can be a corrupting influence on the American psyche, Powers's fiction is incredibly relevant to our own time. These are issues the Church, and American culture at large, continue to grapple with, and Powers's work can be an important interlocutor in these discussions.

Powers resisted the idea that because of his clerical subject matter the themes of his work were only relevant for a limited audience. When a reviewer described *Morte D'Urban* as "a book for Catholics," Powers responded by asking, "Would you say that *The Wind in the Willows* is a book for animals?" (Malloy 8). Powers claimed he wrote about priests because "I want to deal with things I find important, like life and death. Officially, the priest has to believe those things are important. Every man should" (8). In this sense, the main themes of his work are similar to O'Connor's, who claimed that "every great drama naturally involves the salvation or loss of the soul," and "the writer operates at a peculiar crossroads where time and place and eternity somehow meet" (*Mystery* 167, 59). Powers writes about priests not in order to appeal to a uniquely Catholic audience, but because he wants to explore the juxtaposition of day-to-day reality and this kind of eternal vision; as he wrote, "[Priests] are officially committed to both worlds in a way most people officially are not" (Malloy 8). As discussed in the previous chapter, O'Connor's stories usually end with a moment of insight, where the formerly unaware individual gains a new perspective on transcendence; Powers's stories about priests, though, often begin with this insight as a given, and he explores whether this kind of mindset really affects how people act.

And ultimately this question of how one's faith interacts with one's behavior is what interests Powers and plays a central role in his fiction. For Powers, this was not an academic question. The tension between faith and the world played an important role in his own life as well. Powers lived a rather undramatic life,[3] but one aspect of his biography that stands out is how his early commitment to a radical understanding of Catholicism affected the way he engaged with the world. Katherine A. Powers, Powers's daughter and the editor of *Suitable Accommodations: An Autobiographical Story of Family Life: The Letters of J. F. Powers, 1942–1963*, notes how her father's faith was shaped by the Detachment movement, which she describes as "possibly the most forgotten strain in the nearly forgotten American Catholic countercultural religious and social ferment of the mid-twentieth century" (xvii). Detachment preached the importance of "detaching oneself from unnecessary material things and earthly desire"; Powers was particularly drawn to the movement's "criticism of American materialism and militarism, and its rebuke to complacent middle-class Catholics, who, for all their manifest religiosity, put 'business sense' first" (xvii). Both Katherine Powers and John Hagopian, author of the first monograph on Powers, note that Powers's Catholicism was particularly influenced by a 1943 retreat led by Fr. John Hugo, the same priest whose retreats played an important role in Dorothy Day's faith.[4] Robert Ellsberg, who edited Day's journal and letters, writes that Hugo's retreats, "which emphasized the universal call to holiness, intensified [Day's] already demanding spirituality" (viii); Powers's exposure to the retreat seemed to have a similar, radicalizing effect. During World War II, Powers declared himself a pacifist and refused to appear for military service. After being refused conscientious objector status (pacifism was not recognized as a legitimate option for Catholics until 1965), Powers was "sentenced to three years at Sandstone Federal Penitentiary in Minnesota," though he only served a little over a year (*Suitable* 4).

His letters from these years contain a number of references to the plans he and a few fellow COs were developing for a communal farm; he described it as a place where "we will get our living from the earth. A living is not so much as the light companies and grocers try to make city people think. It will be a risk of course. I'm dead sure 'risk' is the magic word. The condition of the cities is due to the fact that people will not risk anything to live. They would rather die for not living" (*Suitable* 8). Eventually, in his fiction, he focuses this critique of contemporary Americans unwilling to risk their own comforts primarily on the institution of the Catholic Church, both its clergy and parishioners. In part, this is because he comes to realize that all of society—secular and religious alike—suffers from a kind of blindness. As he writes in a later letter, "I used to give the businessmen a rough go [in fiction], and the mistake was in limiting such treatment too much to them" (9). He writes that his time in the penitentiary "matured" him, and by this he means he lost his naivety about what holiness and sanctity look like: "the innocents I find are ever harder to find than before. I am thinking of alleged pacifist societies and related groups. . . . I was somewhat taken in by 'do-good' organizations" (9). He does not turn his back on the Church, or even on the sorts of pacifist societies he associated with, but both in his life and in his fiction he comes to view them with a more nuanced eye. He is able to celebrate what is unique about them, while still acknowledging their shortcomings. And it is this nuance that appears in his fiction and makes it continually relevant, and affecting. As the literary critic Paul Giles notes, Powers's "work ironically surveys the contradictions between spirit and matter, rather than simply relapsing into that easier satirical mode of denigrating all secular interests. . . . Consequently there is a lack of certainty and closure in Powers's texts that most Catholic critics, too keen to pick out satirical moralizing, have been oblivious to" (437).

"Prince of Darkness": "Not Peace but a Sword"

This lack of closure is one of the reasons Powers's fiction is worth revisiting. In both of his novels and in many of his short stories he directly takes on the question of how the Catholic Church should engage with the modern world, and he resists easy answers. Although, as I argue below, I believe *Morte D'Urban* to be Powers's true masterpiece, many readers and critics respond most strongly to his short stories. His stories contain a spark and a vitality that hold up to close reading and invite reflection, and his best stories can continually surprise and affect the reader. Like his Catholic contemporaries, Powers does employ strategies of disruption to unsettle and upend readers' and characters' expectations, leading to moments where new insight, and grace, are present—though often overlooked. As soon as we think we have a clear read on who is "right" in a given story, Powers tilts the perspective ever so slightly, leaving us second-guessing our too-easy conclusions. In this way, his stories work to create a more attentive and thoughtful reader. He continually aligns our perspective with protagonists who seem to subscribe to reasonable—even correct—views of the social order, only to reveal in a final, subtle twist that they have been self-deluded all along.[5] In so doing, his stories force the reader to think about the ways that we also subscribe to false narratives about what truly matters in life. As the powerful closing lines of "Prince of Darkness" state, his work offers the reader "not peace but a sword" (*Stories*, 213).

Despite the violence inherent in this image (a reference to Matthew 10:34), Powers's work is not saturated with the kind of violence we find in O'Connor, or even in Percy's novels (though it is often still present, albeit in comical form). Some stories do focus on death (as in "Lions, Harts, Leaping Does"), or violence against nature (as in "The Lord's Day"), or the violence of nature (as in "Look How the Fish Live"), but for the most part his stories are more focused on the personal suffering that comes from experiencing broken dreams and worldly disappointments. In Powers's work, the "sword" of disappointment helps prune the soul, and the violence and cruelty of the world can lead to contemplation, if not always to clarity. Below I focus on how a small moment of somewhat comical violence does function as a key turning point in *Morte D'Urban*, but it is worthwhile to spend time unpacking "Prince of Darkness" first, because this story can serve as a helpful introduction to Powers's themes and methods.

"Prince of Darkness" follows one day in the life of Fr. Burner, a disappointed priest who has been continually passed over for promotion to pastor of his own parish. He spends his time "brood[ing] upon his failure as a priest. . . . He was forty-three, four times transferred, seventeen years an ordained priest, a curate yet and only. He was the only one of his class still without a parish" (192–93). Why, exactly, he has been continually passed over and moved around the diocese is never explicitly stated. For the contemporary reader, a story about a mid-twentieth-century priest being transferred from parish to parish immediately calls to mind stories of abusive, predatory priests, and the Catholic Church's shameful practice of shuffling them between parishes, but Powers does not take the story in this direction.[6] Rather, it seems—at least initially—that Fr. Burner's failure to thrive in the priesthood is tied to his unwillingness, and inability, to engage in the kind of political maneuvering that is required for advancement. Since this is the primary critique directed at a priest like Fr. Urban in *Morte D'Urban*, Fr. Burner's rejection of this kind of politicking might initially lead the reader to think his lack of worldly success is a mark of his holiness, but Powers demonstrates that this is not the case.

By the end of the story, the reader comes to understand that the reason Fr. Burner fails to advance is not because he is too pure for worldly success, but rather because he is not a particularly good priest. On some level, Fr. Burner understands this about himself, even if he fails to recognize that this is why he is not given his own parish. His belief that he deserves a promotion is not tied to a deep commitment to his vocation, but rather to the simple idea that after a set amount of time in any position, one deserves to advance. He acknowledges that for him the priesthood is a job like any other, "a temporal part to be played, almost . . . a doctor's or lawyer's" (196). And over the course of the story, we see him, for the most part, play this role half-heartedly. He spends his days golfing, drinking, and flying a plane, rather than in prayer or ministry.

Despite the "prince of darkness" nickname, though, he is not depicted as an overtly sinister figure. There are a few places in the story where Powers shows Fr. Burner acting uprightly. He goes to visit his friend who is sick in the hospital; he spends time thinking about themes for homilies and offering up prayers (albeit in a rote fashion). The story opens with him rejecting an insurance salesman's offer because he is able to see that this salesman represents immorality (or at least amorality): "In [the salesman] he sensed free will in its senility or the infinite capacity for equating evil with good—or with nothing—the same thing, only easier" (172). By tying the narrative perspective closely to Fr. Burner, Powers invites the reader to sympathize with Burner's point of view. Only when we come to the end of the story do we fully realize that this indictment—the inability to differentiate between good, evil, and nothingness—is what truly defines Fr. Burner's character (just as, for Powers, it defines many of his readers as well).

In the final movement of the story, Fr. Burner has been asked to hear confessions at the Cathedral. Since it is "common procedure . . . for the

Archbishop to confer promotions by private interview," Fr. Burner assumes that this is the real reason he is being summoned to the Cathedral. Because of his preoccupation with whether he is going to be promoted, he is an inattentive confessor. Powers uses this moment to perfectly encapsulate Fr. Burner's failure as a priest. At the last possible moment, a young woman enters the confessional; she is hesitant and nervous, but instead of taking the time to understand what has brought her back to the Church for the first time in years, Fr. Burner is impatient and disinterested. He badgers her with questions about her sex life and use of birth control, which leads her to shut down. What could have, should have, been an encounter that leads to grace and mercy instead turns into a scene of disconnection and frustration. Fr. Burner does not recognize his failure here, but the reader does.

On the heels of this failure, he meets with the Archbishop. Throughout the interview, Fr. Burner continually says whatever he thinks the Archbishop wants to hear, while repeatedly failing to hear what the Archbishop is actually saying to him. The Archbishop says, "'Today there are few saints, fewer sinners and everybody is already saved. . . . As for villains, the classic kind with no illusions about themselves, they are . . . extinct. The very devil, for instance—where the devil is the devil today, Father?'" Fr. Burner can offer no insight, leading the Archbishop to finally say, "'I think we should look—to ourselves, the devil in us.'" Fr. Burner agrees, but only because he "knew the cue for humility when he heard it" (210). If he were able, in this moment, to actually take the time to reflect on how his whole idea of himself is filled with illusions and delusions, this might be a turning point for him. But throughout the exchange all he is focused on is "the really important thing, to kiss the Archbishop's ring and receive his blessing" (212). As in the earlier confessional scene, this encounter is an opportunity for grace, but it is one that Fr. Burner is missing out on because his attention is elsewhere. He is consumed by his interest in temporal affairs, and so is unaware of the possibility for true insight and change.

The story ends with Fr. Burner opening the appointment letter from the Archbishop, which notifies him of his transfer to another parish assistant position; the letter (and the story) closes with the line "'I trust that in your new appointment you will find not peace but a sword'" (213). Based on everything we have seen from Fr. Burner, there is little reason to believe that this fresh disappointment will actually lead to new insight into his failings as a priest, or the ways the devil may, indeed, be inside of him. But by paying close attention to the ways that Fr. Burner has earned this sort of temporal rebuke, we as readers might come to be more attentive to the ways that we too carry around our own illusions, and how these illusions interfere with our ability to recognize or accept our own moments of grace. Powers's stories are subtle, and they call for careful readerly attention in order to fully grasp what he is up to. They help create a reader who is patient and aware, character traits that Fr. Burner is noticeably lacking, and ones that—if fully developed—can help us as individuals to be less focused on kissing the ring and more attentive to opportunities for true connection and communion with those around us.

Morte D'Urban and the Modern World

Fr. Burner is a failure of a priest on a number of levels. Powers's first novel, *Morte D'Urban*, focuses on the fortunes of Fr. Urban Roche, who is outwardly successful in ways that Fr. Burner could only dream of, though one of the main themes of the novel is what, exactly, true success actually looks like (indeed, the novel functions, in part, as a thorough indictment of most readers' conventional ideas of success). Urban is the most charismatic and outgoing member of the Clementines, an Order "unique in that they were noted for nothing at all" (15). He is a gifted speaker and fundraiser, but his efforts to improve his Order are, for the most part, unappreciated by his superiors. At the beginning of the novel he is hoping to be named provincial of the Order but is instead exiled to the community's retreat house in the hinterlands of Minnesota. Once there, he undergoes a series of comical trials, as he attempts to improve the run-down retreat house (mainly by buying up nearby land and building a golf course, so that they can attract "people who really mattered" to come as retreatants [99]), while continuing to fundraise for the Order by resuming his preaching and traveling retreat work. He experiences a number of successes on these fronts, only to ultimately be brought low after being struck in the head by the local bishop's errant golf ball. After this, most of the apparent progress he had made, both in terms of the material success of the Order, as well as in personal relationships with a few wealthy benefactors, is undone. In a final twist, the novel ends with him finally being elected provincial, though by this point his head injury has severely debilitated him, and he "wasn't himself" (312). Whether he is ultimately a better person and priest by the end of the novel is a question I return to later.

When I first read the novel, shortly after graduating from college, I had a similar sensation to when I first read O'Connor: I felt disoriented by the actions of the plot. In the novel, a seemingly "good man" comes to experience an unlooked-for downfall, and I wasn't quite sure why it happened, or what it was supposed to mean. As H. Wendell Howard notes, because of Powers's unwillingness to explain character's motivations, or to pass authorial judgment on what happens, "it is easy for [the reader] to be bewildered about Powers's intent" (85). This was certainly my initial experience of the work. Is Urban a hero brought low by the incompetence of the people around him, and then by a meaningless, freak accident, or is there something else at work? Clearly, Powers intends for it to be the latter, but it took time and attention for me to understand this. Indeed, shortly after reading the novel for the first time, I told a priest friend of mine that he reminded me of Urban, and I meant it as a compliment. This priest was excellent with people, and a bit of a mover and shaker in his religious Order, and I saw in Urban's virtues the things I admired in my friend. It was only on a reread of the novel that I understood why my friend did not seem to view the comparison as purely a compliment.

I returned to the novel after coming across Thomas Merton's review, "J. F. Powers—*Morte D'Urban*: Two Celebrations," in his *Literary Essays*, in which Merton is highly critical of Urban's character. As I read his critique of Urban, I barely recognized the man whom Merton was describing; I had to ask myself if I had totally misread the novel. Indeed, in large part I had; but even upon revisiting the book, I am not sure that I find Merton's critique to be totally accurate, and this is what makes the book so compelling. It resists easy classifications.

In Merton's view, Urban is "the kind people like to call a 'good priest' without reservation and without resentment because his zeal is just the kind they have been taught to admire. He is not trying to be holy. He is not trying to encourage crackpot movements. He is not mixed up with radicals, pacifists, or integrationists. He is just a great guy with people, particularly if they happen to have money" (150). Of course, for Merton, these are not traits that actually define a good priest. He goes on to point out the emptiness at Urban's core: "We find in him empty gregariousness, not friendship. Verbalism, but not much to say. Cleverness, not talent or intelligence. His clerical zeal, though energetic, is based on an assumed equation between his own enlightened self-interest and the interests of the Church. He owes it to the Church to be a 'winner,' doesn't he? How else is the Church going to be respected in a competitive and affluent society?" (150). Merton is right that many readers view Urban as a good priest because he succeeds at integrating the Church into mainstream American society, but this is precisely why, in Merton's view, he is a failure for the majority of the novel—because integration into, and acceptance by, American society is not what the Church should be striving toward.

Merton's reading of the novel is in line with the general critical consensus; the most common interpretation claims that the novel traces an arc in which Urban loses his urbanity, and "recovers his vocation and is reborn, a sadder and wiser priest" (Meyers). Hagopian spells it out in even starker terms: "The plot can be seen as the experience of a man who uses the priesthood as an instrument for worldly success until a traumatic event shocks him into awareness that compromise with the mammon of iniquity is morally and spiritually degrading. Then, as his mortal self declines, he gradually sets his own soul in order, without false piety and even without conscious deliberation" (134). This is also more or less how Powers himself understood his text; he describes the Urban of the end of the novel as "a wiser man and a better man" than he was earlier in the novel, since "he has lost this aggressive 'be a winner' kind of thing" (Malloy 13).

Although *Morte D'Urban* can certainly be read this way, I contend it is actually a more complicated novel than this; rather than offering such a stark contrast between worldliness and holiness, it instead poses a series of unanswered questions. What is the proper relationship between the Church and contemporary society? What amount of worldly success should the Church, or even the individual, strive for? Can one be both holy and successful, or holy and powerful? These were particularly timely questions for the American Catholic Church in the 1950s, when, as Jay Dolan makes clear, the Church had achieved a new level of mainstream acceptance. He writes that "Catholics seemed to sit at the top of the world during these years. Every index suggested that they had embraced the American way of life and still remained staunchly Catholic" (182). But Paul Giles indicates that, as the decade progressed, "social conformity" became a defining trait of midcentury American Catholicism, and he notes that this posed a problem for the Church; in the 1950s a common critique of Catholics was that they "were becoming just too conformist, too patriotic" (429). *Morte D'Urban*, through the character of Fr. Urban, foregrounds this tension between conforming to American ideas of success and maintaining a distinctly Catholic identity.

Powers said that in his initial vision for the novel, by the time Urban gets his desire to be named provincial of the Order, he would be "out of his mind" because "anyone who became provincial of the order would just naturally be deficient or else how could he ever be elected—you know, like the presidency. How, having the public we have, can they throw up anybody but one of themselves, since they vote?" (Malloy 13). This deep distrust of public power and authority does come through in the novel. The bishop is depicted as a petty tyrant, obsessed with his own power and authority. Fr. Wilf, who is in charge of the retreat house when Urban arrives, also revels in the little authority he has, using it poorly. In fact, Powers does not give the reader any models of powerful people using their authority wisely. At the same time, he also fails to give us any true depictions of holiness, unless the reader believes, as several critics—including Merton and Hagopian—have claimed, that the Urban of the final pages has acquired a new level of sanctity. I am not fully convinced of this, as I discuss below. But before assessing the novel's final turn, it is worth examining in more detail how Powers constructs his indictment of Urban's worldliness.

Disorientation and Reorientation in *Morte D'Urban*

To appreciate what, exactly, Powers is up to in *Morte D'Urban*, it may be helpful to return to his more famous contemporary Flannery O'Connor and contrast their approaches. Although Powers's work does not share many surface-level similarities with O'Connor's stories of small-town farmers or backwoods "freaks," the two Catholic writers do share a few important traits, particularly in terms of theme and technique. The most obvious structural similarity between *Morte D'Urban* and much of O'Connor's fiction is the significance of violence as a turning point in a character's narrative arc. As discussed in the previous chapter, O'Connor famously stated, "I have found that violence is strangely capable of returning my characters to reality and preparing them to accept their moment of grace" (*Mystery* 112). In a similar vein, Powers claimed Urban needed the physical violence of the "hit on the head" from the bishop's golf ball, because "nothing else could have slowed up a man like Urban" (Malloy 13). But unlike most O'Connor stories, where the moment of violence either ends the story (see, for instance, "A Good Man Is Hard to Find" or "Greenleaf"), or is followed by a denouement where the character clearly arrives at a moment of insight (as in "Revelation"), Urban's story continues on for another eighty-five pages after he is knocked unconscious by the bishop's golf ball, and he is not consciously aware that this moment of violence has changed him. The attentive reader, though, will recognize that even though this particular moment is a form of triumph for Urban (the bishop decides not to claim the golf course for the diocese, largely—it seems—out of guilt over injuring Urban), this is the last "worldly" success he has, until he is named provincial of the Clementines. After his injury, he suffers a series of setbacks, and the careful reader is forced to ask why this happens, and what Powers is up to here.

These questions lead to the other important connection to O'Connor's work. The moment of violence within the text, which leads to the character's change, is really just a precursor to the change that takes place within the reader. The reader needs to reevaluate his or her expectations—not only about what the author is doing, but about the entire world of the text—in order to understand what is happening. Paul Ricoeur provides a helpful framework for this process of disorientation and reorientation in *The Symbolism of Evil*, where he describes a necessary movement from a first to second naiveté. The movement between these stages requires that we gain a critical distance, where we become disabused of our false views of existence.[7] Powers, like O'Connor, uses the moment of violence as the means of achieving this critical distance, for his characters and for the reader.

Ricoeur's theory of reading prioritizes both the way the text is constructed by an author and the role of the reader in constituting the meaning of the text. For Ricoeur, the true meaning of a text is produced via the encounter between the differing worldviews of author/text and reader: "Only when the world of the text is confronted with the world of the reader . . . does the literary work acquire a meaning in the full sense of the term, at the intersection of the world projected by the text and the life-world of the reader" (*Time* 2:160). The reader comes to the text with a set of assumptions, just as the writer does. Productive engagement takes place when these assumptions rub up against each other and get rearranged. For Ricoeur, reading literature that provokes, shocks, offends, or disorients results in a struggle with the text, which can "lead the reader back to himself" ("Between" 395). This disorienting encounter with a strange and hostile text can lead to "a dynamics of reorientation" for the reader, and it is just this process of orientation, followed by disorientation, culminating in a final reorientation that is at work in *Morte D'Urban*.

The novel begins with a process of orientation to a familiar world—midcentury American Catholicism. Jay Dolan notes that in most parishes in the 1950s, the priest still "represented the authority of the church, and few questioned his role as the parish chieftain" (183). As Merton observes, Urban initially fits this model and strikes the reader as an embodiment of a "good priest." We assume that the worldview of the third-person narrative voice, which paints him in a mostly positive light, is reliable. The reader becomes disoriented once he or she realizes that this assumption is incorrect. It may take the reader quite some time to figure out that the third-person point of view is not an objective, disinterested perspective, but is in fact being focalized through Urban. Powers is a master of controlling point of view, and he uses it to ironize Urban, although it is not always clear where the irony begins or ends. Some of Urban's judgments are clearly meant to be misguided, but in other instances it seems that although he has a biased perspective on people or events, his version of reality is not entirely off base. We see this right from the start of the novel, in the aptly titled "Overture." In this opening section, as in a symphonic overture, we are introduced to most of the key themes of the work that will be developed in more depth and detail throughout the rest of the piece.

The first sentence of the Overture is, "It had been a lucky day for the Order of St Clement the day Mr Billy Cosgrove entered the sacristy of a suburban church after Mass and shook the hand of Father Urban" (*Morte* 7). The reader initially has no reason to doubt that this is a true claim; indeed, as the novel progresses we come to learn that Billy is rich, and generous with his money. His support allows the Clementines to move to a "prestigious address" in Chicago (12), a location that Urban believes will both help the Order to attract other wealthy benefactors and entice "superior lads" to join the Order (16). This drive to improve the Clementines seems to be a good one, since we as readers have no reason to doubt Urban's assessment that "the Order of St Clement labored under the curse of mediocrity" (15). The Overture concludes with Urban's assessment of the state of the Order: "The Order wasn't up to the job of being an effective influence for good on the near North Side, or anywhere else in the fast-changing world of today. . . . There had to be a new approach" (16).

Once we realize that Urban's perspective is not necessarily Powers's, we need to go back and rethink these passages. How much of Urban's indictment, if any, is still true? There is a temptation, once the reader discovers that the narrative point of view is not totally reliable, to discard all of Urban's assessments, but this would be a mistake. Even after completing the entire novel, there does not appear to be any reason to doubt Urban's assertion that the Order is mediocre.[8] Indeed, his final claim about the Order—that it needs to adapt or die—seems to be prescient. Powers clearly does not endorse Urban's initial desire to improve the Order by cultivating wealthy donors and aligning it further with mainstream American ideas of success, but as the epigraph of the novel states, "The life of every man is a diary in which he means to write one story, and writes another . . ." (3). The story Powers meant to write is an indictment of Urban's worldliness, but with time and distance it is possible to see that, despite all his many flaws, perhaps Urban was on to something after all.

Certainly, Urban is too caught up in ideas of power, success, winning. He is, undeniably, too worldly. But in his embrace of the other side of the equation—in his outright rejection of worldly standards—Powers may have gone too far. As his collected letters make clear, Powers himself was a man who refused to engage with the world's expectations. As Katherine Powers's introduction notes, "'We have here no lasting home' was his constant refrain," and she indicates that he seemed to think this concept excused his refusal to settle down and provide for his growing family (xx). She writes, "While Jim prided himself on having a clear, unillusioned perception of how things really worked, when it came to adapting to reality, he was not one for making suitable accommodations himself" (xx). While I don't want to read too much of his own personal life into his fiction (though the letters do make it clear that he often mined his own experiences for his stories), there does seem to be a parallel between his own rejection of the modern age in favor of the world to come and his final depiction of Urban's total disengagement as a victory over "mammon."

The novel clearly shows that Urban's pursuit of worldly success was misguided and divorced from spiritual perfection and holiness, but the events of the plot also indicate that there is something worthwhile in Urban's early actions. There is a line between being holy and being ineffectual. If no one goes to the retreat house, if no one listens to a preacher's sermon (or if no one reads the book), then no one will be changed. Hearts and minds cannot be won if the ones out there trying to win them are terrible at the work they do. This is Urban's repeated claim throughout the book, and while Powers does his best to undermine this kind of worldly thinking through the structure of the novel, it remains a persuasive argument. To read the Urban of the end of the novel, who is diminished in nearly all ways and seems to be entirely uninterested in finding a "new approach" for leading the Order in the modern age, as a model of wisdom and sanctity seems to be more about finding in the text what we expect to find, rather than what is actually there.

And this is, ultimately, what makes *Morte D'Urban* one of the great Catholic novels. It is not simply an amusing tract against American ideas about worldly success. It acknowledges the contradictions at the heart of the Church in the modern world. The Church is a worldly institution, and it needs to be one in order to be effective. There is a common phrase, that Christians should be "in the world, not of the world"; but while many critics have focused on how the novel ultimately makes the case for not being of the world, it is important to note that it also, at the same time, acknowledges the need to be *in* the world—engaged with people where they are.

In this light, the Urban we see at the end of the novel serves as a demonstration that rejecting the ways of the world is not enough. It is true that he is no longer obsessed with gaining power, or promoting his own brand, but while it is undeniably good that Urban has let go of these particularly American concepts of what success looks like, it would be a mistake to think that in doing so he has automatically become saintly. Renunciation of worldly desires and pursuits is not sufficient. Most critics assume that Urban has replaced his false idols with true sanctity. For instance, Robert Benson, in his essay "Purgatory in the Midwest: The White Martyrdom of Urban Roche," makes the case that in his "removal from the world [Urban] finds peace and his true vocation" (184), and Hagopian describes the final version of Urban as a "humble and even saintly figure" (136). But the text does not really show this. Catholic readers are trained to expect that the protagonist will come to reorient himself to a right and true idea of the good, but we should not let our expectations about what we will find blind us to what is actually present in the text. Urban comes to reject worldly materialism, but he does not seem to replace it with anything transcendent, or immanent.

Powers writes that, as provincial, Urban is viewed as a failure: "Seldom had a new Provincial so badly disappointed the hopes and calculations of men" (*Morte* 333). We might expect that this is yet another incident of viewing Urban's actions through the lens of worldly success, and that his failures in this regard are actually triumphs. Indeed, Urban gains a "reputation for piety," which Powers tells us is "not entirely unwarranted" (334), though this tepid endorsement is not particularly backed up by Urban's actions. He gains the reputation for holiness because the aftereffects of his concussion cause him to spend lots of time with his head bowed and eyes closed, waiting out the pain of the attack, which leads others to think him lost in prayer. But it does not appear that this is really the case; rather, he is, as others in the Order suspect, "not well" (334). Merton counseled that modern Christians trying to bring about change should "not depend on the hope of results" but should instead foster real connection with other people, because "in the end . . . it is the reality of personal relationships that saves everything" (*Hidden* 294). The Urban of the early parts of the novel is clearly too focused on results, but if Merton is right, and personal relationships are truly at the heart of Christian practice, then Urban is still failing here as well, since, as provincial, "he did his best to see as few people as possible" (*Morte* 334). The Urban of the end of the novel is a sick and diminished figure. He may no longer be committed to a false idea of the good, but there is little reason to think that he is now reoriented toward true holiness.

If we reject the traditional American model of worldly success, we need to replace it with something, but Powers does not offer us a clear model of what this might look like. It is worth noting that this is not necessarily a failure on Powers's part, since simply by raising the issue he leads his readers to consider the problem. Ricoeur claims, "The moment when literature attains its highest degree of efficacy is perhaps the moment when it places its readers in the position of finding a solution for which they themselves must find the appropriate questions, those that constitute the aesthetic and moral problem posed by the work" ("Between" 407). In *Morte D'Urban*, readers are led to ask themselves just these sorts of questions. If Urban's initial driving focus is misguided, how then should he act? Rejection and renunciation are not enough.

"An effective influence for good": *Morte D'Urban's* Vision of Success

And here is where the novel does connect, again, to the contemporary moment, and the state of the Catholic Church under Pope Francis. Although he is the exact opposite of Urban in many ways, Pope Francis is committed to a vision of the Church that is engaged with the world, and he recognizes the need to reach people by meeting them where they are at in life, using a pastoral approach to find common ground with them. In one of his first interviews after being elected pope, Francis laid out his vision for the Church: "This church with which we should be thinking is the home of all, not a small chapel that can hold only a small group of selected people. We must not reduce the bosom of the universal church to a nest protecting our mediocrity" (Spadaro). He goes on to say, "The thing the church needs most today is the ability to heal wounds and to warm the hearts of the faithful; it needs nearness, proximity." He calls for a Church that, like Urban in the early parts of the novel, goes out into the world to meet people where they are: "Instead of being just a church that welcomes and receives by keeping the doors open, let us try also to be a church that finds new roads, that is able to step outside itself and go to those who do not attend Mass, to those who have quit or are indifferent."

Clearly Urban is not a perfect model of this type of evangelization. His preaching is directed not at the marginalized, but at the well-heeled, and he is too dedicated to trying to make inroads with what he considers "people who really mattered" (*Morte* 99). He embodies what Pope Francis, in *Evangelii Gaudium*, condemns as "spiritual worldliness," a mentality focused on "social and political gain" and "a concern to be seen," which leads to an embrace of "a social life full of appearances, meetings, dinners and receptions" (95). But Pope Francis, in the same document, also declares that the missionary heart of the Church "never closes itself off, never retreats into its own security, never opts for rigidity and defensiveness" (45). And this is something that Urban also sees and critiques about the Clementines; he does recognize the flaws in the insularity of his Order and his Church.

While some critics look to his behavior as provincial as the mark of his spiritual triumph, his most telling success in the novel is really found in the parish of St. Monica's. It is here, when he is working as a substitute pastor, that he is able to, in his own words, "live and work as a *priest*" (*Morte* 117, emphasis in original). For Urban, this means administering the sacraments, but also going out to meet with parishioners and planning for a renovation and expansion of the church and its parish hall. Powers sets up a dichotomy between Urban and Monsignor Renton, a more conservative priest, who believes that "any time not spent at the altar, or in administering the sacraments, was just time wasted for a priest" (151). Renton goes on to lament, "'Forty years ago, we weren't expected to do so much selling, nagging, and hand-holding'" (152). Powers seems to think that Renton has the right perspective here, since the monsignor, acting as Urban's confessor, is able to give penetrating and necessary advice to him: "'Whatever else we do, let's not put ourselves between God and the people—or let them put us between them and Him as too often happens nowadays'" (151). Urban certainly is guilty of putting himself forward and mistaking his own personal successes as successes for the Church, but this does not mean that Renton is necessarily right about the role of the priest. Another character in the novel describes this as a conflict between a "priest-promoter" and a "priest-priest" (154). Urban contends that "'a man *has* to be both,'" and that fulfilling both roles means being concerned about both "the spiritual welfare of [a priest's] people" and about the priest's "own soul" as well (154–55, emphasis in original).

The skeptical reader might see this as Urban simply justifying his own role as "priest-promoter," but his actions as acting pastor at St. Monica's indicate that he is on the right path. While we do need to read his interpretation of what happens under his guidance at St. Monica's with a skeptical eye, since he is apt to see his actions in the most positive light, it does seem that his active role in the parish community leads to a number of positive outcomes, including "attendance at daily Mass up 150 percent" (though this still only means ten parishioners); the "most successful [mission] in the history of the parish"; "parish life now a reality"; and the young parish curate also becoming more active and engaged, helping end what he called "the aridity in his spiritual life" (176–77, 162). Even the bishop, who is not a particular fan of Urban, praises the work he's done there: "'I've heard good things about you, Father, since you've been at St. Monica's. I understand you've done more than hold the line'" (187).

In his time as a parish priest, Urban actively lives out his priestly vocation. He celebrates the sacraments, preaches, evangelizes, and visits his parishioners in their homes. He demonstrates that one can be both a "priest-priest" and a "priest-promoter" and that the combination of prayer and action together is what makes for a truly successful priest. As Pope Francis declares, the successful parish is "in contact with the homes and the lives of its people, and does not become a useless structure out of touch with people or a self-absorbed group made up of a chosen few. The parish is the presence of the Church in a given territory, an environment for hearing God's word, for growth in the Christian life, for dialogue, proclamation, charitable outreach, worship and celebration" (*Evangelii Gaudium* 28); or, as he puts it more succinctly later in the same document, "at the very heart of the Gospel is life in community and engagement with others" (177). This is the kind of parish life Urban is developing at St. Monica's.

In the "Overture," Urban claimed that in order for the Church to be "an effective influence for good," there needed to be "a new approach," and it is at St. Monica's where we actually see this approach put into action. When he is finally elected provincial of the Order, he has lost the drive to be a "priest-promoter," and while Powers, Hagopian, and others might see that as a positive development, presumably the parishioners of St. Monica's, where "a number of fathers and mothers told him that he'd given them new hope," would not view the change in such a positive light (*Morte* 166). Fostering hope and a sense of community in the parish community is a worthwhile mission for a priest; in contrast, as provincial, Urban is notable mostly for "badly disappoint[ing] the hopes" of the members of his Order (333).

At St. Monica's, he lays the groundwork for building a new church by canvassing the parishioners and conducting a census; as provincial, "the Clementines moved out [of their prestige Chicago address], and not to another location (many had predicted a return to the Loop), but out to the Novitiate" (331). And even there, one of the principal things "that came to mind when men thought of the new Provincial" was that he oversaw the destruction of "the tribe of elm trees on the grounds" (333). The trees were infected and needed to be removed, and his willingness to do it, despite appearances, does indicate that he no longer cares about superficialities, but perhaps he should care a bit more. He could, after all, plant new trees and give some hope to the future. This physical retreat and diminishment of the Order's appearance reflect Powers's central conviction that "we have here no earthly home," but the lasting image of the novel is that a priest needs to care about both this world and the next, since his parishioners and fellow members of the Order are here, now.

This tension between the mundane and the eternal is central to Powers's work, and it is a continual source of conflict and humor in his fiction. Spending time within his stories helps orient, or reorient, the reader toward this double awareness. His work demands a careful, attentive reader, since it is never immediately clear who or what, exactly, Powers is critiquing in a given story. His artistry works to align our readerly sympathy with a given character, only to then slightly shift his lens and demand that we rethink our initial perspective. As we read his work, we are continually tasked with noting the assumptions we are making, and which familiar narratives we are too easily accepting. He uses his fiction to surprise the reader into an awareness that we, as individuals and as a society, value the wrong things and give our attention and desire to things that will not satisfy us. He is less inclined than O'Connor to rely on "large and startling figures" to get his message across, because, in part, his message is subtler, but it can ultimately be just as surprising and transformative.

3 / Walker Percy and the End of the Modern World

Walker Percy's work occupies a middle point between that of O'Connor and Powers and the more contemporary writers I discuss in the latter half of this book. Kieran Quinlan, in *Walker Percy: The Last Catholic Novelist* (1996), argues that Percy marks the end of an era, because no Catholic writer after Percy could ever be as "immersed in the technicalities of a philosophical and theological Catholicism" that shaped the preconciliar Catholic Church, and that a Catholic worldview such as Percy's "is no longer viable" in the postmodern world (9). Rather than position Percy as the last of the old guard, though, I prefer to see him, like many of his characters, as occupying a liminal space between different worlds and different ways of understanding oneself. He, like O'Connor and Powers, is focused on the state of an individual character's soul, but unlike these earlier writers, Percy's vision of salvation is primarily communal. Percy's characters are alienated searchers after meaning, but they fail to find ultimate meaning in the direct relation between themselves and God. Rather, what insight they come to is relational; they are not, and cannot be, redeemed in isolation. Like O'Connor and Powers, though, he structures his fiction so as to lead his readers to the same types of awakenings that he desires for his characters, and he uses a similar process of disorientation and then reorientation to bring this about.

Quinlan is right that Percy's theology was shaped by the neo-Thomism that was so influential in the first half of the twentieth century and that he had little use for the more progressive, or radical, theology of the post–Vatican II years. In an interview, Percy named Romano Guardini, Jacques Maritain, and Karl Rahner as the "recent theologians who've meant the most to me," and he called Hans Küng and Edward Schille-beeckx "nutty, heterodox priests . . . who I'm not sure are Christians" (*More Conversations* 117–18). But while he is the last exemplar of a certain type of Catholic novelist, formed by pre–Vatican II theologians and philosophers, he is also the first American Catholic writer whom we can consider as being engaged with postmodernist concerns.[1] Percy's theology is not postmodern, but his fictional interests are; we see this primarily in his anxiety over the ability of language to convey meaning,[2] and his preoccupation with, and concern over, the proliferation of media and its effect on consciousness.

Postmodernism is notoriously difficult to categorize, but its generally agreed-upon traits include "fragmentation, indeterminacy, and intense distrust of all universal or 'totalizing' discourses," along with the rejection of "belief in linear progress, absolute truths, the rational planning of ideal social orders, and the standardization of knowledge and production" (Harvey 9). Terry Eagleton writes that postmodernism signals "the death of . . . 'metanarratives,'" and he declares that in the postmodern world, "science and philosophy must jettison their grandiose metaphysical claims and view themselves more modestly as just another set of narratives" (194). While it may seem paradoxical to declare a writer a postmodern Catholic, since Catholicism is clearly a "metanarrative" and postmodernism rejects all such claims to universal truth, Percy's work investigates this very paradox (most notably in *Lancelot* [1977]). Percy repeatedly presents a world in which things are falling apart and where the center has failed to hold, but rather than trying to revert to an idealized past, or gathering together the remnants of a defunct culture,[3] it acknowledges that we must, as a society, search for something new, while resisting top-down solutions that are overtly dogmatic or proscriptive.

This last element is important. Percy's fiction hints that Catholicism offers some solution to the problems of contemporary society, but what Percy champions in Catholicism is not its hierarchical structure and institutions, but rather its sacramentality and the way it provides communion between isolated individuals. Even as he points toward these Catholic elements, though, his work resists the urge to didacticism; his characters are searching for these things, and even when they find them, Percy takes care to not overemphasize the religious aspects of either the seeking or the finding. This is somewhat surprising since Percy, at least early in his career, had a very definitive view of the goals for his fiction. In an early letter to his mentor Caroline Gordon, he stated, "What I really want to do is tell people *what they must do and what they must believe if they want to live*," and he went on to tell her he thought his next novel would "be mainly given to ass-kicking for Jesus' sake" (quoted in Tolson 300–301, italics in original). Part of this claim can be attributed to his zeal as a relatively recent convert to Catholicism, and in his later years he would back away from making such strongly authoritarian assertions regarding his fiction, but throughout his career he maintained a strong sense both for what was wrong with the modern world and how these problems could be overcome.[4] Even as he went about drafting his "ass-kicking" novels, though, he refrained from allowing their religious message to overwhelm the narrative. Percy's novels enact what John Sykes, using Kierkegaard's terminology, describes as "indirect communication," in which the writer "attempts to lead the reader to the verge of a discovery that the reader may or may not make. The discovery is one the writer has already made, and in that sense the writer has led the reader directly to it. But in a deeper sense, the revelation by its very nature is private and invokes the agency of the reader" (114). While it is possible to perform strong authoritarian readings of his work, their form resists such classification. They remain open-ended and ambiguous, thereby allowing, perhaps demanding, that the reader make the final judgment calls regarding what has happened within the framework of the novel.

There is one sense, though, in which Percy's novels are unambiguous. Throughout his fictional oeuvre, he remains consistent in his attempt to diagnose what is wrong with the modern world, and this is where we can begin to witness the specific rhetorical strategies that Percy employs to draw the reader's focus to his thematic concerns. Like O'Connor, Percy often turns to moments of violence to affect both readers and characters alike. Violence pervades Percy's novels, and it comes in two broad categories: the largely impersonal violence that is a product of widespread social and cultural ills, which in turn can be attributed to the ascendancy of the metanarratives of science and dehumanized "progress," and the intensely personal, self-directed suicidal violence that is a product of an individual's feelings of meaninglessness (Lancelot Lamar's homicidal violence, in *Lancelot*, is a manifestation of these same two root causes). Both of these types of violence relate to Percy's critique of contemporary society. Percy explained his vision of modern America in a number of places, and it changes little over the course of his career. In 1978 he wrote,

The American novelists seems to be saying . . . that something has gone badly wrong with Americans and with American life, indeed modern life, and that people are suffering from a deep dislocation in their lives, alienation from themselves, dehumanization, and so on—and I'm not talking about poverty, racial discrimination, and women's rights. I'm talking about the malaise which seems to overtake the very people who seem to have escaped these material and social evils—the successful middle class. What engages the novelist's attention now is not the Snopeses or the denizens of Tobacco Road or Flannery O'Connor's half-mad backwoods preachers or a black underclass. It is rather the very people who have overcome these particular predicaments and find themselves living happily ever after in their comfortable exurban houses and condominiums. Or is it happily ever after? Either the novelists are all crazy or something has gone badly wrong here, something which has nothing to do with poverty or blackness or whiteness.[5] (*Signposts* 36)

Percy's critique of the modern age was shaped by a variety of influences, including his reading of such existentialist thinkers as Kierkegaard, Sartre, Camus, and Dostoevsky,[6] but his worldview was also shaped by the Catholic intellectual tradition. In particular, it is worth looking closely at Percy's use of the German theologian Romano Guardini, who also had a profound influence on O'Connor.[7] There is an important distinction to be made between the way Guardini's work affected both authors, and this distinction will help to clarify my reading of Percy as both a traditional and a new kind of Catholic author. O'Connor most frequently praised Guardini's *The Lord*, which is primarily about the individual's relationship with the person of Jesus Christ; it is an example of kerygmatic theology, a way of understanding God that is based not primarily on doctrine but on a personal relationship "with the living Christ who is present to people of every age" (Krieg 138). In *The Lord*, Guardini writes that, in order for the individual in the modern world to come to know and accept God, faith must supersede intellect; reason leads us astray, but surrender to the divine will and obedience to God are what lead to understanding. If one wants to come to know Jesus, "You must let go; renounce all hope of self-illumination, fling the measuring rod of reason and experience to the winds and venture the call: Lord, come—send me your Spirit that I may be recreated!" or, again, "To become a Christian means to go to Christ *on the strength of his word alone,* to trust solely in his testimony. Blind acceptance of what remains unclear, unreasonable is part of this step and belongs essentially to the 'foolishness' of the crossing over" (149, emphasis in original). One finds this pattern repeatedly in O'Connor's fiction. Her characters do not reason their way to faith. Rather, they live in a world where God's presence becomes a palpable reality. Guardini advocates personal surrender to a reality beyond reason, which entails a vision of the power of God's judgment, or what Guardini calls "the threat of God" (336)—a very O'Connor-esque vision of reality. Both Guardini and O'Connor believe that the modern world can only be redeemed through an encounter with Christ, and they acknowledge this type of encounter can be terrifying. It makes sense that this work resonated with O'Connor, whose own fiction emphasizes the often irrational, frequently terrifying, relationship between an individual and the divine.

Percy, though, used a passage from Guardini's *The End of the Modern World* as the epigraph to his second novel, *The Last Gentleman*, and when Percy writes or speaks about Guardini, he seems to be referring to this work, or at least to the worldview that Guardini displays within it. In a 1984 interview, when questioned about the existential nature of his fiction, Percy steers the conversation to Guardini's worldview, which might be termed a form of Christian existentialism:

He [Guardini] is talking about an existential predicament. He says we are living in a post-Christian world where people are alone but he also says, and this is an important thing, it's the world where there is less deception; people are alone and, yet, they are capable of forming true relationships. One lonely person finds another lonely person. From this very loneliness, this existential alienation, there is possible a true communion, which in a way is even better than it used to be, when everybody lived in the same system, everybody understood one another, say, in the nineteenth century Europe. (*More Conversations* 74)

This description of alienation, loneliness, and possible connection comes directly from *The End of the Modern World*, which in both tone and format is a very different work from *The Lord*. While Guardini's essential worldview remains consistent throughout, the two works serve distinct functions. *The End of the Modern World* is an assessment of the state of society, not of an individual's relationship to Christ. That Percy was drawn to this work of social commentary says a great deal about his fictional project, which is in large part a critique not of the individual but of modernity as a whole, and the way the problems of modernity affect the individual's sense of self. Percy's understanding of the modern age as being defined by the loss of common consensus, loss of faith, and the pursuit of pleasure as the highest good all have analogues in Guardini's assessment of the modern world.

There are a number of places in *The End of the Modern World* where Guardini's words closely parallel Percy's own and thus help to illuminate Percy's fiction. Guardini writes that "the experience of modern man" entails "man's loss of his objective sense of belonging to existence" and that this results in "modern anxiety," which "arises from man's deep-seated consciousness that he lacks either a 'real' or a symbolic place in reality. In spite of his actual position on earth he is a being without security. The very needs of man's senses are left unsatisfied, since he has ceased to experience a world which guarantees him a place in the total scheme of existence" (34–35). This depiction of the anxious, displaced individual is characteristic of all of Percy's protagonists, whose fictional journeys entail the search for both a real and a symbolic place in their worlds. Guardini contends that most anxious, alienated moderns end up as examples of what he terms "mass man," which he defines as an individual who "has no desire for independence or originality in either the management or conduct of his life. . . . To either a greater or a lesser degree mass man is convinced that his conformity is both reasonable and right" (60). Most of Percy's protagonists are "mass men"; Binx Bolling, for instance, describes himself at the beginning of *The Moviegoer* as "a model tenant and a model citizen and [I] take pleasure in doing all that is expected of me" (6).[8] One can read Percy's novels as being primarily about "mass men" who are awoken to self-consciousness, usually through an act of violence, and who subsequently come to reject conformity but struggle to find an adequate replacement.

For Guardini, as both *The Lord* and *The End of the Modern World* show, the only adequate and sufficient source of meaning in the contemporary age is grounded in a total reliance on God. Guardini sees a renewed form of Christianity as the solution to the problems of the new age, but in his view this new Christianity will be distinct from contemporary Christianity, for while it is contiguous with the traditions of Christianity, it will "once again need to prove itself deliberately as a faith which is not self-evident; it will be forced to distinguish itself more sharply from a dominant non-Christian ethos. . . . At the forefront of Christian life, man's obedience to God will assert itself with a new power" (106–7). Man's faith and obedience to God will ground him and "permit him to remain a vital person within the mounting loneliness of the future, a loneliness experienced in the very midst of the masses and all their organizations" (108). Percy is particularly adept at depicting this loneliness, but while his novels usually show his protagonists finding a way beyond this loneliness, they do not have the same surety of religious vision that Guardini demonstrates. Percy's novels usually end with some instantiation of faith, but it is tenuous at best, and lacks the assertiveness that Guardini indicates is necessary to combat the modern malaise.

WALKER PERCY / 59

The End of the Modern World concludes with a vision of a smaller, more committed Christian society, where love is revitalized, primarily because this love is grounded in a personal devotion, and obedience, to God. Percy uses a selection from this conclusion as an epigraph to *The Last Gentleman*:

> We know that the modern world is coming to an end. . . . At the same time, the unbeliever will emerge from the fogs of secularism. He will cease to reap benefit from the values and forces developed by the very Revelation he denies. . . . Loneliness in faith will be terrible. Love will disappear from the face of the public world, but the more precious will be that love which flows from one lonely person to another. . . . The world to come will be filled with animosity and danger, but it will be a world open and clean.

This epigraph is a collage of passages culled from *The End of the Modern World*, ranging over more than fifty pages of text.[9] What Percy chooses to include here, and what he leaves out, are informative. Percy selects passages that emphasize the sense of an ending and the existential loneliness that this entails, along with a corrective to this loneliness found via the love "which flows from one lonely person to another" ushering in a new, "open and clean" world; these selections encapsulate Percy's thematic concerns, while eliding one of, if not *the*, central theme of Guardini's work: the coming importance of man's "unconditional obedience to God" (107), which makes possible the love between individuals of faith. Guardini's original sentence reads, "Love will disappear from the face of the public world, but the more precious will be that love which flows from one lonely person to another involving a courage of the heart born from the immediacy of the love of God as it was made known in Christ," and this is but one of many passages where Guardini foregrounds the inextractibility of God and Christ from the only hope he sees for the future. Percy, though, hints at a different solution, one that includes the possibility, but not the necessity, of faith. Percy's fiction, like Guardini's work, emphasizes what has gone wrong with the modern world, but Percy points toward relationships, rather than the total surrender of one's will to God, as the primary solution to these problems.

This dynamic is most evident in the conclusions of his novels, where Percy repeatedly demonstrates an uneasy accommodation between faith and doubt; within his fiction there is no such thing as absolute certainty. Faith is clearly important for Percy, and for his characters, but it is primarily relational. John Desmond, in *Walker Percy's Search for Community*, persuasively makes the case that "all of Percy's fictions show a movement toward some genuine community as the novel ends, even if only between two people, a *solitude a deux*, which is for Percy the bedrock of all human community" (4). Desmond goes on to explain that, for Percy, community is an ontological necessity because "we are structured to fulfill our natures not individualistically, but through relationships, through community" (17), and that all true communities are an imitation of the mystical communion embodied in the Trinity. Many of Percy's novels end with moments of community, or shared love between lonely individuals, and it is possible to view this community as an instantiation of a sacramental communion, but this connection is never fully explained. While Percy's novels do point to community and communion as solutions to the problems of modernity, we never see his protagonists surrendering their will in obedience to God.

Percy's resistance to Guardini's position on unconditional obedience to God might strike us as surprising, since he repeatedly cited Guardini's worldview as an influence on his own writing,[10] but it is actually perfectly in keeping with Percy's postmodern fictional concerns. While Flannery O'Connor saw the individual's inflated sense of self to be a central problem of modernity, for Percy, the problem was not that individuals put too much faith in themselves, but rather that they were too willing to surrender their autonomy to systems of belief that they spent little to no time interrogating.[11] In particular, Percy was critical of what he saw as the modern tendency to believe that science could explain everything, and while this "scientism" was his primary target, Percy's work is critical of all unreasoned, fundamentalist beliefs, or what Eagleton calls "metanarratives." Percy's novels are about the search for meaning and understanding, and fundamentalist beliefs (including religious ones[12]) preclude any such searching. In a very real sense, this is why his novels rarely have clear, well-defined resolutions; such a resolution would negate the necessity of a search. Because of their lack of closure, his novels can spur the kind of questioning and seeking Percy sees as an important first step in countering many of the underlying problems of the contemporary age.

To be clear, though, Percy found "scientism" to be the most widespread, and unacknowledged, fundamentalism in contemporary America. Scientism, he explained, "is characterized less by the practice of a method of discovery and knowing than by what can only be called a surrender of sovereignty and a willingness to believe almost as a matter of course that the scientific method by virtue of its spectacular triumphs and the near magic of its technology can be extrapolated to a quasi-religious all-construing worldview" (*Signposts* 297). Percy contends that the individual who believes science can answer all questions and solve all mysteries is a fundamentalist, one who believes without questioning the premises or results of one's belief. Within the world of his fiction, the end result of this blind faith is the malaise that results when a person surrenders one's sovereignty over oneself and eliminates the possibility for mystery.

One object of Percy's fiction, then, is to demonstrate the flaws in the faith of scientism, and one way he does this is by showing the violent outcomes of this belief—most memorably in the "Fedville" complex that appears in *Love in the Ruins* and *The Thanatos Syndrome*, which includes "the Behavioral Institute, the Geriatrics Center, and the Love Clinic" (*Ruins* 14). In these centers, individuals who are unhappy are subjected to behavioral conditioning in order to recondition them to be exactly like other, "normal" individuals. These clinics are places where individual human lives have no inherent meaning, because the focus of scientific thinking is not about the individual but about the group. Both *Love in the Ruins* and *The Thanatos Syndrome* portray the clinics as totalitarian machines, willing to dispose of those individuals who will not conform. This is particularly apparent in *The Thanatos Syndrome*, where pedeuthanasia and gereuthanasia have been legally sanctioned by the Supreme Court, and pharmacology is the new widespread means of controlling human behavior, leading to decidedly subhuman results.

One of the central set pieces of *Love in the Ruins* illustrates Percy's condemnation of scientism. Tom More and the behaviorists of Fedville hold a debate about whether to euthanize Mr. Ives, an elderly man who refuses "to participate in the various recreational, educational, creative and group activities" at his geriatric community, the Golden Years Center, and instead "defecate[s] on Flirtation Walk" and "utter[s] gross obscenities to Ohioans" (223), until finally lapsing into a mute, catatonic state. Given his unwillingness to participate, and his resistance to reconditioning via the Skinner box, the Fedville doctors want to send him to the Happy Isle Separation Center, where he would be euthanized. More is able to save the man by demonstrating that his unwillingness to speak or act does not indicate an absence of "selfhood" (228), and that his decision to "refuse to respond at all" to the Skinner box is the only possible response to reconditioning (234). In *The Thanatos Syndrome*, Percy takes his critique of the kind of scientism embodied by Fedville one step further, linking the work of the Fedville scientists to Nazi Germany. Fr. Smith, Tom More's friend and the conscience of the novel, tells More that he is part of the "first generation of doctors in the history of medicine to turn their backs on the oath of Hippocrates and kill millions of old useless people, unborn children, born malformed children, for the good of mankind" and he warns that, inevitably, "you're going to end up killing Jews" (127–28). For a readership that (presumably) aligns itself with science, progress, and rationality, seeing the scientific community linked to the atrocities of the Nazis is a shock, but of course this is Percy's point—he wants to shock us, because this then leads to questions and reflection; it can be the start of the search. For Percy, scientism leads directly to institutionalized murder because it devalues individual human life; it also contributes to the personal sense of meaninglessness that he calls the "modern malaise."

A Pattern Established: Violence as Precursor to Search in *The Moviegoer*

This connection between scientism and malaise is evident in Percy's earliest published work, *The Moviegoer*, where Binx explains that in his youth, "I stood outside the universe and sought to understand it. I lived in my room as an Anyone living Anywhere and read fundamental books. . . . The greatest success of this enterprise, which I call my vertical search, came one night when I sat in a hotel room in Birmingham and read a book called *The Chemistry of Life*. When I finished it, it seemed to me that the main goals of my search were reached or were in principle reachable" (*Moviegoer* 69–70). But at that moment he realizes the limits of this "vertical" approach to understanding: "The only difficulty was that though the universe had been disposed of, I myself was left over" (70). In other words, nothing that he learned could explain himself, or as Percy described the predicament in a 1984 interview, "What people don't realize is that the scientific method has no way of uttering one word about an individual creature. . . . Science is only interested in you so far as you are like another class of people. But science itself cannot utter one word about the individual self in so far as it is individual. It leaves a huge leftover" (*More Conversations* 73).

Binx, rather than beginning a new search for an understanding of himself as an individual, turns away from this sort of existential question, and instead "went out and saw a movie called *It Happened One Night*" (70). He turns to the movies because they allow him to elide the question of meaningfulness; they provide him with a model for living that is all surface and no depth. By escaping into the movies, he negates the need to answer the questions that linger below the surface, such as "what does it mean to be alive";[13] for most of his life, before the action of the novel, Binx has been content to ignore this lingering question in favor of a life lived easily on the surface. It is only when he is confronted by the coming death of his brother and his cousin Kate's suicidal urges that he begins to search, again, for an answer to the question that he did not want to face: "why am I here?"

Part of Binx's difficulty is that he inhabits a liminal space; falling between various communities and identities, he lacks any place to truly feel connected to the world. Binx dwells in a middle ground between the aristocratic, stoic gentility of his father's family and the faith-filled, down-to-earth sensibility of his mother's. He lives in a kind of nowhere, in-between space that he values for its anonymity and lack of charm (*Moviegoer* 6). And so, like Percy's Man on a Train, "he is both in the world he is traveling through and not in it . . . [in a place where] a partition exists . . . between oneself and one's fellow commuters, a partition which is impenetrable by anything short of disaster" (*Message* 87). And, like Percy's commuter, it is only after disaster strikes that Binx comes to himself and comes to see himself as "a wayfarer and a pilgrim." Percy contends that this is the modern condition: that truly self-aware people are alienated from themselves and their communities, and that modern man is continually searching for ways to reintegrate into the world. But, on some level, this quest to feel at home in the world is an impossible one because the metanarratives that lead to a feeling of belonging and groundedness are no longer viable. They have been discredited, and so the self-aware cannot embrace them.

Percy's first novel, then, is a diagnosis not only of Binx Bolling's life but also of the culture that produces him. Percy's depiction of midcentury American culture (and in particular the southern culture out of which he is writing) is of a society that is structured such that it prevents the individual from asking the questions that Binx eventually comes to ask, and that it requires some shock to the system—something startling, disorienting, violent—to lead the individual to question this system. Binx is surrounded by a number of individuals who espouse worldviews that they subscribe to without much interrogation, from Aunt Emily's stoicism to Uncle Jules's business-savvy bonhomie to his mother's unreflective faith. While it is tempting, given Percy's stated religious affiliation, to claim his mother's Catholicism as the "correct" mode of living within the novel, Percy is critical of her faith as well: "sometimes when she mentions God, it strikes me that my mother uses him as but one of the devices that come to hand in an outrageous man's world, to be put to work like all the rest in the one enterprise she has any use for: the canny management of the shocks of life" (*Moviegoer* 142). Like the movies that Binx frequents, all of these characters represent ready-made answers to the problems of modernity, and Binx's "search" is about the necessity of circumventing these easy solutions in search of something more difficult to articulate.[14]

The malaise that afflicts Binx Bolling, and indeed all of Percy's protagonists in one form or another, is about a crisis of meaning, something
that Charles Taylor expounds upon in *A Secular Age*. Taylor defines the
secular age as "one in which the eclipse of all goals beyond human flourishing becomes conceivable" (19), and he writes that this eclipse of the possibility of transcendence brings about, for some individuals, "a sense of
malaise, emptiness, and a need for meaning" (302). Percy's work focuses
almost exclusively on these types of individuals, because he believes that
this should be the way that all individuals feel. In Percy's view, if a
person does not feel this way, then he or she is most likely simply not
aware of his or her own condition, and part of Percy's goal as a fiction
writer is to initiate this feeling in his readers. His goal, though, is not to
point out the absurdity of life, but rather to push his characters, and his
readers, past this feeling. He wants to initiate in them (in us) a search
for meaning.

For Taylor, one of the defining characteristics of contemporary society is that most people live in a "middle position," between complete dis-
belief and real religious conviction—where we "strive to live happily with
spouse and children, while practicing a vocation we find fulfilling, and . . .
which constitutes an obvious contribution to human welfare" (7). It is a
place where the highest goal is "human flourishing," and there is no possibility (or desire) for anything more than this. Binx's is an interesting
case, because in many ways he fits this middle position, which Taylor describes as "a way to escape the forms of negation and emptiness, without
having reached fullness" (6); this is how Binx envisions himself. His search
is for some way beyond the middle ground of "human flourishing" into
a more rich and fulfilling life. Of course it is important to note that at the
start of the novel he does not have a spouse or a fulfilling job, which might
contribute to his discontentment, but that is quite explicitly not how he
understands his predicament. He sees himself as a searcher, in Taylor's
sense of the word.

So if the novel is about the process of circumventing the modern malaise, which is itself a by-product of a mode of unreflective living dictated
by modern American culture, then it is worth questioning how Binx
comes to question, and finally reject, the prepackaged ideological systems
of his culture. Significantly, his journey toward insight begins with a moment of violence. Binx says he first became aware of his alienation, or of
"the possibility of the search" (13), after being wounded in the war; only
after he was knocked unconscious could he come to see things anew: "only
once in my life was the grip of everydayness broken—when I lay bleeding in a ditch" (145). This is one of the recurring themes of *The Movie-*

goer, that in the depersonalized modern world we need tragedy and pain, like Kate's fiancé's death or Binx's car accident, to break through the malaise, the everydayness of life, and begin to look for more out of life than simply being alive. This idea, that an individual will only become aware of his condition when he or she suffers violence, is found throughout Percy's fiction.[15] The same sentiment is uttered in *The Last Gentleman*: "The certain availability of death is the very condition of recovering oneself" (372); *Love in the Ruins*, "One morning . . . my wrists were cut and bleeding. Seeing the blood, I came to myself, saw myself as itself and the world for what it is, and began to love life" (97); and *The Second Coming*, "Is it possible for people to miss their lives in the same way one misses a plane? And how is it that death, the nearness of death, can restore a missed life?" (124).

Percy makes this claim in a number of his nonfiction pieces as well. As noted above, in "The Man on the Train" he describes how violence is needed to bring about awareness and connection between isolated individuals. In "The Loss of the Creature," he claims that one of the few ways to make an individual aware of one's position, not as "a consumer of prepared experience" but as "a sovereign wayfarer," is "by ordeal . . . in these cases, the simulacrum of everydayness of consumption has been destroyed by disaster" (*Message* 60). "Notes for a Novel about the End of the World" contains Percy's most extensive explanation of his fictional technique: "How does he [the Christian novelist] set about writing, having cast his lot with a discredited Christendom and having inherited a defunct vocabulary? He does the only thing he can do. Like Joyce's Stephen Dedalus, he calls on every ounce of cunning, craft, and guile he can muster from the darker regions of his soul. The fictional use of violence, shock, comedy, insult, the bizarre, are the everyday tools of his trade" (118). And he concludes the essay with an even more concrete claim for why violent and startling imagery features so prominently in his fiction, and it points toward fiction's transformative role on the individual reader's consciousness: "Perhaps it is only through the conjuring up of catastrophe, the destruction of all Exxon signs, and the sprouting of vines in the church pews, that the novelist can make vicarious use of catastrophe in order that he and his reader may come to themselves" (118).

Percy not only believed that moments of violence can shake the individual out of the malaise and open the way for insight, but he also, like O'Connor, linked this thematic concern to his fictional method itself. Percy, like many midcentury American artists, believed that he was running up against the limits of what fiction could say or do.[16] Percy found this to be a particular problem for the Christian writer, because while all language was, in a sense, exhausted, the language of religion was particularly worn out. In "How to Be an American Novelist in Spite of Being Southern and Catholic" (1984), he explained the "serious impediments in the current historical manifestation of Christendom" that make it particularly difficult to write about God and religion in a way that is fresh and interesting:

> It has to do with the devaluation of the Christian vocabulary and the media inflation of its contents. The old words, God, grace, sin, redemption, which used to signify within a viable semiotic system, now tend to be either exhausted, worn slick as poker chips and signifying as little, or else are heard as the almost random noise of radio and TV preachers. The very word "Christian" is not good news to most readers. (*Signposts* 180)

In order to overcome this malaise within the very language itself, the Christian novelist must adopt the position not "of edification but rather that of challenge, offense, shock, attack, subversion" (181). As O'Connor did before him, Percy argues that the Christian writer must use a sort of literary violence in order to prevent his Christian vision from being subsumed within the predefined parameters of what qualifies as "Christian." Paradoxically, only by appearing *not* to be Christian can the work reveal its Christian message, and only through these aesthetic techniques of alienation and disorientation that the writer can truly reach and affect his audience.

This helps to explain Percy's reticence within his fiction to provide clear, edifying endings. As Binx states at the end of *The Moviegoer*, "As for my search, I have not the inclination to say much on the subject" (237), which is a rather coy position to take since he has been detailing the progress of this search for more than two hundred pages. We know that he has entered into a somewhat strange but certainly necessary and fulfilling marriage to Kate, and has decided to become a doctor, in order to "listen to people . . . [to] hand them along a ways in their dark journey and be handed along" (233). What he has achieved in the end looks, to use Taylor's terminology, an awful lot like human flourishing, not existential transcendence, and yet Percy intimates that the final destination of Binx's journey is a place beyond this human flourishing. The conclusion of the novel contains subtle hints that Binx has found some sort of meaning in a return to the Catholic faith; John Desmond describes Binx at the end of the novel as finally living "in communion with others" (*Community* 78), particularly in his "commitment to Kate in marriage," in his work as a doctor, and in his faith in the Catholic "belief in the resurrection of the body" (55), which he affirms when he tells his relatives that his half-brother Lonnie will be made whole "'when Our Lord raises us up on the last day'" (*Moviegoer* 240). The most explicitly Catholic aspect of the conclusion takes place on Ash Wednesday, when Binx watches a man walk out of Catholic mass and he wonders if the man truly "believes that God himself is present here at the corner of Elysian Fields and Bon Enfants" (235). Binx's unanswered question leads the reader to consider this possibility, though no definitive answer is forthcoming in the text. It also indicates that this is a question that Binx himself will continue to ponder. So while, in Binx's words, "It is impossible to say" what, if anything, he has accomplished through his quest, we know he has been changed over the course of the novel, and we are left to reflect on the nature of this change. By leaving the ending ambiguous, Percy leads his readers to ask a series of questions: Did Binx finish his search? Did he find what he was looking for? Is it just a matter of time before he once more succumbs to the malaise of everydayness? By asking them of Binx, we might ask them of ourselves.

As Gary Ciuba explains, "The deliberate irresolution of Percy's novels, in which love is so often imperfect and faith seems so unfinished, rejects any completely realized eschatology. His novels always intimate that there is more to come and often express this incompleteness by looking to some future consummation. But since this end is ultimately unspeakable, his novels have more to say about the hope and love that must begin in the present" (22). John Sykes concurs, indicating that "the revelation Percy strives to bring about is one that happens off the page, so to speak, in an existential encounter that happens after the reader closes the book," but since the "grace-filled events in Percy's fiction are nearly invisible," they are "therefore easily missed" (5–6). Percy does not provide answers because answers preclude the necessity of a search, and his primary goal is to initiate this search for the reader, to make the individual question his or her assumptions, no matter what they may be. Percy believes that such questioning will result, as it did for him, in the embrace of faith, but he is unwilling to impose that system of belief on his readers.

A Pattern Revised: Violence and the Failure of Insight in *Lancelot*

Percy's use of ambiguity and misdirection is evident throughout his fiction, but his most nuanced engagement with it is found in his fourth novel, *Lancelot*. While the threat of apocalypse hangs over *Love in the Ruins*, the killing of the old and the young has become legalized in *The Thanatos Syndrome*, and Will Barrett's graphic memory of his father's suicide functions as a focal point of *The Second Coming*, *Lancelot* is Percy's darkest and most violent novel. It is the only one of his novels to dwell on personal violence, directed from one individual toward another; the novel is narrated by Lancelot Lamar, who is incarcerated in a "Center for Aberrant Behavior" after murdering his wife and her lover, along with two others. *Lancelot* is Percy's most extreme treatment of his principal themes; in this novel he depicts the violent outcome of both the personal anguish of the alienated individual and the dehumanizing tendencies of totalizing narratives. The novel also calls into question many of the beliefs regarding society that Percy himself espouses in his essays and other novels; *Lancelot* gives voice to Percy's condemnations of the modern age, but in Lance's mouth these critiques become just one more example of the dangers of extremism and the inherent risk of subscribing too fully to any one worldview.

Lancelot is, in many ways, a reenactment of the themes and events of *The Moviegoer*, but while the earlier novel is a mild comedy, Lance Lamar's story is thoroughly dark. Both novels feature protagonists who profess a belief in scientism, who suffer from the modern malaise, and who are subsequently shocked out of this condition into quests for knowledge, but in each instance Lance's experience is more extreme than Binx's, and his quest(s) lead to much more sinister results. Even in their broader arcs, the two novels share similarities: for instance, both novels are heavily invested in the concept of the movies, but whereas Binx merely watches them, and is content to observe how the form of the movies provides a template for one's life, Lance's life becomes completely enmeshed in them. His home becomes a movie set, and his wife and daughter become romantically involved with the movie actors and producers; he himself enacts the role of the jealous husband character from a B movie as he uses a Bowie knife to carry out the revenge plot. Both novels critique the way the movie business creates a simulacrum of the world, which in turn becomes more real for the consumers of the movies than anything else,[17] but *Lancelot* questions the very idea of "the real" by drawing attention to the way in which one's conception of reality is shaped by the images one consumes. As Lance observes, "What was nutty was that the movie folk were trafficking in illusions in a real world but the real world thought its reality could only be found in the illusions" (152). Percy not only indicts the community surrounding Belle Isle for falling prey to the illusions being manufactured by the movie industry, he also condemns Lance for subscribing to a different set of illusions that pervert his sense of reality as well.

In *Lancelot*, Percy turns the well-established pattern of violence/shock leading to insight/grace on its head. Twice in the narrative Lance is shocked out of his preconceived notions about reality, but in neither instance does this shock and reorientation lead him toward anything resembling a moment of grace. Before the beginning of the events in his narrative, Lance is a man beset by the malaise of everydayness; he tells Percival, "Do you know what happened to me during the past twenty years? A gradual, ever so gradual, slipping away of my life in a kind of dream state in which finally I could not be sure that anything was happening at all" (57). He is awakened from this stupor by the shock of discovering that his daughter is actually not his biological child, and this discovery spurs him toward a search. In order to reinforce the parallel between Binx and Lance, Percy recycles the language of *The Moviegoer*; Lance claims that after the shock of discovering Siobhan was not his child, "I had the feeling I was on to something, perhaps for the first time in my life" (140), a direct echo of Binx's description of the search: "To become aware of the possibility of the search is to be onto something. Not to be onto something is to be in despair" (*Moviegoer* 13). But unlike Binx, who eventually eschews his scientism in favor of a "horizontal search" for community and a sense of belonging in the world, Lance begins "a quest for evil" (*Lancelot* 136), and he does so in a scientific manner. We see this in his reaction to the blood test that proves Siobhan cannot be his own child: "There was a sense of astonishment, of discovery, of a new world opening up, but the new world was totally unknown. Where does one go from here? I felt like those two scientists . . . who did the experiment on the speed of light and kept getting the *wrong* result," and, like a scientist, he demands objective proof of what has happened: "One must see for oneself. . . . I had to be absolutely certain" (42–43). Lance's understanding of his quest is self-defeating, though; he believes he is "on to something," but instead of looking around and attempting to reorient himself, he limits himself to looking from a preconceived vantage point, thus precluding any possibility for insight.[18]

Throughout the first arc of the story, which carries Lance from the shock of his discovery to the acts of murder that lead to his imprisonment, he holds himself at a distance from the events of his life; he views his life as if he were a character in a movie: "for the first time, I saw myself and my life just as surely as if I were standing in the dark parlor and watching myself" (57). Even in his search for evidence, his "quest for a true sin," he inhabits a predetermined narrative; he envisions himself in an Arthurian quest narrative—"So Sir Lancelot set out, looking for something rarer than the Grail. A Sin" (140)—and in his search for evidence he too becomes a moviemaker, filming his wife's actions in an attempt to capture some sort of evidence, more real and true than the proof of his daughter's blood type. But what he does not consciously realize is that, in his quest for proof of evil, he ultimately comes to embody the evil for which he is searching. In a very literal sense, he performs the science experiment, but fails in his observations.

His quest for sin ends in his performing the sin he is searching for, as he murders his wife's lover with a Bowie knife, but he misinterprets the result. He claims that when he murdered Jacoby he felt nothing, only "numbness and coldness . . . a lack of feeling," and he contends that this lack of feeling proves that there is no such thing as evil, that there is no "unholy grail just as there was no Holy Grail" (253). But rather than disproving the existence of evil, this absence that he experiences as he commits the murder substantiates the Augustinian (and Thomist) definition of evil as a deprivation, as the absence of good.[19] The end result of the search initiated by the shock of his wife's betrayal is Lancelot's total isolation. But, within the framework of the novel, this moment of violence also serves as the possible beginning of a new search.

When Belle Isle explodes, Lance claims "for the first time in thirty years I was moved off the dead center of my life" (266),[20] another instantiation of Percy's claim that catastrophe reorients one's sense of self, but for Lancelot this new orientation is just as inverted as his murderous compulsion. After this second shock, the second narrative arc begins; this one entails Lance's quest for a new, pure beginning. It is in this aspect of the novel that we see how much of Percy's own beliefs about the modern world have made it into Lancelot's character. Rather than seeking a reintegration into the world, or atonement for his horrific actions, Lance begins to plot an even grander plan—a "new order" for the world, based not on "Catholicism or Communism or fascism or liberalism or capitalism or any ism at all, but simply on that stern rectitude valued by the new breed and marked by the violence which will attend its breach" (158). Although Lance claims that this new order is not based in any "ism," it is clearly a form of totalitarianism grounded in a twisted union of the kind of stoicism espoused by Binx's Aunt Emily and the most extreme elements of Percy's own condemnations of modernity.[21] Lance's vision for the future is Percy's clearest indictment of all types of fundamentalism, even one based in beliefs that he is sympathetic too, for it must be said that Lance's critique of modernity is, in large part, Percy's. Lance condemns contemporary American society for its vices, its ambiguities, and its lack of coherence and order, and his proclamations about the new society he will build in Virginia are the (almost logical) endpoint of the line of reasoning Percy espouses in his essays. But while Lance's vision of modernity is similar to Percy's, his response to the end of the modern age is not the same as Percy's, or Guardini's, for that matter. Where Guardini saw total humility and obedience to God as the solution, and Percy finds a way beyond the modern malaise in the embrace of community and a tentative but sincere return to the sacraments, Lancelot seeks to impose his vision on the world, and the center of Lance's vision is his own sense of right and wrong. *Lancelot* is Percy's demonstration that such a grounding is not, cannot be, adequate. In *Lancelot*, we can see that Percy recognizes the seduction of believing that one is right; by putting many of his own attacks on contemporary culture into the mouth of a character like Lance Lamar, Percy undermines his own didactic tendencies. In place of the imposition of metanarratives, Percy champions subtlety and ambiguity; he positions Percival's silent transformation as the counterweight to Lance's violent ideology.

Through Lance's journey, Percy critiques the trope that moments of shock and violence lead to real insight, and shows that critiquing the modern world is not the same thing as changing it. But while the novel demonstrates the inherent dangers in trying to remake the world as you see fit, it does offer an understated hint of how things might change; in rebuttal to Lance's all-encompassing monologic worldview, Percy offers Percival's nearly total silence. Numerous critics have noted that the story is just as much Percival's as it is Lance's;[22] the true journey of insight that takes place happens almost entirely off the page. Although we do not hear his voice until the final page of the novel, we know that Percival has changed from a position of disengaged detachment to a recommitment to his priestly vocation, lived in service to the poor. As Lance says, dismissively, "You plan to take a little church in Alabama, Father, preach the gospel, turn bread into flesh, forgive the sins of Buick dealers, administer communion to suburban housewives. . . . What's the new beginning in that? Isn't that just more of the same?" (256–57). Lance's final question is also the reader's question, and perhaps it is Percy's as well. Can such actions really serve as an effective counter to both Lance's totalitarian urge for control and to the despair at the heart of the modern age? Percival does not explain how this can be so, but his final "Yes" indicates that he believes it to be true. The question lingers long after the reader closes the book.

Once more, Percy offers Catholicism as a possible answer to the troubles of modernity, but, as in his other novels, the Catholicism that he champions is not hierarchical and bureaucratic, but rather a form of Catholic subsidiarity, which practices direct service and humility.[23] Percival's role in the text is similar to that of Mrs. Flood in *Wise Blood*; he is a reader surrogate who, when faced with the disturbing actions of the protagonist, is forced to respond. Although we do not hear Percival's account of how he has changed, or what has changed him, we can infer that it was his encounter with Lancelot's narrative that precipitated his reorientation. So what the novel finally reinforces is, once again, how encountering violence (even narrative violence) can serve as the precursor to change. Within Percy's worldview, we need to be "moved off the dead center" of our lives in order to truly live; if we are not shocked into the awareness of our condition as individuals who must choose a way to be in the world, we are (perhaps unknowingly) in despair.

And so he uses his fiction to spur his readers onto the journey, hoping that we, like Percival, will be led to reflection, and this reflection will lead us not only to insight, but ultimately to a life lived in humble service. It is important to note the form that Percival's transformation takes. In his role as servant priest, Percival will not be putting himself first. In this novel, Percy is offering a different vision for how the alienated individual will find meaning. Rather than in the single community of love formed between two people, which is the ending found in many of Percy's other novels, here Percy demonstrates that to love is to serve, to value something, or someone, more than oneself. This is the most overtly Christian message in Percy's work, and it stands in sharp contrast to the doctrinal ideology condemned by the novel. The "Yes" which ends the novel is a vision of meaning that transcends the self, and it comes about because Percival hears the story of violence and is transformed.

Or at least that is my interpretation of Percy's fictional project, but the ambiguity of his novels allows, even necessitates, that each reader determine this on his or her own. Any critical attempt to summarize, moralize, or sermonize is diametrically opposed to what I see as Percy's primary goal for his fiction, which is to initiate in each reader his or her own reflection on the source of ultimate meaning. For Percy, the goal of fiction is to spur the reader toward a search for insight, because to search is to be onto something, and not to be onto something is to be in despair.

4 / Tim Gautreaux and a Postconciliar Approach to Violence

The work of Tim Gautreaux provides a particularly revelatory entry point for my discussion of the post–Vatican II Catholic imagination because, as a southern Catholic writer, Gautreaux has concrete ties to the two most influential American Catholic fiction writers, Flannery O'Connor and Walker Percy. Gautreaux has repeatedly acknowledged his debt to both Percy and O'Connor, even going so far as to incorporate two of O'Connor's own characters—Julian, from "Everything That Rises Must Converge" and O. E. Parker, from "Parker's Back"—into his short story "Idols." He also studied fiction under Walker Percy at Loyola University New Orleans in 1977. Before taking this course, Gautreaux thought of himself as a poet, and has said that his experience with Percy helped put him on the path to writing fiction (*Conversations* 41).[1] Although he consciously engages with the themes and form of their work in his own writing, Gautreaux's fiction emphasizes postconciliar Catholic thinking, both in its emphasis on the significance of community and in his prioritization of the importance of social action. Rather than using violence to shock the reader (as O'Connor does), or employing carefully controlled point of view to unsettle and surprise the reader (as Powers does), or writing fiction to diagnosis the modern condition (as Percy does), Gautreaux crafts stories that lead the reader to reflect on how to live ethically and act morally in the world.

Gautreaux's stories often hinge on questions of moral imperatives, and the most righteous course of action is not always immediately obvious.[2] The dramatic tension in his work often hinges on the conflict between doing what one thinks is right and just, and having compassion and mercy, and sometimes we need to see how these elements play out in a real scenario (even a fictional one) in order to help us think through what we should do. In this sense, the stories can become a sort of ethical training ground.[3] Gautreaux's stories present the reader with complex ethical scenarios, and he invites us to contemplate, along with the characters, how best to respond.

One main tool that he uses to accomplish this—perhaps unsurprisingly, given his connections to O'Connor and Percy—is the fictional use of violence. My goal in this chapter, though, is not simply to list similarities and differences between Gautreaux and his Catholic predecessors or to provide an influence study, but to construct a narrative of how Gautreaux, as a writer shaped by the postconciliar Catholic Church, reimagines the role and function of violence in literature. For O'Connor, violence was a tool used to identify and make visible the role of the transcendent in a secular age. As I discuss in my analysis of "A Good Man Is Hard to Find," the violence in her fiction often does arise from the social dynamics of the postwar South, but her primary aim is spiritual, not social, critique. But in the post–Vatican II world, the emphasis on personal salvation—the individual's journey toward salvation or damnation—is recontextualized into a communal setting. One's salvation or damnation has everything to do with one's relationships, not only with a transcendent God, but with the people of God on earth, and post–Vatican II Catholic fiction reflects this dynamic. Consequently, the violence in postconciliar fiction takes on a different valence; instead of primarily serving as a means of breaking through the secular wall between the human and the divine, it (often) breaks through the walls that separate individuals, or conversely, the violence serves as an obstacle that prevents the union of individuals that is a precursor to grace.

As discussed in the previous chapter, we can begin to see this change in the fiction of Walker Percy, whose fictional oeuvre begins almost immediately before the opening of Vatican II in 1962, with *The Moviegoer* (1961), and ends in the post-*aggiornamento* world of 1987, with the publication of *The Thanatos Syndrome*. While the primary focus of Percy's work is always on an individual who is alienated from himself (all of Percy's protagonists are male) and his society—and who usually must come to reject his society in order to reclaim his sense of self—Percy's depiction of this process of alienation and recovery is united with an increasingly overt social consciousness. Throughout his work, Percy strikes a balance between emphasis on the individual and emphasis on community until the two become practically inseparable; the sickness of the one is indicative of the sickness of the other, and the cure of the one hints at the possible cure for the other as well.

In the work of Tim Gautreaux, whose entire fictional corpus is post–Vatican II, we find the scale beginning to be tipped in the other direction. Although his focus is still on the individual (one of his great strengths as a writer is strong characterization), Gautreaux's work does not primarily concern itself with the individual's pursuit of salvation, but rather with the interactions between the individual and their community—how a person is shaped by the culture in which they live, and how they in turn can reshape their community with their choices. Nevertheless, his work is still deeply Catholic, since the broad themes of his novels are profoundly shaped by Catholic social teaching, particularly the Church's stance on war and violence. His fiction is emblematic of the American Catholic Church's post–Vatican II position vis-à-vis the modern world, which Jay Dolan describes as "an era when issues of social justice became paramount" (201).

Gautreaux's stories feature moments of violence that are, on the surface, very O'Connor-like, yet they have a different underlying significance, both for the characters and for the reader. Ultimately, Gautreaux's work, drawing on post–Vatican II Catholic social teaching, critiques violence as both a social and a literary tool. In particular, the structure of his 2009 novel *The Missing* creates a dynamic in which the reader expects, and even desires, a violent climax, but instead of fulfilling this desire it leaves us questioning both why we desire to see violence carried out and why the violence that is present is not necessarily transformative or redemptive. While in O'Connor's work, violence is almost always an opportunity for grace, Gautreaux's fiction seems to operate on an inverse principle, where the withholding of violence becomes a moment of sanctification. At the same time, while Gautreaux's fiction portrays a more palatable understanding of violence, it often lacks much of the truly transformative properties that are found in O'Connor's and Percy's work. In Gautreaux's fiction, existential questions about the meaning of life and humanity's proper relationship to God are elided in favor of more practical ones; for Gautreaux, the fundamental question he wants his readers to contemplate is not "Why are we here?" but "How should I live?"

Gautreaux's Early Work: Using and Revising the Literary Patterns of Catholic Fiction

In a number of interviews, Tim Gautreaux has identified himself as a Catholic novelist, in large part because he writes about questions of morality from a Catholic perspective: "I consider myself to be a Catholic writer in the tradition of Walker Percy. If a story does not deal with a moral question, I don't think it's much of a story" (*Conversations* 11). But while he repeatedly acknowledges his debt to, and admiration of, both Percy and O'Connor, he also draws a clear distinction between his work and theirs: "I'm not a philosopher like Walker Percy. . . . I'm just a Catholic from the bayou" (23). For Gautreaux, Catholicism is both a source of morality and the cultural system in which he and his characters operate: "It's impossible to write about South Louisiana culture without writing about the Catholic Church, because it permeates everything—from wedding ceremonies to industrial fishing to the sugarcane industry to the way people think about eating on Friday. A lot of my stories have priests in them or references to going to Mass or confession, and that's because of what I'm writing about" (18). But Catholicism provides more than the cultural milieu for his stories; it is also the guiding principle for his characters. When asked why his characters repeatedly intervene to help in the lives of their neighbors, or even strangers, he responds, "All of that comes from being raised Catholic where we have been taught to help people who are less fortunate than we are, not just by praying for them but by actually going out and fixing their busted air conditioners and stuff" (147). For Gautreaux, more than for Percy or O'Connor, Catholicism is manifested in the practical activities of everyday life; in his work, Catholicism is the driving force for social action rather than an answer to metaphysical concerns.[4]

Gautreaux's work also offers a much more hope-filled vision of humanity than that found in his fellow American Catholic writers. His characters are still beset by troubles, and evil and violence still threaten them, but more often than not they respond to the obstacles of life with love, service, and kindness, and they do this out of a Catholic sense of justice. Gautreaux does write stories in which characters act cruelly toward the innocent or the helpless ("Little Frogs in a Ditch" and "Sorry Blood," with its O'Connor-like title, come to mind), but even in these stories, the vision of human cruelty is countered by other characters' acts of compassion. And it is far more common in a Gautreaux story for one character, when faced with another's suffering, to work to rectify it, as in "The Bug Man" or "The Piano Tuner." These characters are not always successful in transforming the lives of those they seek to help, but their effort does have a significant impact on the one who acts; it is a mark of grace.

Gautreaux's Catholic fiction does not deal with existential questions about the meaning of life, and his story arcs do not call for the violent inbreaking of grace to change his characters.[5] Rather, his Catholic sensibility champions the value of community and the presence of grace in the everyday. But while his fiction embodies a different notion of what Catholicism means, vis-à-vis the modern world, it still follows the structure for Catholic fiction laid out by O'Connor and Percy. We can see these parallels, along with the thematic differences, by looking at two of Gautreaux's earliest works: his first novel, *The Next Step in the Dance* (1998), which parallels *The Moviegoer* in a number of ways, and the title story of his first collection, "Same Place, Same Things,"[6] which, in its depiction of a violent encounter between strangers, follows the structure of any number of O'Connor's stories. In both instances, though, while the structure is similar, the way Gautreaux depicts the movement of grace within the human community is radically different.

The Next Step in the Dance is set in the small coastal town of Tiger Island, Louisiana, and focuses on a young married couple, Paul and Colette Thibodeaux. Paul divides his time between working as a mechanic and going to movies, drinking, and basically living an aimless, goalless existence, while his beautiful wife, Colette, desires something more from life. Fed up with Paul's fecklessness, Collette leaves him and heads out to California,[7] to find "people who sparkle" (23), and eventually Paul follows to win her back. After finding good jobs and making a fair amount of money they become disenchanted with the superficiality of California and end up back in Tiger Island, where the economy has tanked because of the oil bust of the 1980s. They have a number of trials and tribulations that eventually lead them both to realize they still love and need each other. It is, in many ways, a standard love story; it is also a story about Cajun culture in a specific time and place, and when the novel has been reviewed, this is often the critics' focus. But by reading the novel in connection to *The Moviegoer*, we can recast Gautreaux's work in a more complex light. Both novels are versions of the coming-of-age story. They revolve around young men who are trying to figure out how to live well in the modern world—a world in which traditional standards of moral and ethical behavior are being challenged or discarded.

Gautreaux said that in his course on fiction writing, Percy

was not very opinionated as to what we should write about, but he was very adamant in letting us know that we're all on some kind of quest. The writer is always looking for something, the characters are always looking for something. . . . For Percy, it was, at least in part, always spiritual. We are looking for what makes us happy, and the characters are looking for what makes them happy. And for Percy it wasn't money, and it wasn't fame. So what was it? Well, he never really told us, but you could guess. (*Conversations* 112)

Gautreaux is right to draw attention to Percy's decision not to tell his readers (or his students) what it was that they should be seeking, but I think Gautreaux's substitution of happiness as the goal of the search helps to differentiate the student's work from the teacher's, because Percy's novels are not really about happiness. They might initially appear to be, and the characters might even think this is what they are looking for, but Percy is actually interested in pushing his characters and readers to look beyond worldly happiness toward a more transcendent orientation. As Percy biographer Jay Tolson points out, for Percy, "the true character of evil" is "the despair and emptiness that drive people toward the endless pursuit of happiness in the first place; the despair, moreover, which can only be healed by its acknowledgment, and by acknowledgment of its cause—man's radical alienation from his soul and his creator" (456). Both *The Next Step in the Dance* and *The Moviegoer* are, in a sense, quest novels, but the natures of these quests differ. Binx is trying to figure out if it is possible to live a *meaningful* life, while Paul and Colette are trying to live *happy* lives.

For Percy, modern men and women are alienated because they lack community, but Gautreaux's novel challenges this position and contends that community is still present (usually in small, isolated pockets); since this community exists, in Gautreaux's fiction the deep existential angst we find in Percy is not a universal given. Whereas Percy contends that there is a "breakdown of the consensus, of a common language, a shared discourse denoting a common set of referents" (*Signposts* 157), Gautreaux's work is focused on a community that is built around common language and referents. Paul and Colette do not need to seek for a sense of self because their true identities are to be found in relation to the community of Tiger Island, where everyone holds similar customs and beliefs; they share a culture. Outsiders, whether they are Texans or Californians, can threaten this culture, but this threat does not turn Paul and Colette into alienated individuals. They may not know what they want out of life, and they may make poor life decisions, but Paul and Collette are not afflicted by Binx's existential dread that perhaps there is nothing worth wanting in life and that nothing truly matters.

When we first encounter Paul, though, he is in a similar state to one of Percy's protagonists—he is sunk in everydayness. In the first scene he is at a drive-in movie; he is, in a possible homage to Percy's work, literally a moviegoer. And, like Binx, he is content to be a spectator in his own life. Although Binx is certainly more introspective than Paul, neither young man is particularly engaged in the life they are living at the start of their novels. Both need to be shaken out of their apathy, and both novelists use moments of violence and shock to accomplish this. The initial shock to Paul's system that wakes him out of his malaise is Colette's leaving him; this incident is not violent or life threatening, so it does differ in extremity from the shocks administered in O'Connor's and Percy's work, but it is a form of suffering and leads to a similar outcome. Soon after Colette leaves for California, Paul drives around Tiger Island, and he is quite obviously truly *seeing* the place for the first time. Binx says that the search allows a person to actually see their life for what it is, with fresh eyes: "I felt as if I had come to myself on a strange island. And what does such a castaway do? Why he pokes around the neighborhood and he doesn't miss a trick" (Percy, *Moviegoer* 13). Paul does exactly this, as he drives around town, and instead of the familiar people and places, he sees anew his "drunk relatives, unusual dogs, weather-ruined houses. It seemed that the town he'd become used to like an old pair of pants no longer fit him" (Gautreaux, *Next Step* 68). His moment of pain and loss opens up the possibility of his own search, which leads him to leave the comforts of home to pursue his wife in California.

The episode out west in California is Colette and Paul's attempt at what Percy, drawing on Kierkegaard, called a rotation—an attempt to go somewhere new to find meaning in life. Gautreaux's interest in this section is primarily about contrasting Paul and Colette's wealth of family and friends in Tiger Island with the depersonalized, materialistic world of Los Angeles. But, in what is an unsurprising turn of events for readers of O'Connor and Percy, what ultimately challenges both Paul and Colette to reevaluate what matters in their lives is a series of violent accidents and near-death experiences. The second half of *The Next Step in the Dance* repeatedly dramatizes Percy's claim that violence leads to insight and self-awareness, as both Paul and Colette continually come close to dying. Paul is locked in a steam boiler and nearly murdered by Colette's new boyfriend; Colette falls out of her boat, is knocked unconscious, and nearly drowns; Paul's shrimping vessel is shipwrecked in a storm and he is presumed dead. In each of these instances, both characters come away from the experiences with new insights about what matters in their lives—namely, they come to actually see and appreciate the reality of the unique personhood of the other, and the necessity of reintegrating into the community of Tiger Island. This leads to the happy reunion that ends the novel.

The overall structure of *The Next Step in the Dance* follows a similar pattern to that found in *The Moviegoer*, in which characters who are living aimless lives are shaken out of their malaise and begin searches for something more out of life, and both novels end with a vision of domestic harmony. That being said, there is a key difference between the horizons of expectations found in these two novels: Percy's fiction points beyond mere happiness and fulfillment toward a horizon of transcendence, whereas Gautreaux is interested in bringing his characters to a place where they achieve immanent fulfillment, not existential transcendence. Paul and Colette, in Charles Taylor's terms, are failing to achieve the position of "human flourishing," which he describes as the goal for most moderns; at the beginning of the novel they do not "strive to live happily with spouse and children, while practicing a vocation they find fulfilling . . . which constitutes an obvious contribution to human welfare" (7). Initially, they are not finding contentment in their routines of work and marriage, and their journey is toward a place where these things do give them some sort of fulfillment. While Binx is searching for something beyond the limits of "human flourishing," Paul and Colette are just trying to achieve it in the first place. But what is most interesting about these different horizons of expectations for the main characters is that both novels end in the same place. Paul and Colette's journey culminates with them reunited in a happier, more fulfilling marriage, working more meaningful and important jobs, and firmly embedded in their community and culture; a position that is very similar to that of Binx and Kate at the end of *The Moviegoer*. But while the endings are similar, they leave the reader with radically different sensations. We respond to Gautreaux's work with a happy, contented sigh. The ending is tidy and unambiguous; it is what we have expected and longed for all along. Because there is no ambiguity about the outcomes, and there is no hint that there is more to life than this sort of happiness, Gautreaux's novel, though satisfying, is not ultimately a transformative one for the reader. It does not leave the reader with unanswered questions; it will not lead one to initiate Percy's existential search. There is something to commend about Gautreaux's approach, though, since the struggle to live a good life does not need to be attended to by existential angst. Perhaps living a life of deep human flourishing, connected to one's family, friends, and community, and being aware that one is doing it is to be "on to something" after all, and the depiction of such a life is worth championing in its own right.

While his first novel is, perhaps, ultimately unchallenging for the reader, Gautreaux's short stories do call for a more complex response. Many of them are crafted around complex ethical scenarios that defy clear and obvious solutions. For instance, I often teach the story "Deputy Sid's Gift," in which the precipitating action is a man having his pickup truck repeatedly stolen from out in front of his house, but the story itself is constructed around the man confessing to a priest that he had not done enough to help the thief. It's an excellent story to teach, because it leads to animated conversations about the nature of justice and the question of how much we owe to our neighbors, particularly ones who cannot (or will not) help themselves.

"Same Place, Same Things," one of Gautreaux's earliest published stories, also interrogates the theme of what we owe to others, and if outcomes matter nearly as much as the effort we put forth. The story portrays a similar worldview to that found in *The Next Step in the Dance*, in which a commitment to doing good, meaningful work, and an inherent sense of moral decency, serve as countermeasures to the evil and violence of the world. I am going in depth on this particular story because it is, in many ways, a prototypical Gautreaux story: it features a working-class protagonist who, in the course of doing his work, encounters an isolated individual who is in need of help; it is also very reminiscent of O'Connor's fiction,[8] both in its depiction of the violent collision between strangers and in the parallels it makes between the natural world and the dramatic action of the story. Harry Lintel is a pump repairman who travels throughout the drought-ravaged Depression-era South doing "repairs . . . that no one else could manage" (5); on one house call, he finds the man of the house dead at the pump, the victim of an apparent accident, and soon thereafter the widow, Ada, begins to follow Harry on his repair runs. She wants to escape from the emptiness of her life, and she thinks that going on the road with Harry will provide her with that freedom. Initially, the story follows a familiar pattern often found in Catholic fiction: a sudden, shocking death leads an isolated individual to question and change her life. Ada, in the immediate aftermath of her husband's death, confesses, "'Sometimes I think it's staying in the same places, doing the same things, day in, day out, that gets me down. Get up in the morning and look out the window and see that same rusty fence. Look out another window and see that same willow tree. Out another and see that field. Same place, same things, all my life'" (13). She appears to be suffering from the same affliction that besets most of Percy's characters, "the malaise of everydayness," and, as in a Percy novel, a moment of violent disruption, in this case the death of her husband and the simultaneous appearance of the outsider, will provide her with the opportunity to reinvent her life, to wake up to the possibility of more than just empty routine.

But, in a refreshing twist, that is not the story that Gautreaux is telling. In fact, he is subtly critiquing that narrative convention, for it turns out that Ada has actually murdered her husband, most likely after seeing Harry's ad and deciding that she could take care of two problems at once by ridding herself of her husband and then using the traveling repairman to escape from her situation. She views violence as the easiest means of reinventing her life; by removing the obstacles in her path she thinks she can change her circumstances without actually changing herself. In Gautreaux's story, though, this violence is not ultimately transformative for any of the characters. Harry is intrigued by Ada's offer of accompaniment; he is a widower, and the possibility of having a companion on his travels is clearly appealing to him, and he also wants to do what he can to "heal what was wrong" with Ada (13). But he also realizes the limits of his abilities and knows that some broken things cannot be fixed. He intuits that something is not right about Ada and her situation, so he returns to her house and discovers that she left the pump switch on in order to electrocute her husband; after this discovery, "he put his face down into his hands and shook like a man who had just missed being in a terrible accident" (14). He sees his brush with Ada as an encounter with his own mortality, and he thinks that in discovering her secret, and subsequently avoiding her, that he has escaped a terrible fate. In this, too, he is mistaken.

Harry, like many an O'Connor protagonist, has a high opinion of his own abilities (and, oddly enough, his automobile): "He gazed fondly at his Ford. . . . It could take him anywhere, and with his tools he could fix anything but the weather" (7). In an O'Connor story, the protagonist would ultimately be disabused of this sense of surety and be forced to recognize his or her limitations, or, if the protagonist fails to recognize these limitations, then the reader at least will be alerted to the ways in which the protagonist has failed.[9] And although the story follows the pattern so often used by O'Connor, in which the protagonist is assaulted, robbed of his automobile, and left for dead, the lingering effect of the story is neither one of condemnation of Harry Lintel for his foolish pride, nor of wonder at the presence of transcendent grace amid tragedy. Harry, at the end of the story, is not remarkably different from Harry at the beginning of the story. Perhaps the difference between Harry and an O'Connor protagonist can be attributed to the qualification that the narrator places on Harry's sense of his own mastery: Harry knows that although he is able to fix the pumps, and therefore provide some measure of relief from the drought, he cannot address the source of the problem. He cannot fix the drought, and in a similar fashion, he recognizes the limits on his ability to "heal what was wrong" with Ada. After he discovers that she has stowed away in his truck in order to accompany him out of town, he tells her as much, "'Where you want to go . . . I can't take you,'" and "'If I could help you, I'd bring you along for the ride. . . . But I can't do a thing for you'" (15–16). Throughout the story, Harry has been aware of the severely limited horizons available to Ada and he is sympathetic to her situation, so much so that he does not turn her in to the police, but at the same time he recognizes that "she was a woman who would never get where she wanted to go" (17). Ada seems to believe that by escaping from her home she will be able to reinvent herself and escape her malaise, but Gautreaux's story indicates that such a reinvention is impossible, because what troubles Ada is internal and thus inescapable.

Ada uses violence to get what she wants—she knocks Harry unconscious with his own tools and steals his truck, but this moment of violence is not transformative or redemptive. Ada, we learn, has already murdered three husbands, and there is no reason to believe that her encounter with Harry has changed her; she is fleeing to a new situation that will be no different from her earlier ones. At the same time, there is no reason to believe that this experience has changed Harry either. Harry has been a decent man throughout the story, and the mark of grace that concludes the story—the "dove singing on the phone wires" over Harry's head after he regains consciousness (16)—is not indicative of newfound grace or insight that Harry has gained as a result of his encounter with Ada; instead, it confirms the grace that has been present in Harry all along. In Gautreaux's story, the character who suffers violence does not need to do so in order to change his or her worldview; in this instance Harry proved himself to be a good man long before Ada attacks him and leaves him for dead.

"Same Place, Same Things" shows Gautreaux using the pattern of violence established by his Catholic predecessors, but for a different end. Harry is, like most of Gautreaux's protagonists, a decent human being who is doing his best to reach out to others and help them in whatever way he can, while recognizing that he is a limited, fallible person, and that he cannot help or redeem everyone. His job is to fix what he can, and then move on. This is entirely within keeping with the Catholic vision found in Gautreaux's work, in which love and service are valued over existential questions about ultimate meaning. The Catholicism of Gautreaux's work is more practical than that of his literary predecessors, and he is more committed to depicting how Catholic principles can be embodied in day-to-day life. For Gautreaux, love and service are the way to move oneself, and perhaps one's neighbor, beyond the malaise of the everyday, and toward some possible awareness of an immanent, sacramental reality. His fiction invites the reader into these relational dynamics; by asking us to engage with these thorny ethical questions, he leads us to reflect on how we, too, can and should act. In a very practical way, his stories work to create, in Ricoeur's words, "a reader who responds" ("Between" 395).[10] Often, particularly in Gautreaux's novels, the ethical scenarios the reader must contemplate and formulate a response to involve the use—or avoidance—of violence.

Gautreaux's Novels: Engaging the Literature of Violence

Gautreaux's fiction, like that of Percy and O'Connor, maintains a steady focus on violence in the modern world, but Gautreaux is more interested than his predecessors in exploring the root causes of violence. Margaret Donovan Bauer, the author of the first book-length study of Gautreaux, notes that in both *The Clearing* (2003) and *The Missing* (2009), "Gautreaux continues his deconstruction of romantic notions of war and his exploration of the ravages of war that persist after peace is declared" (175). L. Lamar Nisly's articles on *The Clearing*, "Presbyterian Pennsylvanians at a Louisiana Sawmill, or Just How Catholic Is Gautreaux's *The Clearing*?" (2005) and *The Missing*, "Tim Gautreaux's *The Missing*: Journeys of Vengeance or Belonging?" (2011), focus predominantly on Gautreaux's treatment of violence, and Nisly makes a compelling case that Gautreaux's work is reflective of Catholic social teaching, which "affirm[s] the centrality of nonviolent responses in the face of evil action" ("Vengeance" 196).[11] Nisly's work provides a helpful overview of the turn toward nonviolence within the contemporary Catholic Church, noting the appearance of "a strand of Catholic social thought [that] rejects the common assumption that redemptive violence is needed to redress a wrong or that vengeance is the necessary response to an evil act" (197).

As *Gaudium et Spes* makes clear, the Catholic Church advocates an understanding of peace "which goes beyond what justice can provide" and acknowledges that "since the human will is unsteady and wounded by sin, the achievement of peace requires a constant mastering of passions and the vigilance of lawful authority" (78). The document goes on to note, "We cannot fail to praise those who renounce the use of violence in the vindication of their rights" (78). While the drafters of the document stop short of embracing pacifism as the only response to war, they do recognize the rights of conscientious objectors to war and condemn all weapons of mass destruction (79, 80). Pope John XXIII, in *Pacem in Terris*, indicates that one of the sources of the violence of the modern age can be attributed to the lack of proper moral formation, and that one of the failings of modern society is that Christians are not taught how to be moral and virtuous:

> We consider too that a further reason for this very frequent divorce between faith and practice in Christians is an inadequate education

in Christian teaching and Christian morality. In many places the amount of energy devoted to the study of secular subjects is all too often out of proportion to that devoted to the study of religion. Scientific training reaches a very high level, whereas religious training generally does not advance beyond the elementary stage. It is essential, therefore, that the instruction given to our young people be complete and continuous, and imparted in such a way that moral goodness and the cultivation of religious values may keep pace with scientific knowledge and continually advancing technical progress. Young people must also be taught how to carry out their own particular obligations in a truly fitting manner. (153)

Much of Gautreaux's work turns upon this very question of how individuals in the modern world should go about carrying out their moral obligations, and how the failure to do so contributes to the pervasive violence of modernity. Within his fiction Gautreaux repeatedly depicts scenarios that call for a moral response, particularly in his portrayal of the moral complexity surrounding the use of violence, and asks that his characters, and his readers along with them, ponder the most virtuous course of action; indeed, his stories can function, in part, as the kind of "particular training" in moral action that Pope John XXIII calls for. Although Gautreaux never reveals any "correct" answer to the dilemmas he poses, his positioning of the issues does reflect the nuanced position of post–Vatican II Catholicism.

This is best encapsulated in a minor but significant character from *The Clearing*, Marshall Merville. As a lawman, Merville must often use force to keep the peace, but he never does so recklessly or without remorse. Early in the novel, he articulates the moral conundrum that runs throughout the book: "'You know, I got a friend who's a priest. He says it's a sin to kill. I got no problem with that, but what if I don't kill one, and that one kills two or three? Did I kill that two or three? I can't figure that out, me'" (59–60).[12] Gautreaux does not give a clear-cut solution to this problem; it is something that all of the characters, and the reader, are left to wrestle with. The novel does indicate that Merville's most heroic action resides not in his use of violence but in his work to prevent it. Throughout his life, every time he disarms a man or confiscates a weapon, he discards it behind a dresser in his room, and "this disposal was what he enjoyed most. It took away from all evil that he had done and felt" (218). It is active act of reparation, which has a concrete impact on the lives of the people in his community. After he dies, the cache of weapons is discovered, and the men who find it reflect, "'Think of all the things that were not done'" (272). In a novel that demonstrates that acts of violence almost always beget retaliatory violence, Merville's act to remove weapons from the fray is one of the only ways to break the cycle. He cannot stop the human propensity for violence any more than Harry Lintel can help or change Ada; Merville simply does what he can to prevent the fallen people from carrying out the worst aspects of their nature.

Gautreaux is interested in more than just the question of justifiable violence, though. While most of Gautreaux's characters do not ruminate over the theological arguments regarding peace and nonviolence in as explicit terms as Merville, the experiences of the Aldridge brothers, Randolph and Byron, in *The Clearing*, and Sam Simoneaux, in *The Missing*, reflect a developing engagement with war, suffering, and nonviolence, one that reflects the nuanced Catholic position on these issues. In Gautreaux's later novels, those who experience violence are scarred, physically and emotionally, and Gautreaux's description of these scars calls into question any facile link between violence and the experience of grace.

In *The Clearing*, the trauma of World War I hangs over all the action, and its effects are felt both by the protagonists and antagonists. Byron Aldridge returned from the war "neither elated nor somber but with the haunted expression of a poisoned dog, unable to touch anyone or speak for more than a few seconds without turning slowly to look over his shoulder. . . . After France, Byron spoke to people with his eyes wide, sometimes vibrating with panic, as if he expected them suddenly to burst into flames" (11). Clearly suffering the effects of posttraumatic stress, Byron is unable to return to civilized life; he leaves his family and drifts around the country, eventually winding up in a lumber mill in Louisiana, where he works as a constable. Byron's father, a Pennsylvanian lumber merchant, purchases the mill and sends his younger son Randolph down to manage it and to reclaim his brother. The mill is an uncivilized place[13] where violence is ever-present, both in intra-camp feuds between the lumbermen and in the actions of the local mobsters who run the camp saloon. The leaders of the Mafia, Buzetti and Crouch, are ruthless, violent men, but Gautreaux indicates that they, like Byron, have been shaped by their experiences in the war. Buzetti saw three of his brothers bayoneted in one day (174), and Crouch was both tortured by his captors and forced to execute his fellow prisoners (269). Although Gautreaux does not use these traumatic events to entirely excuse the men's actions, he does indicate that their experience of violence and suffering has warped their sense of the value of human life, and the violence of the novel originates from this distorted sense of human dignity.

In contrast to these men who have been deformed by the war, Randolph stands as the emblem of detached civilization, and he is thus initially shocked and horrified by the casual violence of the Nimbus mill. He commands his brother to "'Shoot to wound,'" not to kill, but when his brother points out that even though he values the precept "'Thou shall not kill,'" the men he is trying to control do not, Randolph has no response (126, 123). Randolph has no solution to the moral complexity surrounding the use of violence and is forced to admit, "'I don't know. I just don't know'" what the correct course of action is. After his friend dies a meaningless death as a result of a saloon fight, he tries to rationalize the loss, telling his lover, "'I guess I was trying to find something redemptive in his death'" (128), but there is no such redemption to be found.

Randolph is unable to remain above the violence of the world he inhabits. The novel turns on the question of whether violence is ever necessary and demonstrates that even justifiable violence begets more violence. Randolph shoots and kills a mafioso in an act of justifiable homicide, but even though Randolph had a legitimate reason to shoot the man, the act changes him.[14] Immediately afterward, he boasts to another mobster, "'Tell Buzetti I didn't want to shoot his cousin. . . . But let him know that if he makes more trouble for me I'll make damned sure he never eats another meatball'" (177). Byron, who has more experience of violence than Randolph, tells his brother, "'I've seen this before. . . . It's how it all starts. . . . With posturing. With one shot. . . . What starts small gets bigger'" (177). He is right, of course, as this shooting leads to retaliation by the mobsters, which initiates an ever-escalating cycle of violence that culminates in a chaotic shoot-out between the Aldridge brothers and their lumbermen and the members of the mob, which leaves Byron partially crippled and most of the mobsters dead. But even this violent confrontation does not end the cycle of violence because Crouch, the one member of the mob who escapes from the shoot-out, returns to the mill camp where he murders a man, shoots Randolph, and nearly murders his wife before being killed by Randolph's housekeeper. Violence begets violence.

After the shoot-out, Randolph wonders "if he would be punished by God for shooting men, or if the killing itself was the punishment" (292), but in one of the novel's few weak points, we, as readers, do not really participate in Randolph's internal suffering over his own violent actions. He is conflicted over them, but within the logic of the novel they seem like the only possible actions for him to take, and they have almost universally positive results. Although all of the protagonists of the novel, including the children, suffer or are threatened with violence over the course of the story, in what is perhaps too harmonious a conclusion they all manage to survive and flourish, and the novel ends on an uplifting note. Randolph has matured, and Byron has reconciled with his family. *The Clearing* demonstrates the endlessness of the cycle of violence and repeatedly condemns the use of violence as an easy solution to life's complexities, but in its larger arc it still hints that violence can, in fact, be redemptive. Both Byron and Randolph begin the novel as broken, incomplete men, and it is in the violent swamp of the Nimbus mill that both men learn to love and sacrifice for each other; there is a connection between their use of violence to end the threat of the Buzetti clan and the final triumphant reconciliation of all members of the Aldridge family. While I agree with L. Lamar Nisly that it is the "refusal to accept violence easily—on both the local and the international levels—as even a necessary evil in our fallen world that affirms *The Clearing*'s Catholic sensibilities" ("Presbyterian" 114), I think the overall structure of the novel still unites violence and redemption in a way that the actions of the individual characters seem to want to resist.

In his subsequent novel, *The Missing*, though, Gautreaux's depiction of both the use and effect of violence provides no such correlation. Repeatedly throughout the novel, only those who refrain from using violence are redeemed. Gautreaux explains why this is so:

> It was a delight to write *The Missing* because it goes against contemporary American culture, and against our worst nature. It goes against everything on American television, where cops and bad guys alike are blowing people apart with pistols and assault rifles every hour, on the hour. *The Missing* goes against almost everything Hollywood teaches. . . . *The Missing* builds toward the expectation of a big shootout. When it didn't happen, I know some readers were disappointed. I expected this from day one. Americans have been programmed to a template of offense followed by justified violence. This is a cliché, and a simpleminded notion. (*Conversations* 160)

Instead of following the Hollywood formulation, which is in large measure the widely accepted American notion of how violence does and should function, Gautreaux follows the Catholic teaching on the use of violence, dramatizing that the only way to end the cycle of violence is to cease repaying violence in kind. Marshall Merville's act of removing weapons from the environment and thereby deescalating the cycle of violence is carried forward in Sam Simoneaux's decision not to use force against the Cloat clan, who murdered his family when he was an infant.

The Missing, like *The Clearing*, is a little too systematic in its ideological positioning, since Gautreaux uses both dominant plot lines in the novel—Sam's search for Lily Weller, a little girl who was kidnapped from the store where he was working as a sort of security guard, and his quest for some measure of closure over the murder of his family—to reinforce the notion that all forms of violence are ultimately destructive.[15] The novel is not a polemic screed against all forms of violence, but Gautreaux does perhaps overemphasize his theme. Time after time, those who take up arms are destroyed, and those who refrain from doing so are redeemed. The diverse set of encounters between the Skadlocks, who kidnapped Lily, and those who seek to get her back illustrates this pattern. Sam first finds the Skadlocks after they have sold Lily, and it is only because he approaches them unarmed that he is allowed to leave their compound alive. Lily's father, Ted, approaches them armed with "his knife and pistol" (114), and he ends up being mauled by their dog; he eventually dies from these wounds. Lily's brother August then seeks them out to avenge his father; Sam follows to dissuade him. Sam offers a long list of reasons that August's quest for revenge is misguided: he almost surely will be killed before he is able to carry out his act of revenge, and even if he is not, any act of revenge will simply start another cycle of violence, in which more Skadlock relatives will come to avenge themselves upon August and his family. Sam advises August to let divine justice take its course: "'down the line, when he does die, he'll have to pay up then. I don't know what will happen, exactly, but it probably ain't good'" (257). Sam's rhetoric persuades the boy not to shoot, and this act of restraint is immediately repaid when the first person who steps out of the Skadlock house, the person August would have shot, is his own sister Lily.

But the Skadlock story is really only a precursor to the central confrontation of the novel, between Sam and the Cloat clan. Throughout the novel, Sam is told that he must seek revenge as a matter of justice and manliness, and that failure to do so makes him a coward and an unfaithful son. August tells him, "'Sam Simoneaux, you're just a coward with all sorts of excuses'" (253), and Sam's bunkmate Charlie repeatedly calls him a coward, "'a little pudding,'" and "'chickenshit'" for not taking revenge (159–60). In Charlie's eyes, taking vengeance is the only form of justice for what happened to Sam's family, and in an echo of the moral dilemma of preventative violence posed by *The Clearing*, Charlie claims Sam's vengeance will also remove the danger of the Cloat menace from the world: "'Kill a snake, and the next man on the trail won't get bit'" (160). Against this rhetoric of retaliatory violence, Gautreaux positions Sam's uncle

Claude, who offers a Catholic perspective on the situation, telling Sam, "'It's what the priest says, Sam. Sin is its own punishment. They got to live with what they did. . . . Baby, what they did is who they are. It makes them cripples. Half-people'" (183). Sam listens to his uncle, but he still feels the necessity of confronting the Cloats, if not to extract revenge then to at least gain some sense of closure. The readers, too, desire to see this confrontation, and we expect the Cloats to get what they deserve. As Nisly points out, Gautreaux humanizes the Skadlocks, but the Cloats are depicted as essentially subhuman, and since "The novel sets up the Cloat clan . . . as the personifications of evil, people without any redeeming qualities . . . the reader is primed for a glorious scene of redemptive violence when Sam confronts the killers of his family" ("Vengeance" 203).

When Sam does finally confront the Cloats, though, we do not get a climactic showdown. Gautreaux subverts our expectations, because this denial of what we have been prepared for leads the reader to reflect on what did *not* happen. When we do not get the ending that we have been led to expect, we ask why, and this lingering question ultimately leads us back to Claude's position, that a life of violence extracts its own payment. The Cloats embody this precept, perhaps too perfectly. Their once-large clan has been reduced to only three ruined members; as Sam questions them about what has happened to their family, we learn that they have been decimated both by revenge killings and disease brought about by their unclean way of living. Sam's final reflection on the "mystery" of the Cloats is that "the worst thing that ever happened to them was each other" (361). Their final, depraved way of life is the inverse of the community that Gautreaux's Catholic fiction champions.

Both Bauer and Nisly draw attention to the fact that since the Cloats are already suffering and close to death, Sam's extracting of violent revenge is unnecessary; instead, Sam's interrogation of the remaining Cloats is a more effective punishment for them. By forcing Molton, the surviving Cloat patriarch, to relive his crimes, Sam initiates a visceral response; the man's "eyes blinked and watered with the pain of retelling" (356). Although Molton maintains there is no eternal judgment, Sam's insistence that "'One way or the other, when you die, there's always something to find out'" is the final message of the chapter (357). But the novel indicates that this postdeath judgment is not the only way people like the Cloats pay for their actions; by depicting them living out their final years in fetid squalor, Gautreaux condemns them to a form of death in life. In what is perhaps too neat a conclusion, the Cloats have truly reaped what they have sowed. In this sense, Gautreaux stacks the deck in favor of his moral vision; a more nuanced denouement, in which Sam is actually in danger and his opponents are not totally debilitated before he meets them, would call for a more complex ethical decision about the use of violence.

But while I do think that Gautreaux might provide an overly simplistic conclusion to the moral dilemmas raised in his novel, his depiction of nonviolence as the most moral and virtuous course of action certainly challenges widespread cultural assumptions, and his replacement of the myth of redemptive violence with the nuanced Catholic vision of ethical restraint adds a compelling and necessary voice to the discussion surrounding the use of violence. In both *The Clearing* and *The Missing* he demonstrates Catholicism's countercultural positions on issues beyond the normal flashpoints of the American culture wars. Gautreaux's work draws on Catholic social teaching to question the values inherent in contemporary American culture, and to provide an alternative way of thinking about how to think and act morally. As Claude tells Sam, "'What you do will say who you are'" (314). In his novels and his stories, Gautreaux uses this emphasis on one's deeds, which has its roots in his experience of Catholicism, to challenge his readers to think about questions of morality that they might not otherwise encounter. He uses the fictional tools of his literary predecessors, particularly the prominent use of violence, to shift the emphasis of the Catholic novel from questions of existential meaning to questions of moral action, and in so doing he keeps the Catholic novel alive and vital as a form of cultural discourse.

5 / Belief and Ambiguity in the Fiction of Alice McDermott

As discussed in the previous chapter, there are numerous connections between Tim Gautreaux's work and that of O'Connor and Percy, and his engagement with Catholic social teaching is robust, but to my mind Alice McDermott's fiction best represents the state of contemporary Catholic literature. No one better captures the rhythms and routines of daily Catholic life; her stories demonstrate the ways in which faith informs and shapes ordinary lives. Although dramatic things do happen in her novels, for the most part the plotlines are less extreme than what we find in O'Connor, Percy, and Gautreaux. Indeed, the closest analogue to her work is that of J. F. Powers. Although Powers wrote primarily about priests, his work, like McDermott's, is primarily focused on the routines of domestic life, and his stories explore how Catholic faith and culture help give shape and structure to these routines. Like Powers, McDermott uses her work to lead her readers into a reflection on the nature of suffering; her novels capture the various ways that practicing Catholics rely on their faith to help them make sense of the suffering they endure, even when their faith is not always up to the task. McDermott's fiction, though, reflects a postsecular mindset; she is more interested in posing questions for her readers than in providing answers, and within the world of her fiction, faith is just one choice among many. As she notes in an essay titled "Faith and Literature": "Complete certainty, total adherence to dogma, to foregone conclusions, to the glib reply, cuts us off—in art as well as in faith—from revelation, from the discovery of what we didn't know we knew" (*What* 183). In her fiction, she uses narrative ambiguity and carefully controlled point of view to lead her readers toward moments of possible revelation.

Although she won the National Book Award (for her novel *Charming Billy*), McDermott was still, for many years, largely overlooked by the Catholic literary community. Paul Giles does not mention her in his magisterial *American Catholic Arts and Fictions*; she is not included in Mary R. Reichardt's *Catholic Women Writers: A Bio-Bibliographical Sourcebook* or Nick Ripatrazone's *The Fine Delight: Postconciliar Catholic Literature*; and Ross Labrie, in his *The Catholic Imagination in American Literature*, dismisses her as a Catholic author, saying she writes about "Catholicism . . . with historical detachment rather than through the eyes of faith" (277). This critique is echoed by Paul Elie, who acknowledges that she is one of our "most accomplished novelists of belief" ("Criticism"), but also claims that her fiction does not address "questions of belief as they're felt in the present time" because "she writes about the 50s and 60s" (O'Brien). In his *New York Times* piece, Elie explains that he is looking for contemporary Christian literature in which "the writers put it all together," and where the writers stop "refus[ing] to grant belief any explanatory power" ("Fiction").[1]

Elie's desire is understandable, but perhaps impossible to fulfill in the contemporary, postsecular age. Although he longs for a literary depiction of belief as whole, unified, and clear, numerous scholars writing on belief in the contemporary world describe it as partial, fragmented, and ambiguous. As Charles Taylor's *A Secular Age* explains, the contemporary moment "consists, among other things, of a move from a society where belief in God is unchallenged and indeed, unproblematic, to one in which it is understood to be one option among others, and frequently not the easiest to embrace" (3). Taylor goes on to explain that we have moved from "a society in which it was virtually impossible not to believe in God, to one in which faith, even for the staunchest believer, is one human possibility among others" (3). This is what we find in contemporary literature that makes any mention of the possibility of belief; whether to believe is but one more choice amid many decisions that individuals must make. It is one that can provide some measure of comfort, solace, or insight, but one that falls short of "putting it all together."

The state of the contemporary literature of belief is well covered in both John McClure's *Partial Faiths: Postsecular Fiction in the Age of Pynchon and Morrison* and Amy Hungerford's *Postmodern Belief: American Literature and Religion since 1960*, both of which discuss the partialness of contemporary faith and the ambiguities of modern belief. McClure's description of "postsecular narratives" as ones that "affirm the urgent need for a turn toward the religious even as they reject (in most instances) the familiar dream of full return to an authoritative faith" aligns with the worldview most often found in McDermott's novels (6). In her fiction, traditional, orthodox Catholic belief and practice are often depicted, but they are not authoritative. Rather, as in McClure's postsecular texts, they are shown to "fall short of the gifts of absolute conviction and secure dwelling identified with traditional experiences" of faith (6). Hungerford's study helps provide context for why this might be true. Her work focuses, in part, on depictions of belief in which "the content is the least important aspect of religious thought and practice" (xiv); this is an accurate description of McDermott's treatment of Catholicism.

As in Powers's stories, McDermott's characters' observance of and commitment to Catholic ritual and practice matter a great deal in the overall shape and substance of the novels, but she is not interested in exploring Catholic dogma, or the mysteries of transcendence and immanence, in the manner of, say, Graham Greene or Flannery O'Connor. McDermott has repeatedly acknowledged that the Catholic nature of her fiction is not in any way doctrinal, writing, "As a fiction writer, I am not interested in conversion, transubstantiation, the mystical body of Christ, the infallibility of the pope, Aquinas, or Augustine" ("Lunatic"). And while she often writes about the importance of her faith in the creation of her art, she is not overly invested in a strictly creedal explanation of what she believes or why she believes it, claiming, "I am not a Catholic novelist if the label means a writer who is out to convince or convert, a writer whose point is that what Catholics believe—the Incarnation, the Redemption, Everlasting Life—is certain and true" ("Redeemed" 16). Nevertheless, many of McDermott's novels, particularly *Charming Billy* and *Someone*, do address the central question of how belief functions in the modern age, which is exactly the question Elie is looking for contemporary writers to address.

McDermott writes about Catholicism from a position of inquiry, not certainty. In her work, she poses the question "Do we really believe it? Christ's death bringing us to everlasting life—heaven? Really?" ("Redeemed" 15). And, she asks, if we do believe this, how does this belief affect how we live our daily lives? This question runs through her fiction and is central to any exploration of Catholic identity in the twenty-first century. Elie wants to find "the writer who can dramatize belief the way it feels in your experience, at once a fact on the ground and a sponsor of the uncanny, an account of our predicament that still and all has the old power to persuade" ("Fiction"). I argue that McDermott accurately fits this description,[2] except for Elie's final phrase. Her work does dramatize the experience of belief, but it does so by reflecting the postmodern predicament, which is that religious faith no longer has "the old power to persuade." It may still have power, but it is certainly not the *old* power. In McDermott's novels, belief in God can disrupt an individual's sense of surety and awaken her or him to new ways of seeing the world, but it does not impose a definitive narrative of meaning on existence.

McDermott's novels allow for the possibility of the divine presence at work in the world, but this presence does not always bring clarity or security. Her characters' struggles over what to believe and how to act on these beliefs reflect the tensions inherent in any declaration of belief in the modern age. This is a central animating concern in her work; as she writes in *Commonweal*, "I attempt to create characters . . . in order to discover what they believe, or hope, or long for. I write stories not to weigh the validity of these beliefs but to figure out how, given such beliefs . . . they live their daily lives in the ordinary, onrushing world" ("Redeemed" 16). Many of her Catholic characters know exactly what they believe about God, salvation, heaven, and hell; at the same time, her novels demonstrate that these beliefs are not necessarily adequate for dealing with the ambiguities and tensions of modern life, and this potential inadequacy of faith is an essential aspect of contemporary religious belief.

For McDermott, one important way this tension plays out is in the way she juxtaposes Catholic belief and ritual as a counterpoint to the finality and meaninglessness of death. She has claimed that Catholicism "is a mad, rebellious faith, one that flies in the face of all reason, all evidence, all sensible injunctions to be comforted, to be comfortable. A faith that rejects every timid impulse to accept the fact that life goes on pleasantly enough despite all that vanishes, despite death itself" ("Lunatic"). She goes on to claim that being Catholic is "a mad, stubborn, outrageous, nonsensical refusal to be comforted by anything less than the glorious impossible of the resurrection of the body and life everlasting" ("Lunatic" [*sic*]). This conceptualization of Catholicism is central to McDermott's fiction, so much so that ten years after these comments, she reiterates the claim:

> What makes me a Catholic writer is that the faith I profess contends that out of love—love—for such troubled, flawed, struggling human beings, the Creator, the First Cause, became flesh so that we, every one of us, would not perish. I am a Catholic writer because this very notion—whether it be made up or divinely revealed, fanciful thinking or breathtaking truth—so astonishes me that I can't help but bring it to every story I tell. ("Redeemed" 16)

Her fiction is often animated by the tension between accepting the truth of this "glorious impossible" and questioning its validity. Although McDermott repeatedly writes about death,[3] her focus is not primarily on the characters who die, but rather on how those who survive try to make sense of death, both of those who have died but also of their own. Her novels pose, implicitly and explicitly, the question of what, if anything, is an adequate response to the fact of one's inevitable mortality. McDermott presents the reader with two possible solutions, art and faith, neither of which is shown to be entirely up to the task. This dynamic is at the heart of the interplay between text and reader in a McDermott novel: she offers up a scenario in which we expect the characters' faith to provide them with solace, and at times it does, but never quite in the manner we expect.

Perhaps surprisingly, McDermott's characters, although they are almost universally Catholic, do not display much in the way of the "mad" faith that she claims defines her own Catholicism. Her characters, particularly her narrators, do not strike us as unreasonable, although they do manifest the sensibility that McDermott claims undergirds the Catholic faith—they refuse to accept loss and death easily. Her narrators, when faced with the very real possibility that life itself might be meaningless, construct narratives of belief that assert order within existence, and yet neither they nor those who hear their stories are particularly comforted by them. They hold out hope that there is something more than narrative that can be offered to ameliorate their pain and fear.

Child of My Heart (2002) is McDermott's most focused depiction of an individual's attempt to use narrative to hold death at bay,[4] but the novel demonstrates that although this desire is understandable it is ultimately both childish and fruitless. The novel is structured as the adult narrator Theresa's remembrance of an idealized summer, and although the novel is littered with traumatic events—including the statutory rape of Theresa by the artist whose child she babysits; a number of marital infidelities, divorces, and neglected children; and the impending death of Theresa's cousin Daisy, who is suffering from undiagnosed leukemia—Theresa's narrative of the summer manages to minimize these traumas. The entire novel functions as the grown-up Theresa's continued attempt to keep death at bay through assertion of story; even though she, as an adult, realizes the implications of her cousin's sickness, as well as the pervasiveness of pain in the lives of the people around her fifteen-year-old self, she refuses to let this trauma overtake her story.

Within the narrative, her fifteen-year-old self acknowledges the presence of death but refuses to grant it any permanent power. Although intimations of mortality repeatedly bubble up in the novel—from the graphic death of the neighborhood cat, to Theresa's claim that she remembers meeting her dead brother in heaven before being born, to Theresa's uncle's story about a ghost father and son who inhabit the attic—the youthful Theresa repeatedly transforms these unsettling events into magical stories. In one early example, Theresa spins a story about a couple who honor the memory of their dead son by creating a lollipop-filled tree in their front yard (10–11). When faced with the profusion of death, both literal and in artistic form, Theresa thinks, "I wanted them banished, the stories, the songs, the foolish tales. . . . I wanted them scribbled over, torn up. Start over again. Draw a world where it simply doesn't happen, a world of only color, no form" (180). Theresa seeks a world where "all dark things [are] banished, age, cruelty, pain, poor dogs, dead cats . . . all the coming griefs, all the sentimental, maudlin tales fashioned out of the death of children" are forbidden (180).

She attempts to use her own stories to fashion this world without pain and death, but while these stories provide transitory relief, they are ultimately powerless. They cannot stave off the inevitability of Daisy's death any more than Theresa's blind refusal to accept the number of signs that point toward her illness. The reader knows that Daisy is going to die even as Theresa refuses to see or acknowledge it. Although Michiko Kakutani identifies "Theresa's failure to get her cousin to a doctor" as one of the more "bizarre aspects of her behavior," I see this not as bizarre but as a very real and human flaw on the part of Theresa. McDermott purposefully makes the reader aware of Daisy's condition even as the youthful Theresa, and her grown-up counterpart, refuse to recognize it, so that we ultimately come to view Theresa's unwillingness to acknowledge reality as a mistake—a foolish, dangerous one, but also a very human one.

In McDermott's view, we are all in some way Theresa; we refuse to acknowledge our own mortality and the mortality of our loved ones, so we spin stories that minimize death or transform it into something manageable. We do not want to contemplate the memento mori in our midst, so we pretend that they are not there. McDermott indicates that this is understandable when we are children, like the fifteen-year-old Theresa, but when we continue to embrace these narratives into adulthood, like the now-grown Theresa, then we are holding onto a mistaken view of existence.

Child of My Heart indicates that we cannot use our stories to entirely rob death of its power, but McDermott's National Book Award–winning *Charming Billy* (1998) takes a different approach to the relationship between narrative and death. McDermott uses this novel to see if we can use narrative, not to ignore death, but to explore and to try to make sense of it.

Charming Billy—Telling Stories in the Face of Death

For McDermott, control of one's narrative is a synecdoche for faith in general, so her exploration of the ways in which narrative responds to mortality is also an exploration of the adequacy of faith to deal with death. In *Charming Billy*, she indicates that a faith that refuses to acknowledge death is essentially meaningless, whereas a faith that faces death and attempts to make some sense of it has value. McDermott makes this connection between narrative and faith explicit in an interview with Elizabeth Farnsworth, stating, "It seemed to me if you're telling a story about faith, you're also telling a story about telling stories, the things that we believe in—our stories that we hear and are told." She goes on to describe her work as being "ultimately . . . about faith, about what we believe in, and, above all, what we *choose* to believe in" (Farnsworth, "Interview," emphasis added). McDermott's prioritizing of the choice involved in this process is central to her conceptions of faith in the modern world; we are defined, in large part, both by what we choose to include in our narrative and what we choose to leave out. While McDermott illustrates that many moderns cannot simply accept an understanding of existence handed down by fiat, her fiction also acknowledges that what we choose to believe about our lives and our place in the world determines the way we carry out our lives. Our belief system structures our lived experience; the two are inextricably linked.

McDermott, like the Catholic writers before her, structures much of her fiction around suffering and death because she knows that how an individual chooses to make sense of these difficult yet inescapable elements of life goes a long way toward defining both what one values and how one acts. Her fiction often contains scenes of pain and violence because she focuses her imagination upon scenarios in which her characters are forced to choose how to make sense of these moments, and what they choose to believe about their underlying significance in a very real way defines who they are and how they live. Although this dynamic is present in almost all of her novels,[5] her treatment of this theme is most masterfully handled in the National Book Award–winning *Charming Billy*. The novel centers on the family of Billy Lynch as they attempt to come to grips with his death from alcoholism, but it is fundamentally about the power of the stories we tell and are told. The novel is structured as a long monologue delivered by the narrator to her husband, and it is a record of the narrator's attempt to inhabit and reimagine the various stories that she has inherited from her father's generation in order to construct a coherent account of where her family has come from, and by extension, who she herself is and where she might be going.

Storytelling is an integral part of the Irish imagination, and *Charming Billy* is filled with various stories and reminiscences recounted by the mostly male members of the older generation during the wake for the narrator's uncle Billy. Through these stories, Billy's family attempts to make sense of his life and his gruesome death; they want to impose a narrative upon his death that will give them some sense of closure. Billy was an alcoholic, and certain members of his family, particularly his cousin Dan Lynch, would like to fashion a romantic tragedy out of his life. The elements of romantic tragedy are present—the death of a young lover (Eva), followed by the downward spiral of alcoholism. This is the narrative arc the readers initially believe, but the narrator undermines this familiar, mawkish story by revealing that Eva did not actually die; she simply took Billy's money and returned to Ireland. Billy's cousin Dennis (who is the narrator's father) invented the story about Eva's death to save Billy's pride, and the power of this romantic narrative was so persuasive to Billy that he allowed it to shape the course of his life. He embraced the maudlin role of doomed lover, and like the hero of so many tragic love stories, he turned to alcohol as a form of solace. The novel then becomes not one more tragic love story but rather a meditation on how susceptible individuals are to the power of narrative.

The narrator does not reveal much about herself, but the little she does say indicates how she was shaped by a desire to resist the dominant narrative of the Irish Catholic girl: "take a look at an unmarried Irishwoman's attachment to her old dad if you want to see something truly ferocious. It was, I suppose, the very image I'd fought against myself, in the years after my own mother died, when I went off to Canisius instead of staying home" (132). She rejects the model of submissive femininity but ends up inhabiting another traditional Irish Catholic identity: the role of family storyteller. What is significant about this role for the narrator, though, is the way that she reimagines the stories she hears. She does not simply recount others' versions of the stories; she tells them as if she herself were present. She reveals other characters' thoughts and emotions in situations to which she would have no legitimate access; her role as storyteller frees her to tell not only her own story but everyone else's as well. This appropriation of others' stories is an example of self-consciously imaginative narrative power. McDermott indicates that every individual's worldview is formed by the stories that we allow others to tell us or that we tell ourselves, and she asks us to pay attention to which stories we embrace as formative ones.

This is where the reader's agency comes into play. The careful reader of a McDermott story knows that the story we are hearing is just one more re-creation of the past, and that while it is engaging, nothing about it requires that we passively accept this vision of events or outcomes. Just as we realize that Billy was mistaken in his submission to the tragic-romantic view of his own life, we know that the true significance of the narrator's story is not authoritative but creative. The narratives we tell and are told are important, but as the narrator acknowledges, no story, "when you came right down to it, was unbreakable, unchangeable" (222). This freedom from the authority of narrative can be liberating or terrifying—the characters in the novel who realize that this creative power is available to them struggle with the concept of God and the afterlife, recognizing that these might simply be more stories that we tell ourselves. Since, for McDermott, narrative and faith are inextricably linked, acknowledging that all narratives can be reshaped, or discarded, is tantamount to accepting that faith itself is essentially a choice, and as such, it holds no definitive claim to objective truth.

The novel ends with the narrator taking on this existential dread. What are we left with if we cannot trust the literal truth of the narratives we inherit and pass on? She acknowledges that we cannot tell the difference between "what was actual, as opposed to what was imagined, as opposed to what was believed," but she goes on to state that these distinctions do not make "any difference at all" (243). The novel ends with an assertion of the power and significance of storytelling and, by extension, of belief, but the entire novel has demonstrated that an important aspect—perhaps the most important aspect—of these stories is the ability to place oneself into them, and to become a co-creator in the process. McDermott supplies an important corrective to views of narrative that are hierarchical and require submission to the stories being told. In her fiction, anyone can become the storyteller and thus can reshape the contours of one's own narrative.

In this sense, then, her work can be read as a commentary on the practice of belief itself. What we believe is a matter of deciding what stories to accept and which to reject. Her characters have chosen to accept the tenets of Catholicism, but their Catholic faith does not inoculate them from fear and doubt. As the narrator says of her family, "All their hopes, in the end, their pairings and procreation and their keeping in touch, keeping track, futile in the end, failing in the end to keep them from seeing that nothing they felt, in the end, has made any difference" (212). Her repeated use of "in the end" foregrounds the mortality that everyone must ultimately face; all of the narratives of the novel circle around the fact that everyone is going to die eventually, so her narrator, characters, and readers are all forced to contemplate the significance of their own lives. Immediately after this passage, her father claims that his feelings of despair were "'only a brief loss of faith,'" and that once again he "'believe[s] everything now'" (212). The narrator and the reader remain unconvinced, knowing that "there was no way of telling if he lied" (212). The question posed by the novel is an essential one for the believer: is faith an adequate response to the fact of one's inevitable death? McDermott's answer is an equivocal "perhaps."

But, while *Charming Billy* foregrounds the ambiguity of belief, and the inability of the Catholic narrative to provide surety and comfort, the novel does indicate that there is something, beyond the power of the stories we tell ourselves, that can offer solace in the face of death: religious, specifically Catholic, ritual. During the central set piece of *Charming Billy*, when the family is holding the wake, Billy's wife, Maeve, is overcome with grief and despair and laments to the priest, "'It's a terrible thing, Father . . . to come this far in life only to find that nothing you've felt has made any difference'" (154).[6] While McDermott does not offer a definitive counternarrative of faith that will assure Maeve that her feelings have essential worth, she does give Maeve the presence of the priest, whose authority allows the mourners to turn their grief and despair over to someone else. The narrator states that once the priest arrives, "We all felt it, felt the tremendous relief that we finally had among us someone who knew what he was doing" (151). The priest speaks "with an authority that superseded all our experience of Billy" (152–53), and for the moment, the mourners are relieved to surrender to this authority. They lay aside their own attempts to construct a narrative of meaning and allow the priest to impose one upon them. This surrender to ritualized authority provides them with the solace they need. But while the priest does provide a narrative that "life goes on, in Christ," his story of salvation is less reassuring to Billy's family than the Catholic sacramental ritual of the Rosary:

> Abruptly, before Maeve could say another word, the priest asked us all to say a Rosary with him, understanding (of course) that there was only so much more that could be said, that the repetitiveness of the prayers, the hushed drone of repeated, and by its numbing repetition, nearly wordless, supplication, was the only antidote, tonight, for Maeve's hopelessness. (155)

In the Rosary, the priest provides a counternarrative to despair—one that is sacramental, in that it unites both word and action. It is an instantiation of faith that is more powerful than narrative alone. It is not the priest's attempt to make sense of Billy's death that matters in that moment, but rather the embrace of ritual. This moment, which is echoed throughout

McDermott's oeuvre by similar sacramental scenes (such as the wedding that closes *After This*), demonstrates that even in the postmodern age, when the necessity of choice is prioritized, the tradition of Catholic sacramentality, which unites belief and practice, remains lasting and significant. This sacramental sensibility is most evident in McDermott's novel *Someone*.

Someone—Patterns of Grace in the Postsecular Age

While *Charming Billy* self-consciously emphasizes the significance of what we choose to believe and how this affects how we act, *Someone* is more interested in depicting the patterns of grace that are present in our life, whether we are consciously aware of them or not. The Catholic sacramental view of reality indicates that the world, and everything in it, can lead one to experience grace or to have an experience of the divine, and it is this sacramental sensibility that informs the novel. Although grounded firmly in realism, *Someone* is suffused with moments that point beyond purely rationalist explanations of existence; these hints at a transcendent, supernatural presence undergirding reality are often found in both Catholic and postsecular fiction. Literary critic Mary Reichardt argues that "a defining feature of a Catholic vision and one that sets it apart from strictly deterministic theories is that it is open to supernatural mystery, the existence of another world beyond that of the senses to which human beings are ultimately oriented" (4). John McClure claims something similar for the postsecular characters he writes about: "these characters are transformed and steadied . . . by the sense that the world is seamed with mystery and benignity" (6). While in postsecular novels the characters are never quite sure of the source of this mystery or benignity, in Catholic fiction—including McDermott's—the characters who do sense this presence are able to align it with their Catholic worldview. But even in Catholic fiction, at least in contemporary Catholic fiction, these moments of grace and presence are not definitive; they are subjective, open to interpretation and even dismissal. In *Someone*, McDermott uses the form of the novel to lead the reader into a reflection on their significance.

Spanning most of the twentieth century, the novel tells the life story of Marie Commeford, a first-generation Irish American. Her life is, for the most part, unremarkable (she experiences romantic heartbreak in her teens; her father dies young; her brother, Gabe, enters and then leaves the priesthood under somewhat mysterious circumstances; she unexpectedly marries late in life, and has healthy and successful children), and it is just this relative ordinariness that McDermott wants to explore. The novel is not structured chronologically, or even thematically, but certain elements and themes recur throughout the work,[7] which help to give shape and meaning to Marie's life. Catholic philosopher and literary critic William Lynch defines the religious imagination as the individual's attempt to "literally . . . imagine things with God. Again and again, therefore, it finds itself rearranging patterns of facts and evidence into new patterns, according to its own information, its own forms, its own history" (23). Lynch's emphasis on how the religious imagination arranges information into patterns is especially applicable to *Someone*; the novel circles around a number of repeating tropes, including an emphasis on blindness/vision, the significance of falling, and the concept of mystery.

Throughout her life, Marie struggles with vision problems, which are both a literal and metaphorical issue in the novel.[8] Marie's poor vision leads her first lover to leave her, because he wants to marry someone who has "no flaws that he could see," and so the "'blind'" Marie will not do (McDermott, *Someone* 78). Part II of the novel opens with Marie suffering an acute eye injury, which leads to temporary blindness as she recovers from surgery. McDermott connects this moment of literal blindness to Marie's mortality; for Marie, the hospital room calls to mind "Something of Calvary Cemetery, of Gate of Heaven" (96). In this moment of blindness, when Marie's fear and mortality are emphasized, McDermott presents us with the "someone" of the title. Marie fears she is all alone in the dark, literally and metaphorically, and she reaches out, hoping and trusting that someone will be there with her, and the reader is slightly confused but also pleasantly surprised when she is met by the reassurance of her husband, Tom (because of the disjointed narrative structure, when Tom first identifies himself, the reader is not sure who he actually is). It is a moment where McDermott beautifully demonstrates the comforting presence of grace; the reader, along with Marie, is moved from a place of disorientation to insight and comfort.

A similar moment in the novel takes place when Marie, as a child, first encounters mortality face-to-face at the wake for her neighbor and friend Pegeen. Rather than being a frightening or disorienting experience, Marie describes the moment as one of clarity and insight:

I felt a pair of large hands slip themselves under my arms, warm and strong. And then I was aloft. *The light grew brighter and the darkness fell away.* I clutched the hard edge of the box, resisting even as I gave in, put my face to the moon-colored brightness of Pegeen's cheeks, kissed her, and then saw my own white face briefly reflected in the dark glass of the bay window as I was returned once more to the pooled shadows of the floor. (24–25, emphasis added)

In a novel that uses the interplay between sight and blindness, and light and darkness, as two of its most important and unifying symbols, it is significant that young Marie's initial encounter with death is light filled and provides her with a limited moment of self-awareness, glimpsed, as it were, "through a glass darkly."

These moments show that in this novel, death is not an enemy that needs to be resisted. Unlike the narrators of *Child of My Heart* and *Charming Billy*, Marie does not need to use storytelling as a way to construct a narrative of meaning that will invalidate the finality of death. *Someone* does contain a rather telling scene of this—the old women who spend their time above the funeral home providing overly simplistic accounts of people's lives (119ff.)—but the entire novel functions as a counterpoint to these kinds of narratives. Marie's life could easily be summed up and dismissed in a couple of lines; she recognizes that if she passed away, these same women would tell a brief story of her life: "I suspected my poorr father would be mentioned (there would be the gesture of a raised glass), my poorr mother, yet another widow in her top-floor aviary (the rubbing, perhaps, of finger and thumb)" (130 [*sic*]), but the novel demonstrates that these few lines of summary would be inadequate. McDermott's novel reveals the complexity and richness of what we normally think of as unremarkable lives. *Someone* is not about seeking to impose meaning on existence, but rather is an attempt to locate the meaning that is already there; in this sense, it is her most Catholic novel. The novel rejects the premise, which McDermott grapples with in many of her earlier works, that perhaps nothing matters at all. The moments of insight and grace in Marie's life, slight though they may be, serve as evidence that meaning is inscribed in our day-to-day lives, present in the daily mysteries and in the light amid the shadows.

Perhaps the most significant and powerful image of mystery and presence comes in the third section of the novel. Marie's brother Gabe comes to stay with Marie and Tom after he is released from the hospital where he was being treated for a mental breakdown. As Gabe struggles to readjust to life outside the psychiatric institution, they open their house and take him in. While Gabe is staying with them, Marie dreams of her oldest son's death—another scene where the line between reality and belief is blurred. Although the scene is presented as a dream, Marie insists that something else is actually at work here. She sees it as a supernatural event, and feels she has experienced an inbreaking of grace: "it had not been a dream at all. I had asked [that it not be real] and it had been given to me. Time had relented, doubled back on itself, restored what had been lost" (230). In the aftermath of the dream, she is consoled by Gabe, and in that moment of communion between the two siblings, Marie removes Gabe's medication from the nightstand, subconsciously fearing that he will purposefully overdose. She claims, "I might have saved my brother's life that night. I don't know. I might only have dreamed the loss of my first child" (231). What is real and what is imagined and how they connect to each other blend together, and are ultimately indistinguishable for both Marie and the reader.[9]

In that moment, Marie is present for Gabe, to catch him *before* he falls. The novel ends less than a page later, with Marie's recollection of Pegeen asserting, "I'll pretend to fall, see, and he'll catch me and say, Is it you again?" (232). These images—of the individual falling and either being caught or picked up—serve as bookends for the novel, and the middle of the book contains two scenes of people falling and being caught as well. Both instances point toward the existence of a transcendent presence that undergirds the often violent nature of reality. The first is Tom's brush with death. As an airman in the war, his plane was shot down and he was forced to parachute out: "he dropped into the worst nightmare anybody ever had: cloud, smoke, the thick smell of the fuel. A dream's endless falling" (163–64). He lands in enemy territory and ends up in a POW camp. He tells Gabe and Marie that one thing that "'gave me hope'" (163) was a sermon Gabe had preached during his short time as an acting parish priest. Significantly, given the novel's emphasis on blindness and vision, the homily was on the man born blind (John 9:1–12), whom Gabe describes as the only person "'in the New Testament who Jesus cures without being asked. Without a profession of faith'" (162). This idea—that we don't necessarily need to ask, or even believe, in order to benefit from God's mercy—comforts Tom, and it is an idea that suffuses the novel as well.

It resurfaces in what is the last chronological moment in the novel, which is another moment where vision, falling, and mystery all come together to provide a sense of presence and comfort. At this point in the novel Marie is almost totally blind and resides in an assisted living facility. The line between past and present seems to be blurring for her, and she is seeing visions of things that are not really there: "strangers, children in old-fashioned clothes, sometimes nuns in long habits or women with babies in their arms. A clean and lacy light all about them" (176). As readers, we cannot be sure what to make of this. It seems to be the delusion of age and illness, and this is how Marie's family responds to it, but Marie is not so sure. She asks them, "'Why do you think every mystery is

just a trick of the light?'" (177). Marie's question is a perfect encapsulation of Reichardt's claim that Catholic art points toward "the existence
of another world beyond that of the senses to which human beings are
ultimately oriented" (4); the events of the novel hint at a level of mystery
and presence beyond normal everyday reality.[10] Marie's caregiver calls her
visions "consoling angels that appeared to only the few, in their old age"
(McDermott, *Someone* 177), and in the context of the novel this explanation is entirely plausible. The caregiver himself takes on a Christ-like aspect in the scene; he provides comfort and support for Marie in her hour
of need. He tells her he will always be there for her: "'If you ask . . . you
know I will do it for you. You only have to ask'" (177). Significantly, Marie does *not* ask for his help, but as with Jesus in the parable of the man
born blind, asking is not actually a prerequisite for his presence and aid.
The chapter ends with Marie stating, "I suppose I stood then, because he
caught me as I fell" (177).

This is the lasting spiritual vision of McDermott's fiction: whether we
ask for it or not, someone will be there in the end to catch us when we fall.
This is the "glorious impossible" that she repeatedly invokes in her work.
It is not a reality that individuals in our secular age spend much time
thinking about; it does not necessarily define most people's daily existence. Nevertheless, as *Someone* beautifully demonstrates, it is a central
aspect of McDermott's creative imagination, and the form of the novel
can lead the reader to a renewed awareness of these moments of mystery
and grace in his or her own life as well.

The Ninth Hour—"The Peculiar Gnosis of Trains"

I began this chapter by connecting McDermott to J. F. Powers, noting
that, on the whole, these two writers mine the same vein of domestic Catholicism. This being said, there are also connections to be made to the
work of Flannery O'Connor; although their themes and styles are, for
the most part, quite different, there is a reason that they both are celebrated as (arguably) the greatest American Catholic writers of their re-
spective generations. O'Connor's primary theme is "the salvation or
loss of the soul" (*Mystery* 167), whereas McDermott is more interested in
tracing out how the rhythms and practices of faith shape one's life. There
are places in her fiction, though, where she is explicitly interested in exploring this drama of salvation; this is most pronounced in her novel *The
Ninth Hour*, which is widely considered her most explicitly "Catholic
novel."[11] Here she turns her gaze onto the legacy of sin and the cost of
virtue, and explores whether sacrifice, and even damning oneself to save

another's soul, is the right thing to do (in this respect, the novel echoes Graham Greene's fiction as well).

Rather than exploring all of the Catholic elements in the novel, I focus here on the ways in which one particular scene from the book parallels a scene in O'Connor's work, both in content and theme. Both scenes feature moments of disorientation and violence that reveal fundamental aspects of a fictional character, which in turn shape the reader's overall understanding of the work. By exploring these similarities, we can see how McDermott's treatment of the scene works as a palimpsest laid over O'Connor's own, and we can appreciate the nuances in the approaches taken by these two masters.

The midpoint scene in *The Ninth Hour* bears a strong resemblance to the opening scene of O'Connor's *Wise Blood*. In both instances, the authors place their protagonists on trains in order to draw contrasts between these characters' essential natures and the rest of humanity. Both scenes feature what Walker Percy, in his own pivotal train scene in *The Moviegoer*, called "the peculiar gnosis of trains... from which there is revealed both the sorry litter of the past and the future bright and simple as can be, and the going itself, one's privileged progress through the world" (184). In both *Wise Blood* and *The Ninth Hour*, the train scenes provide background on the characters' pasts and the things that drive them, and contain moments that will shape the characters' future arcs. Moreover, as Percy's quote indicates, the scenes provide insight into the spiritual mysteries that shape these characters' lives. In both scenes, the characters have upsetting interactions with their seatmates and in the dining car, and in both instances the characters end the scene feeling completely isolated and desolate. Crucially, both of these scenes also shape the reader's empathy, or lack thereof, toward the characters, which impacts our own overall understanding of the novels' contours.

O'Connor opens *Wise Blood* on a train so that the reader can immediately get a sense of who Hazel Motes is—a young man, recently released from the army, who has no connections to other people, no home left, no real plans for the future, and who is obsessed with death (understandably so, since we learn he has lost all of his family members) and the question of salvation. Unlike the more "normal" passengers, he does not know how to interact or make small talk; instead, he accosts his fellow travelers with assertions like, "'I reckon you think you been redeemed'" (14), and, "'If you've been redeemed... I wouldn't want to be'" (16). But while this issue of redemption is a central concern of Hazel's, the other passengers clearly do not care about it, and certainly do not want to talk about it (again, understandably so!). Hazel spends his train ride awkwardly badgering the porter into admitting that they are from the same home-town, and trying to tell other people they are not saved because Jesus is not real; no one listens to him, and the chapter ends with him locked up in his coffinlike sleeping berth. The impression the reader is left with is of a lonely, isolated, disturbed young man, both pitiful and off-putting. The other people on the train clearly dislike him and want nothing to do with him; the reader feels similarly. Over the course of the novel, though, O'Connor shows us Hazel ultimately becoming a compelling figure—someone whose actions and underlying beliefs are profoundly, trans-formatively baffling for Mrs. Flood. He remains, even at his time of death, a lonely, isolated, disturbed young man, but over the course of the novel he changes from someone who feels the need to badger others about his beliefs to someone who is unwilling to explain them at all. But in living them out, he becomes a sort of transformative witness for others. Most readers will not come to like or admire Hazel Motes, but he does hold our attention and lead us to ask the kinds of important ques-tions O'Connor wants her readers to consider.[12]

The Ninth Hour focuses on a broader cast of characters than *Wise Blood*; while O'Connor's novel is clearly primarily focused on Hazel Motes, McDermott's novel follows both the arc of a whole family and the order of sisters (the delightfully named "The Little Nursing Sisters of the Sick Poor, Congregation of Mary Before the Cross") who help them. The novel opens with the suicide of a man named Jim, a trainworker with a child on the way, who has been fired for "unreliability and insubor-dination" (5–6), and then it tracks the life of his widow, Annie, and their daughter, Sally. The narrative also touches on the lives of various mem-bers of the Little Nursing Sisters of the Sick Poor, as well as Annie and Sally's neighbors the Tierneys (one of whom ends up marrying Sally). The sisters give Annie a job in the convent laundry and help raise Sally; Sal-ly's children narrate the novel (though in classic McDermott fashion they do so in a manner that involves providing access and insight into events and interior states that they could not actually know[13]). Like *Someone*, *The Ninth Hour* is a story about ordinary, mostly unremarkable lives, though the latter novel, which contains not only the book-opening suicide but also a murder, is more firmly embedded in the violent traditions of the Cath-olic novel.[14] The title itself invokes the time of day that Catholics reflect on Christ's death on the cross, or what McDermott calls, "the time when even the faithful must hold their breath, wait in the sudden stillness to see if their belief will be justified or defeated" (Domestico).

But while intimations of mortality are central to the book, in some re-spects the most distressing and disorienting scene is Sally's train journey from New York to Chicago. As Mary Gordon puts it, "The train Sally boards seems to be a branch of the Hieronymus Bosch Railroad Company";[15] it is on this journey that Sally comes to question, and ultimately reject, her vocational call. McDermott, in true O'Connor style, peoples the train with a series of grotesques. Sally's seatmate is a woman of indeterminate age (throughout the scene, Sally continually revises her assessment of the woman's age: "she was growing younger and younger in Sally's estimation, growing closer to her own age, which seemed odd given how old she had first seemed" [139–40]), who breathes with "the quick, deep, agitated panting of an animal in distress" (137). The woman, upon hearing that Sally is on her way to join a convent, makes light of Sally's vocation and scandalizes her with crude discussions of her sexual proclivities and disappointments. A young boy with "scabs on his scalp and on his chin and nose" and an "unevenly shaven" head, which "made his skull seem battered and misshapen," wanders the aisles of the train, intermittently pursued—and beaten—by his "stooped, hunchbacked" mother (144, 146). In the dining car, Sally meets a young woman about her own age, who spikes Sally's tea and then hits her up for a handout. Sally, as a result of her religious upbringing and worldview, sees all of these experiences as instances of "her vocation . . . being tested" (151).

As she wanders the train she is overwhelmed by the stench of her fellow passengers: "everything reeked. Of smoke and sweat and the human gas seeping from these mounds of flesh" (155), and she cannot help but question if she truly wants to "giv[e] her life" for these "vulgar, unkempt, ungrateful" others. When she finally gets back to her seat, her sleeping (or sleep-feigning) seatmate will not budge, until Sally finally lashes out and repeatedly strikes the woman. The woman (somewhat understandably) calls her "'a devil,'" to which Sally responds, while staring at her own reflection in the window, "'You are'" (158). Here she seems to be directing the name both to herself and the woman next to her. If the train ride is a test of her vocation, it seems she has failed. Indeed, the chapter ends with her arriving in Chicago and telling the nuns who are waiting for her at the station, "'I've thought better of it'" (159).

But perhaps the train ride is less a test of Sally's vocation than a test of her entire worldview. She set out on the journey as a naive young woman, with little experience of the real world. She has idealized the work of the nuns and her own capacity for purity and goodness. She tells herself that she is "going to give her life to others, in the name of the crucified Christ and His loving mother." Her ruling metaphor for her vocation is, "Love applied to suffering . . . [was] like a clean cloth to a seeping wound" (153). She believes that "One kept oneself, one made oneself, pure— . . . to offer relief to the wretched world, to assuage the seething wound, the lesion, *laesio*, of human suffering" (154). This kind of innocence and naivety cannot last in the real world, any more than Hazel Motes's own naive worldview can persist in the face of the world's indifference. But while the reader instinctively recoils from Hazel, for the most part we find our sympathies lie with Sally. She is certainly overly idealistic, but we find her reaction to this grotesque, violent world to be reasonable. Just as O'Connor complicates matters by staying with Hazel and allowing us to witness his journey, McDermott, too, wants the reader to continually reevaluate our assumptions, and she uses Sally's experience on the train to do just this. McDermott's fiction repeatedly calls upon the reader to question the kinds of stories we tell ourselves, and Sally's experience on the train is a particularly powerful account of how one individual can be disabused of her own limited narrative. In *Wise Blood*, Hazel's train ride sets up the rest of his violent and grotesque journey, leading indirectly, but inexorably, to the murder he will commit and the penance he will embrace; in *The Ninth Hour*, Sally's understanding of her own failure will lead to her own murderous plot (she hatches a plan to murder the invalid wife of her mother's lover, in an attempt to save her mother's soul by sacrificing her own). She believes that since she has not been able to successfully give herself to a calling based upon self-sacrifice and service to the unwashed masses, she should instead damn herself in order to redeem her mother. In the end, she does not end up committing the murder she has planned (though one of the sisters, seeming to sense what Sally has planned, appears to carry out the murder instead).

After her experience on the train, Sally trades in one misguided story for her life only to adopt another. Her experience of suffering and disappointment leads her to reject the initial narrative, but she does not come to understand that the story she has been told, and that she continues to tell herself, is mistaken; rather, she thinks she is failing to live up to the role she has assigned herself in the story, and so she chooses a new one that is, in reality, even more misguided. Her worldview has been so entirely shaped by her Catholic upbringing, and the lessons she has internalized about purity, sacrifice, and duty, that she is unable to escape them. In this, she is—again—like Hazel Motes, who cannot escape from his own religious upbringing and the ragged figure of Christ who haunts the back of his mind. For O'Connor, Hazel's inability to fully leave Christ behind is the mark of his salvation. The same cannot be said for Sally, who even in adulthood never seems fully content or at peace; her children note her "midlife melancholy" (241). It is impossible to say whether this dissatisfaction with life is a genetic predisposition (after all, her father clearly suffered from undiagnosed mental illness, which can certainly be inherited), or whether it should be more directly connected to her failure to live up to her religious ideals. McDermott's novel can be read, in part, as a cautionary tale about how the internalized religious worldview can misshape us, just as much as Hazel's antireligious one. *The Ninth Hour* is not an antireligious book—it celebrates the lives of the nuns, and dramatizes the true joys and consolations of a life lived in devotion and service—but it is entirely realistic about the potential costs of such a worldview.

Throughout her oeuvre, McDermott poses hard questions about the adequacy of faith in the modern, skeptical age. She claims, "I am a Catholic writer because my faith taught me to . . . reflect on our mortality, to rail against our suffering, to consider the grace by which we endure and the love that proposes to redeem us" (*What* 171). We see this in her novels, where she shines her fictional lens on the pain and suffering of the world, and looks at how we attempt to make sense of these traumas. In novel after novel, McDermott says we do so with a story; we submit ourselves to a narrative of existence, or we create our own, that helps us find order and meaning. Sometimes this narrative includes the embrace of religious belief, and sometimes this acceptance of faith provides solace. She makes no definitive claims, though, for the power of narrative, or of faith. The answers she provides in her novels are partial at best, but they do spur the reader toward contemplation of what we do not know; her fiction indicates that partial answers, and glimpses of mystery and grace, are the best options that we have in the modern age. This is not to say, though, that the religious vision of her fiction is in any way lacking; on the contrary, a careful reader of McDermott's novels repeatedly gets the sense that even these partial answers truly are enough.

6 / "Life Is Rough and Death Is Coming": George Saunders and the Catholic Literary Tradition

George Saunders is not often discussed as a Catholic writer, but in both his thematic concerns and his literary techniques, his work does fit solidly within the Catholic literary tradition. Like the other writers discussed in this book, he is interested in affecting his readers and leading them to consider often overlooked moral and spiritual aspects of existence. Saunders is fond of quoting Flannery O'Connor's claim that "The writer can choose what he writes about but he cannot choose what he is able to make live."[1] As it turns out, what Saunders is able to make live in his fiction is remarkably similar to what we find in many of the works discussed in the previous chapters, particularly O'Connor's. Both of these masters of the short-story form are funny and bleak in equal measure. Both frequently write about what O'Connor called "freaks," grotesques or people on the margins of society. Both are intensely moral writers who are upfront about their desire to impact their readers, and they both often rely on moments of violence to bring about a new level of insight or grace for characters and readers alike. One underlying reason for these similarities might be the common background that O'Connor and Saunders share—their formation in the Catholic Church.

On a number of occasions, Saunders has discussed how his Catholic upbringing has continued to shape and affect his worldview. In a 2016 interview with *Image* magazine, Saunders stated, "I was raised in parochial schools. . . . I think I've always had a need, because of that intense period, for mystery and metaphor and beauty—really because of the power of the Catholic Mass. Catholicism was central to my way of thinking and being in the world—a moral system and an aesthetic system" (*Conversations* 142–43). He goes on to state that his faith dwindled in middle and high school, but he notes the lasting significance of that early exposure to the Catholic faith: "Once a person has a glimpse of mystery, he's always going to be seeking that" (143). This emphasis upon, and attempt to seek out, the underlying mystery of existence is an important aspect of the Catholic imagination. In the previous chapter I cited Mary Reichardt's claim that "one [aspect] that sets [a Catholic vision] apart from strictly deterministic theories [of existence] is that it is open to supernatural mystery, the existence of another world beyond that of the senses to which human beings are ultimately oriented" (4). Saunders says something similar, claiming, "We live in an incredibly material time. . . . [We] think that it just so happens that in this generation we are fully equipped to know all that there is, and that we can know it logically and via the senses, period. And this inclination leads us to be very rational and data-reliant and pragmatic and mystery-denying— and yet mystery is real. We have no satisfactory answers for any of the biggest questions" (*Conversations* 149).

As we will see, exploring this mystery is central to his award-winning fiction, but it is a recurring theme in his essays as well. Saunders has written about his Catholic upbringing on a few different occasions; the essay "Hypocrites," published in *The New Yorker*, best encapsulates his youthful faith journey. Here he recounts his experience of serving as an altar boy and coming into the sacristy to find his priest and a nun in the midst of a passionate kiss. It is a slight and humorous piece, but in just a few short pages he traces out an entire arc of religious experience—from unquestioning acceptance of a top-down approach to religious belief, through a moment of disillusionment and doubt, to outright rejection, and finally back toward a more cautious and nuanced acceptance of belief.

After recounting the moment of seeing the kiss, he writes, "By now I knew enough about the time in which I was living to know that one of our fundamental narratives was that a critical moment of disillusion could be followed by a bitter but justified downward slide into decadence. Having seen what I had seen, in other words, entitled me to cry Hypocrites! and leave religion behind forever." He goes on to debate within himself about whether it actually is justified to dismiss all organized religion based on the failures of two of its representatives. He writes, "This vignette proved, in effect, that the whole religion deal was a sham. Didn't it?" But in a surprisingly wise insight for a teenager, he is able to reject this line of thinking: "In a moment of clarity I saw that it did not."

The failure of these people whom he respected as representatives of the religious institution leads him to recognize that "the system, supposedly overseen in even its smallest details by God Himself, via these representatives, [might] actually be just a crude, man-made form, inspired by, but inaccurately addressing, even obscuring, some greater and more difficult-to-discern truth." So his adolescent self comes to the conclusion that perhaps it does invalidate some aspects of organized religion, but not belief in general: "Yes, it's just you and Me now, Jesus said inside me. You can know Me all on your own. In fact, that is how you must know Me." This is both an affirmation of a spiritual reality, while also a rejection of traditional religious forms, which is how Saunders approaches the transcendent in his fiction as well. His depictions of spirituality and grace are often couched in terms of hesitation and doubt, balanced with a sense of wonder, and even awe, at the undeniable reality of a spiritual experience that exists beyond the purely secular. Even though the religious sensibility within his fiction is not necessarily orthodox, it is still possible to see how it has been shaped by his Catholic upbringing.

"Enough. Let Us Speak Honestly": The Confessional Urge in *Lincoln in the Bardo*

One concrete way that Saunders's Catholic upbringing manifests itself in his fiction is through his focus on the necessity of confession, which plays a role in his short stories and is a central concern of his only novel.[2] Saunders has spoken about the importance of the sacrament of confession in his own youthful faith: "I remember going to first confession, which to me meant I was going to be pure for the first time in my life. And I remember feeling that purity, loving it. . . . Once you've had that experience as a young person, it's real to you forevermore. It's not trivial. It's not laughable. And you have a hunger for it thereafter" (*Conversations* 147). This hunger for purity and a kind of innocent, youthful faith is central to the overall structure of *Lincoln in the Bardo*, where the various characters realize that in order to move on from the bardo they need to openly admit and accept their faults. The confessions in the novel lack the forms of the sacrament, but their function is similar.

The novel takes place one February night in 1862; Abraham Lincoln's son Willie has just died, and his body has been interred in a crypt in a Georgetown cemetery. The vast majority of characters in the novel are ghosts who inhabit the graveyard. They are, for the most part, unaware that they are dead; they think, or at least claim to think, that they are merely sick. They spend their nights obsessively re-living and retelling details from their lives—as one spirit says, "to stay, one must deeply and continuously dwell upon one's primary reason for staying; even to the exclusion of all else" (255). It is their inability, or unwillingness, to let go of specific aspects of their lives that keeps them trapped in the bardo. The term comes from Tibetan Buddhism, but it bears more than a passing similarity to purgatory; it is a space between life and whatever comes after death. Once a character comes to the position of being able to surrender their will and let go of whatever is holding them back, they disappear from the bardo and move on, through a process the ghosts call the "matterlightblooming phenomenon." This is unsettling for the ghosts who remain behind, although it is clear to the reader that to be trapped, as the ghosts are, is a form of torture, and—although it is not entirely clear what comes after the matterlightblooming phenomenon— it must be preferable to the sort of backward-looking obsessions that hold these spirits in place. Over the course of the novel, young Willie's presence in the bardo is a catalyst that leads many of the souls who have been trapped there for centuries to finally move on.

For reasons not fully explained, adults can linger in the bardo indefinitely, but it is forbidden for a child to remain behind. A child who does experiences a more overt form of torment. Willie was ready to move on soon after arriving, but once his father shows up in the graveyard to hold the boy's body, this act of physicality leads Willie to want to remain. The other ghosts are moved by this demonstration of love, but also realize that the boy cannot stay. This is the crux of the novel. It is funny and strange and moving, and has important things to say about race and class and the idea of America, and how to live a good and meaningful life. But for our purposes, what is most compelling here is that it is a prize-winning novel that is focused on one of the great mysteries of faith—what happens after we die—and the premise takes it as a given that the spirit will live on, and that our actions in life have some impact upon the disposition of our soul after death. The afterlife depicted here is not strictly Christian, though there is one character (the only one in the cemetery who knows he is dead) who is a Christian minister, and his vision of death and judgment is explicitly tied to his Christian faith. But Saunders makes it clear that he doesn't want to limit his depiction of the afterlife to anything too familiar or dogmatic, stating, "One of the things I tried to do was use the word 'bardo' as opposed to 'purgatory,' partly to help the reader not to bring too many preconceptions to it. Whatever death is, we don't know what it is, so in a book about the afterlife, it's good to destabilize all of the existing beliefs as much as you can" (Prickett).[3]

The afterlife portrayed in the novel *is* destabilizing, but one familiar element, for anyone raised Catholic, is how confession functions here. On a number of occasions, spirits are only able to move on from this place after they admit what they have done wrong in life; this process allows them to be freed from the things that are holding their souls back. As one newly arrived soldier says, "I . . . am trapped here and I see of this instant what i must do to get free./ Which is tell the TRUTH & all shall be/" (138 [*sic*]). He then hesitates, because he doesn't want to tell, to admit his fault. But he continues on, dictating a letter to his wife in which he admits to infidelity and asks her, and God, for forgiveness. His soliloquy ends with him saying, "[I] cry out to you . . . in hopes that you, and He who hears & forgives all, will hear & forgive all and allow me to leave this wretched" (140)—and before he even finishes the confession we see the matterlight-blooming phenomena and he is gone.

We see a more developed version of this pattern toward the end of the novel, when the two primary narrators, Hans Vollman and Roger Bevins III, also go through a form of this confessional process. Bevins tells Voll-man, "Enough. Let us speak honestly" (327), and they finally acknowledge to themselves, and each other, that they are dead, and that they have failed both in life and in the afterlife. They had had a chance to intervene to save another child who was trapped in the bardo, and it is this failure that "had always, in every minute since, gnawed at us./ Our first huge failing." So they go to where the girl is trapped and being tormented and tell her, "We are sorry . . . sorry we did not do more." . . . / "We were afraid . . . Afraid for ourselves" (332). But, as in the Catholic understanding of the sacrament of confession, admission of wrongdoing is only part of the process; they also need to make amends. So Vollman goes into the place where this young woman is trapped and uses the sort of metaphysical explosion that accompanies the matterlightblooming phenomena to free her from her torment, allowing all of them to move on from the bardo. We do not know what comes next, whether it is enough to save their souls or not, or if the whole concept of a "saved soul" is the wrong one to bring to the novel. But it is significant that in this crucial scene Saunders is drawing on his Catholic upbringing to bring about a resolution, demonstrating the central role that contrition, confession, and satisfaction (or seeking to rectify our wrongs and make amends) play in healing the soul. When we finish the novel, we do not have any sense of surety about the immortality of the soul or the "four last things," but—as with McDermott's novels—*Lincoln in the Bardo* points us toward consideration of these themes, and leaves us with the sense that asking these sorts of questions is what truly matters.[4]

From "The River" to "The Falls": O'Connor and Saunders

Saunders's focus on the confessional impulse is the most overtly sacramental aspect of his fiction, but throughout his work there are numerous connections to the broader currents of the Catholic literary tradition. Saunders himself notes how his "moral or ethical sense" provides a through line from his early experience with Catholicism to his fiction and to his current Buddhist practice. In each of these modes, he says, "I had a sense that we ought to be urgently seeking, because we are in some trouble down here: life is rough and death is coming" (*Conversations* 143).

It is in this idea—that life is rough and death is coming—that we can most clearly see how his work echoes that of Flannery O'Connor. As Coleman and Ellerhoff note, when connecting Saunders to O'Connor, one of the defining traits of Saunders's writing is his "metaphysical concerns for the place of short fiction in readers' and writers' lives" along with his sense of "the moral agency of literature" (vii). Like O'Connor, Saunders uses a combination of violence and humor to surprise and disorient his audience, usually in the service of some sort of moral/ethical vision. O'Connor's famous quote about why she uses violence and the grotesque, which was discussed in chapter 1, provides a helpful framework for understanding Saunders's work:

> The novelist with Christian concerns will find in modern life distortions which are repugnant to him, and his problem will be to make these appear as distortions to an audience which is used to seeing them as natural; and he may well be forced to take ever more violent means to get his vision across to this hostile audience. . . . You have to make your vision apparent by shock—to the hard of hearing you shout, and for the almost-blind you draw large and startling figures. (*Mystery* 33–34)

Saunders's stories often employ just these kinds of large and startling figures, to similar effect. As I discussed in the Introduction, Saunders—like O'Connor—views fiction as a medium that has real-world consequences for the reader, claiming that when we read, "something happens. Something big and breathtaking and non-trivial" (*Conversations* 158). In his work, the way this comes about is by "destabilizing us and making us re-examine whatever position we are holding—humbling us, as it were" (159).

While O'Connor's worldview is more closely aligned with Orthodox Catholicism than Saunders's, in the latter's work we can see a similar attempt to disorient and then reorient the reader, to bring his audience to see the world as he does—to recognize that elements of contemporary society that most of us accept as normal are in fact deeply disturbing (in this, his work also parallels J. F. Powers's). This is the source of the absurd and grotesque that we see in any number of his stories. In order to fully flesh out the connections between O'Connor and Saunders, it will be helpful to place two of their stories in conversation. I do not know if Saunders's story "The Falls" is a direct response to O'Connor's "The River," but the number of similarities between the two pieces is striking. Besides the obvious direct connection between the titles, both stories feature a child (or children, in Saunders's story) swept away by a river and put into deathly peril, and an adult man who goes into the water in an attempt to save the child(ren). Both stories are also, I contend, about what it takes to be saved, though they approach it from different angles and with a different primary focus.

O'Connor's story focuses on a young boy named Harry Ashfield, who is the child of thoughtless, careless parents who spend their evenings hosting parties and their days recovering from hangovers. Harry is taken by his babysitter to hear a fundamentalist preacher, who baptizes the boy in a river. The story ends with Harry sneaking away from his neglectful home and going back to the river to try to recover the feeling of meaning and belonging he first felt during the action of being baptized. He is carried away by the river, and (presumably) drowns. Despite this tragic conclusion, critics tend to read the story for its religious significance, connecting Harry's death to the sacrament of baptism. Ralph C. Wood describes the conclusion as a "gift of temporal and eternal salvation" for Harry, and goes so far as to call this final scene a "supremely happy ending to a supremely happy story" ("Scandalous" 204).

While Harry's fate is the main focus of the story, for our purposes, it is also important to trace the arc of a minor character, Mr. Paradise. He is first introduced as a religious skeptic; he has skin cancer, and only shows up at the river to "'show he ain't been healed'" (O'Connor, *Works* 159). Down by the water, while most of the assembled are eager to listen to the preacher, Mr. Paradise openly mocks him and his backwoods baptisms, calling out "'Pass the hat and give this kid his money. That's what he's here for'" (163). O'Connor repeatedly links him to porcine imagery, connecting his character both to literal pigs and to the Bible story of Jesus chasing demons into swine. The cancerous growth on his temple is even likened to devil horns. At the conclusion of the story, when he sees Harry walking alone down the road, he grabs a peppermint stick and "dr[ives] slowly down the highway after the boy" (170). In the final scene of the story, Mr. Paradise is the only one present when Harry goes into the water, and he does go into the water after him. Most critics argue that "he is not trying to rescue him but to lure him into another ugly form of abuse, sexual abuse" (Kilcourse 138). Wood notes that while "humanistic readers may want to see the old man as seeking to save the boy from drowning, O'Connor's symbolism is unmistakable—if only by way of nearly what every schoolchild is taught: 'Do not accept offers of candy from strangers'" ("Scandalous" 201–2). O'Connor clearly structures the story so as to make Mr. Paradise a sinister figure, but at the same time we cannot fully understand Mr. Paradise's intent, because O'Connor does not give us access to his thoughts. We only know for sure that when Harry begins to flounder and "hit and splash and kick the filthy river. His feet were already treading on nothing," Mr. Paradise goes into the river after him, waving his hands and shouting (O'Connor, *Works* 171).

While the rest of the story has tracked Harry's experiences, the story closes on Mr. Paradise instead: "Mr. Paradise's head appeared from time on the surface of the water. Finally, far downstream, the old man rose like some ancient water monster and stood empty-handed, staring with his dull eyes as far down the river line as he could see" (171). This final image works on two levels; symbolically, if Mr. Paradise is a demonic figure, it shows that Harry is now safe from this form of predation. But on the more mundane level, O'Connor's stress on Mr. Paradise's limited vision indicates that he, like many of her readers, is unable to see or recognize what has transpired with Harry. He sees it only as a tragedy, whereas O'Connor claimed Harry "comes to a good end. He's saved from those nutty parents, a fate worse than death. He's been baptized and so he goes to his Maker; this is a good end" (*Conversations* 58). O'Connor's primary focus in this story is on a literal depiction of baptism as a dying and rising in Christ (an image she repeats in *The Violent Bear It Away*, where Tarwater simultaneously drowns and baptizes his cousin). There are, she believes, fates worse than death—and in Wood's words, "life's significance lies beyond life" ("Scandalous" 189). The story invites the reader to contemplate this transcendent horizon of significance.

Saunders's version of the story focuses less overtly on this transcendent significance, but it is still a central concern of the piece. In both stories, a character's apparently meaningless, or useless, death is actually a mark of a "good end." O'Connor makes Harry's pursuit of eternal salvation not a subtext but the main theme of the piece (Harry goes into the water thinking "he intended not to fool with preachers anymore but to Baptize himself and to keep on going this time until he found the Kingdom of Christ in the river" [*Works* 170]). For Saunders, writing in a post-Vatican II world and from a less orthodox Catholic position, salvation—if it is to be depicted—needs to encompass, in the words of J. C. Whitehouse, the horizontal axis of salvation.[5] Redemption is reached not just in the dynamic between creator and individual, but in the way the individual cares for those around him.

In "The Falls," Saunders's primary focus is not on the child(ren) in danger, but rather on the adult trying, vainly, to save them. While we cannot know what Mr. Paradise is thinking when he goes into the water, in "The Falls" we do get this kind of direct insight. The story moves back and forth between two interior monologues. We spend the majority of the story inside the mind of Morse, a neurotic husband and father. He is a classic Saunders protagonist: one who doubts his own self-worth and life's meaning, who is beset by doubts and worries and appears to lack any form of resolve. We also occasionally shift into the mind of Aldo Cummings, an angry, bitter forty-something who lives with and resents his mother, while dreaming of future literary greatness.[6] The contrast between the Morse and Cummings mindsets makes up the majority of the story; the dramatic action—the introduction of the runaway canoe being swept toward the titular Falls—does not happen until about two-thirds of the way through the piece. Like the Wolff and Dubus stories discussed in the Introduction, "The Falls" begins as one type of story and, through the introduction of an unexpected catastrophe, becomes something else.

"The Falls" begins with Morse walking past a Catholic school, worrying about what the schoolchildren will think of him—he doesn't want to smile too broadly lest they think he's "a wacko or pervert"[7] (*Pastoralia* 175). It quickly becomes clear that Morse's concern over what others think of him, not only schoolchildren and passersby on the sidewalk, but also his wife, his kids, and his boss, is almost paralyzing. He has a hard time acting in the world because he is constantly second-guessing himself, worrying over how his actions will be perceived. He is ashamed of his own thoughts and actions (or inaction), and yet also "ashamed of his own shame" (176). He "go[es] about in such a state, pulse high, face red, worried sick that someone would notice how nervous [he] was" that he is caught in a thought spiral (177), where his worries about his worries keep him trapped in his own head.

Cummings, on the other hand, is openly disdainful of what others might think about him. His thoughts, too, tend to focus on how he is perceived by others, but whereas Morse feels shame and embarrassment, Cummings feels anger and resentment. He feels marginalized and overlooked by the "power elite in [his] conspiratorial Village" (178), while at the same time it is clear that he believes himself intellectually and aesthetically superior to the "wage slaves . . . with their feet of clay thrust down the maw of conventionality" who make up the rest of his town (184). Morse's interior monologue is hesitant and recursive; Cummings's is florid and overblown (if this is his literary voice, it is clear that he will never achieve the artistic success he dreams of).

The two men come upon the river, separately, and each sees that two girls have lost control of their canoe and are in imminent danger of being carried over the Falls. We follow both men's internal hesitation about what to do. In keeping with his character, when Morse first hears the girls' desperate pleas for help, he assumes they "yelled something insulting" at him (181); we follow his train of thought as he works through his self-centered worries and finally arrives at the crucial insight: "Morse stopped in his tracks, wondering what in the world two little girls were doing alone in a canoe speeding toward the Falls, apparently oarless" (183). On the heels of this realization, Morse initially hopes others will act to save the girls, but finally comes to realize that no one else will be able to get there in time. If anyone is going to do anything to help rescue them, it has to be him.

Significantly, the reader is aware of at least one other person who could intervene. Cummings, too, sees what is happening. Like Morse, he is initially lost in his own thoughts, but whereas Morse is wracked by self-doubt and therefore not initially aware of what is unfolding on the river, Cummings recognizes the situation at once. Saunders, using free indirect discourse, captures the scene using Cummings's own poetic register: "he rounded the last bend before the Falls, euphoric with his own possibilities, and saw a canoe the color of summer leaves ram the steep upstream wall of the Snag. The girls inside were thrown forward and shrieked with open mouths over frothing waves that would not let them be heard as the boat split open along some kind of seam and began taking on water in doomful fast quantities" (185). The would-be artist cannot help but dramatize the situation, but unlike Morse, he immediately knows "I must do something. . . . I must do something" (185).

Both men spend time dithering, hoping someone else will act. Saunders shows Cummings "stumbl[e] over the berm uncertainly, looking for help but finding only a farm field of tall dry corn" (185). This is where the story leaves him—knowing the girls are doomed without his intervention, but still unable to fully commit to action. For Morse, on the other hand, his actions and his thoughts work at cross-purposes. Once he recognizes the danger, he "began to run" toward the water, even as, in his mind, he hopes others will act before he gets there. Once he reaches the river and sees how close they already are to the Falls, he understands:

> They were dead. They were frantic, calling out to him, but they were dead, as dead as the ancient dead, and he was alive, he was needed at home, it was a no-brainer, no one could possibly blame him for this one, and making a low sound of despair in his throat he kicked off his loafers and threw his long[8] ugly body out across the water. (188)

In the final lines of the story, the perpetually feckless Morse finally takes decisive steps, even though it seems certain that he will not be able to save the girls, and most likely will also be swept over the Falls. It is, then, a seemingly meaningless, fatal action. But, like Harry's immersion in the river, it is anything but meaningless; it is the mark of Morse's salvation.

Morse's attempt to save the girls can only really have meaning if we look for meaning beyond the hope of immediate results. Saunders does not tell us what happens, so it is possible—though certainly improbable—that Morse will be able to rescue the girls. We are told, though, that "no one ever had" been able to swim out to where the girls are foundering, and that Morse is a "mediocre at best" swimmer (187). Earlier in the story we hear about a young man who attempted the feat only to be swept over the Falls (181), which foreshadows the ending. So if we assume that this rescue attempt is unsuccessful, doomed before it even begins, is it still a worthwhile thing for Morse to attempt? As he notes, he has a wife and children; is it not a wasteful decision for him to make this attempt, knowing as he does that the girls "were basically dead" already? (188) The key passage comes right before the long sentence quoted above, which ends the story:

> The girls saw him now and with their hands appeared to be trying to explain that they would be dead soon. My God, did they think he was blind? Did they think he was stupid? Was he their father? Did they think he was Christ? (188)

He is certainly not Christ, but his self-sacrificial act of being willing to lay down his life to save others is Christ-like. And this invocation of Christ ties back to the prominent placement of the aptly named St. Jude's Catholic Church at the beginning of the story. St. Jude, as the patron saint of lost causes, would carry special significance for Morse's heroic, but almost surely hopeless, rescue attempt. When presented with the girls' plight, Morse is shocked into action and is able to transcend the prison of his own consciousness; even if he is unsuccessful, he is saved. He is, like O'Connor's grandmother, able to recognize his own kinship with the suffering Other and to intuit his responsibility to act, even in the face of overwhelming odds.

In Saunders's *A Swim in a Pond in the Rain*, he discusses Tolstoy's "Master and Man," which also features a scene where a character (Vasili, a rich landowner) somewhat surprisingly sacrifices his life in an attempt to save another; Saunders summarizes Vasili's transformation by invoking O'Connor's "A Good Man Is Hard to Find": "He would have been a good man if there'd been someone there to freeze him to death every day of his life" (242). Morse, too, would have been a good man if there'd been someone to throw him over the Falls every day of his life (though apparently the same cannot be said for Cummings). When discussing "The Falls," Saunders notes that extreme circumstances can shake us out of normal routines and lead to moments of true insight: "Maybe we are like eggs, with our shells made of habit and ego, but every now and then little cracks appear and some light comes in and we get a glimpse of how things actually are. . . . Every now and then we get a brief glimpse of our own limitedness—which is, of course, also a glimpse of our limitlessness" (*Conversations* 144).

Saunders's work, like O'Connor's, can help facilitate these little cracks and moments of insight for the reader as well, and they both use violence, and moments of trauma or catastrophe, to open these cracks. Their best stories leave the reader asking questions, and these questions point us toward issues of morality, ethics, and ultimately salvation. Here, the story asks the question, What do we owe to each other? Who exactly is our neighbor, and what are the limits of our empathy and our actions? If we see someone in need, what are we obligated to do? What is the connection, or perhaps disconnection, between our own thoughts and self-conception, and how we act in the world? We do not need to turn to the metaphysical realm to make sense of the story or answer these questions, but the story does invite us to include these aspects in our reflections.

Saunders's Diagnostic Fictions

While I think the parallels to O'Connor are important, there are also strong connections between Saunders and the other most significant American Catholic writer of the twentieth century, Walker Percy. Many of Saunders's stories are, in Percy's terminology, "diagnostic" fictions, which shine a light on the maladies afflicting modern consciousness.[9] Like Percy, Saunders is interested in depicting the isolation and despair of the individual in the midst of contemporary mass society, and (like Percy) Saunders indicates that the root causes of these problems can be traced back to the very structure of our consumerist, technophilic society. As in

Percy's novels, Saunders's stories feature characters who are suffering both physically and metaphysically, and these maladies are tied together. The illnesses and sicknesses that beset so many of Saunders's characters— perhaps most obviously in the "flaweds" from the short story "Bounty"— are not simply pathologies; they are signs of deeper systemic problems in the social fabric and in the way the culture functions.

This is, essentially, the theme of the entire *In Persuasion Nation* collection, where in story after story we see how consumeristic, capitalistic culture is inundating and overwhelming the individual. Each section of the book opens with an excerpt from a book called *Taskbook for a New Nation*—an invented piece of nationalistic social criticism, which makes absurdly grand claims about "prosperity," "freedom," "tradition, family, friends, tribe," and the need for "moral distinctions," while demonizing anyone who dares to question this kind of groupthink mentality. It culminates in the line "we must not be slaves to what we have previously said, or claimed to be true, or know to be true, but instead must choose our words and our truths such that these will yield the most effective and desirable results. Because, in the end, what is more honest than preserving one's preferred way of life?" (181). This is the kind of mentality, a defining feature of late-stage American capitalism, that his stories attempt to both depict and resist.

We find evidence of Saunders's diagnosis of modern society in almost all of the stories he writes; it is one of his most urgent themes. "CivilWar-Land in Bad Decline," the first story in his first collection, can serve as a microcosm for the whole Saunders oeuvre, since many of the key elements that recur throughout his work are already here: we have the somewhat bizarre theme-park setting, the simultaneous presence of humor and despair, the unlikable narrator for whom we nevertheless feel empathy, the overriding stress of economic anxiety (our narrator goes along with his boss's terrible plan to protect the park against roving gangs by arming an unstable employee named Samuel, an ex-soldier who was kicked out of the army for committing atrocities in Vietnam, and he then agrees to help cover up Samuel's murderous behavior because he fears the economic insecurity of losing his job and not being able to get another one). We even have the surprising presence of ghosts, whose appearance is presented to us as readers as being rather unremarkable. And of course we have moments of shocking violence—including Samuel murdering a boy and leaving his severed hand in the narrator's office, and at the end of the story, Samuel stabbing the narrator to death.

From these elements, what kind of diagnosis can we make? First, we can describe this as a fallen world. It is a society with a false sense of its own history and a deep antipathy toward accurately seeing itself (again, this is a trait that is threaded throughout all of Saunders's work). It is a violent world, where violence inevitably breeds more violence, and for reasons of profit and security those in power allow the violence to persist. It is a society where corporate-speak and jargon help mask what is actually going on. It is a society that is devoid of respect for the dignity of the individual.

Our narrator is, in many ways, a pathetic yes-man—unable or unwilling to stand up for himself, to push back against his boss's unethical ideas or his wife's unkindness toward him. And yet he does possess a sense of right and wrong (we see him "express reservations at arming an alleged war criminal and giving him free rein in a family-oriented facility" [15]), and after he buries the dead boy's hand he thinks, "I did a horrible thing. Even as I sit here I'm an accomplice and an obstructor of justice" (20). He goes along with these bad things initially because he worries about losing his job, and then he worries about going to jail and not providing for his family. His fears are legitimate. He lives in a world that makes it hard to be good, and it is clear he does not have what it takes to be a better person.

But what makes the story so exemplary is the final scene, where, as he is being murdered, the narrator begins to gain perfect knowledge. He sees his murderer's past; he sees the pain that he himself has caused, and what he is truly like: "I see the man I could have been, and the man I was, and then everything is bright and new and keen with love and I sweep through Sam's body, trying to change him, trying so hard, and feeling only hate and hate, solid as stone" (26). Here Saunders is gesturing toward what will become one of his central concerns: how we can go about actually changing ourselves and those around us. In this instance, though, the narrator is ineffectual. He cannot do what he wants to do—as in life, so in death.

In this respect, "CivilWarLand" echoes the classic O'Connor story "A Good Man Is Hard to Find";[10] in both, we get unlikable, though not irredeemable protagonists who only come to a full moment of insight as they are being murdered at the end of their story. As noted above, O'Connor closes her masterpiece with the Misfit declaring that the grandmother "would've been a good woman, if it had been somebody there to shoot her every minute of her life." In one sense he is right; it is only when she is faced with her own mortality that she finally sees past the barriers she has constructed around herself and is able to reach out and recognize her kinship with the Misfit, calling him "one of my own children." In a similar fashion, the moment of death has given the narrator of "CivilWarLand" a new level of insight; he gains the ability to feel empathy for his murderer and has a desire to change him.

One of Saunders's critiques of his Catholic upbringing is that "Christianity did a lot of urging one to be good but didn't tell one much about *how* to accomplish that—how to change, how to convert one's way of thinking and being in the world" (*Conversations* 143, emphasis added). Of course, one's experience of Catholicism or Christianity might differ in this respect—surely there are strains of Catholicism that do emphasize practice over theory—but it is a significant aspect of Saunders's diagnostic fictions. He is not interested simply in pointing out what is wrong with society or how we might think differently about our place in the world; he wants to focus on what leads the individual to actually change his or her actions. In this respect, I think it is fair to say Saunders is interested in orthopraxis.

This focus on right action, and how an individual's actions are shaped by their environment and community, is a major focus of Catholic fiction after Vatican II. We can contrast this with, say, O'Connor's work, because while there is some level of social critique in her fiction, her primary focus is on the individual and the salvation of his or her soul. As discussed in chapter 3, Walker Percy's fiction is more emblematic of postconciliar fictions, in that he is more interested in social critique. His novels demonstrate the ways in which society as a whole shapes individuals. Communities are polarized along racial, ethnic, and religious grounds, and the value of individual lives is diminished. Many of his novels feature government-run behavioral conditioning centers, where individuals are reconditioned to be exactly like other, "normal" people. These clinics are places where individual human lives have no inherent meaning, because the focus of scientific thinking is not about the individual but about the group. Percy depicts these clinics as totalitarian machines, willing to dispose of those individuals who will not conform. In response to these social ills, Percy's novels advocate for a Kierkegaardian leap of faith, or the embrace of a transcendent reality that one does not rationally comprehend. And along with this leap into accepting belief, he also continually closes his stories with scenes of communion—of people coming together. One of the core principles underlying his worldview is that the solution to many of the problems facing the individual is to build community.

In this, a strong parallel is present between Percy's vision of a cure and Saunders's own. While Saunders's work does gesture toward transcendence (after all, so many of his stories end not with death but with the moments after death), his writing also foregrounds the importance of human connection, compassion, and empathy as the cure to both personal and societal alienation. This is a particularly resonant theme in the

Tenth of December collection, but really it appears throughout his work. The pervasive reality of Saunders's fiction is that although the world is harsh and difficult for most people—the rich and powerful prey upon the poor and weak, thereby making it more likely for the weak to prey upon their compatriots as well—there is a way beyond this. People can still do good—are, in fact, called to do good, to carry out what (as a product of parochial schooling) Saunders surely knows as the corporal works of mercy: to feed the hungry, clothe the naked, shelter the homeless, visit the imprisoned, comfort the sick, and bury the dead.

The story "CommComm," the final piece in *In Persuasion Nation,* actually hinges, in a way, on this final corporal work of mercy. While excavating the site for a new military base (the pointedly named "Dirksen Center for Terror"), diggers uncover "a couple Potentially Historical corpses" (206), the presence of which threaten to derail the new development. Rather than run the risk of this happening, which would lead to a whole host of problems for the main characters—impending unemployment, exacerbated health problems, the displacement of our narrator's parents' ghosts[11]—one employee, Rimney, convinces the narrator to help him secretly rebury the bodies elsewhere. Their deception is uncovered by their coworker, Giff, which eventually leads Rimney to murder both Giff and then the narrator as well. In some respects the story parallels "CivilWarLand," in that we have a narrator who is not necessarily a bad person but who goes along with increasingly morally objectionable actions because of difficult extenuating circumstances, who is ultimately murdered by a violent coworker. And, crucially, in both stories we stay with our narrator for a moment after they die.

In the final moments of "CivilWarLand," the ghost of our narrator tries to change his murderer but cannot do so; here, something different happens. Earlier in the story, Giff says, "'I had it in me to grow. We all do! I'm not all good, but there's a good part of me. . . . Do you know that good part? Have you met it, that part of you that is all about Truth, that is called, in how we would say it, your Christ-portion . . . [that says] Do what's right, come what may'" (216–17). In this instance, come what may is in fact his grisly murder. But death is not the end.

Giff's ghost comes to the narrator, explaining the revelation that came with his death: that "'There is a glory, but not like how I thought. . . . I had it all wrong. Mostly wrong. Like my mind was this little basket, big flood pouring in, but all I got was this hint of greater water?'" (225). His desire to do good—to reach out to the narrator in order to prepare him for his death and to help free his parents' ghosts—bears fruit. This moment is an instantiation of what a Catholic might call the communion of saints, in which the dead and the living can continue to interact and help save each other. It is a demonstration of how selflessness and true communion can lead to meaningful change. The story ends with one of the more beautiful passages in Saunders's oeuvre (and one that is echoed by a number of different passages in *Lincoln in the Bardo*, which is, in essence, a book-length reflection on these themes):

> All this time we grow in size, in love, the distinction between Giff and me diminishing, and my last thought before we join something I can only describe as Nothing-Is-Excluded is, Giff, Giff, please explain, what made you come back for me?
>
> He doesn't have to speak, I just know, his math emanating from inside me now: Not coming back, he would only have saved himself. Coming back, he saved Mom, Dad, me. Going to see Cyndi, I saved him.
>
> And, in this way, more were freed.
>
> That is why I came back. I was wrong in life, limited, shrank everything down to my size, and yet, in the end, there was something light-craving within me, which sent me back, and saved me. (227–28)

Here we see Saunders demonstrating a faith in something beyond the self—an emphasis upon both transcendence and immanence that aligns with some of the central tenets of Catholicism, and the themes of fellow Catholic writers like O'Connor and Percy. Life *is* rough, and death *is* coming, but we are not alone, and death is not the end.

"Tenth of December" and the Rejection of False Narratives

In "CommComm," as in *Lincoln in the Bardo*, Saunders incorporates aspects of the uncanny in order to illustrate his ideas about the transcendent dimension of existence. In the title story of the *Tenth of December* collection, he eschews these fantastical elements but maintains a focus on the difficulties of life, the reality of suffering, and the ways in which human connection can help save us. Like McDermott's *Charming Billy*, "Tenth of December" is a meditation on mortality and the ways the stories we tell ourselves shape our experiences. The story begins in a close third-person point of view, tracking the thoughts of a boy named Robin as he sets off for a walk in the woods on a cold December day. He is clearly a daydreamer; as he walks he casts himself as the hero of an adventure in which he needs to rescue his classmate, Suzanne Bledsoe, "the new girl in homeroom," from an imaginary race of creatures he calls Nethers. It is clear that he has been engaged in a long-running imaginary battle with the Nethers, and that this is most likely because he is a bit of a social outcast. His thoughts frequently turn to his worries about being overweight (his fantasy version of Suzanne reassures him that "It's cool if you swim with your shirt on"), and his run-ins with real-life "in-school cretins" who mock his name and weight (219, 217). In a heartbreaking passage he reflects, "Sometimes with all the teasing his days were subtenable" (241). Although he does not come out and articulate overtly suicidal thoughts, he does think, "Sometimes in life one felt a feeling of wanting to quit. Then everyone would see. Everyone would see that teasing wasn't nice" (241). In the absence of friends, he takes refuge in the stories he tells himself.

While the story opens and closes with Robin's perspective, the main focus of the piece is really on Don Eber, who at fifty-three is dying from brain cancer. He, like Robin, is out walking in the woods, but whereas Robin is there because he is lonely, Eber has set out on this frigid day because he is planning to end his own life by exposing himself to the extreme temperature. He is terrified of his sickness and of what it will do to him; he does not want his family to have to care for him as his body deteriorates, and he does not want to lose his sense of self as the cancer grows. His solution is suicide, though he realizes he cannot leave a note for his family because of "Insurance. It couldn't seem like he'd done it on purpose" (245). Still, he feels it is worthwhile because by doing so "he would have preempted all future debasement. All his fears about the coming months would be mute. Moot"[12] (232).

Robin's and Eber's paths intersect; Robin finds Eber's discarded coat, and in an attempt to do a good deed and get it back to him quickly, Robin cuts across a frozen pond and ends up falling through the ice. Eber, when presented with Robin's own crisis, abandons his plan and wades into the water to rescue him.[13] This redemptive act leads, eventually, to Eber's recognition that his suicidal tendency was wrong. After pulling Robin from the water he realizes "this [committing suicide] was not him. This was not something he would have done" (245). He realizes that "he still want[s] to live. . . . Yes, yes, oh, God, yes, please" (248). In the broadest sense, "Tenth of December" follows the same arc I have been tracing throughout this book—a character, when faced with a moment of life-threatening trauma, is able to find a sort of clarity of purpose that changes not only their immediate actions but also their overall sense of self. This reorientation opens up the character and the reader to the actions of grace.

This story in particular highlights the ways that individuals are shaped by the narratives they tell themselves, and how these narratives are often unconsciously absorbed from the surrounding culture. In this sense, it connects back to the work of J. F. Powers, who also used his work to challenge readers to see beyond the conventional narrative frames that define particularly American ideas of success. Throughout his oeuvre, Saunders repeatedly draws our attention to the ways that an individual's consciousness is shaped by external forces (usually some combination of commercialism, capitalism, and the emptiness of corporate jargon); his characters demonstrate how these forces circumscribe not just what one thinks about, but even the language one uses to think.[14] Our vocabulary is limited by these frames, and one effect of his writing is to make us, as readers, more aware of this phenomenon. This is a central concern of just about every story in *In Persuasion Nation*, from the mandatory acceptance of targeted advertisements in "My Flamboyant Grandson" to the ways that the test subject teens in "Jon" have their minds and personalities completely shaped by a forced combination of drugs and advertisements. This tendency is also present throughout the *Tenth of December* collection, most overtly, perhaps, in the completely vacuous but undeniably sinister corporate-speak of the Memorandum in "Exhortation." This element might not be the first thing that jumps out to a reader of "Tenth of December" but is nevertheless a central theme of the piece.

Both Robin's and Eber's narrative voices are shaped by the stories they have taken in, which set up idealized expectations of heroic action, of manliness, of a good death. Robin fights his loneliness by telling stories, and these stories are clearly influenced by the narratives he has heard and read. His quest to rescue the damsel in distress is a conventional fairytale plot; the Nethers "tended to talk like that guy in *Mary Poppins*" (216); while on his mission, he directs commentary on his engagement with the Nether back to the mission-control folks at NASA like an astronaut on TV. He sets off across the frozen lake in order to live up to his conventional ideas of bravery: "wasn't this feeling of fear the exact feeling all heroes had to confront early in life? Wasn't overcoming this feeling of fear what truly distinguished the brave?" (229). There is nothing particularly unsettling about a child drawing on these narrative frames, but in Eber's case, where we see a similar dynamic at work, we can see the potential problems that come from having one's consciousness colonized by external narratives.

One reason Eber has chosen this particular method of suicide comes from something he has read in a book, which describes the experience of dying from exposure as a peaceful, even pleasant feeling. He recalls a passage from *The Humbling Steppe*, which reads, "A blissful feeling overtook me as I drifted off to sleep at the base of the crevasse. No fear, no discomfort, only a vague sadness at the thought of all that remained undone. This is death? I thought. It is but nothing" (230). But for Eber, the reality is markedly different from what is described in the book—out in the cold, he is afraid and in terrible pain and is anything but peaceful. There is a disconnect between his personal experience and what he had been led to believe would happen.

Similarly, there is a disconnect between Eber's previous experiences with illness and the death of a loved one, and the social expectations that he has internalized about this. One of the main motivations for his planned suicide is he believes "that's what a father does. Eases the burdens of those he loves. Saves the ones he loves from painful last images that might endure for a lifetime" (224–25). But we learn that Eber has had firsthand experience with the suffering and death of his own beloved stepfather, Allen, who, when dying, underwent a total personality transformation, becoming cruel and violent. Eber fears that something similar will happen to him, and he wants to spare his family from suffering on his behalf. He thinks it is the correct thing to do, even though he personally does not regret or resent Allen for how he acted as he died. On the contrary, he acknowledges, "Oh, Allen. Even when you were THAT you were still Allen to me" (230).

He allows his internalized expectations of what a "good father" would do to outweigh his actual experiences with his own good father. His actions are based not on what he himself experienced, but what he thinks is expected of him. This is partly a result of his own fear, but it is also certainly influenced by American narratives about aging, sickness, and the worth of an individual human life. It is only when he sees Robin break through the ice that this framework is upended and he perceives things in a new light. He is able to discard that narrative, to see it as a false story he was telling himself, and realize, "Good God, there was so much to do. If he made it" (247). He is able to accept that even in his own sickness and death, he can still love and be loved:

the thing was—he saw it now, was starting to see it—if some guy, at the end, fell apart, and said or did bad things, or had to be helped, helped to quite a considerable extent? So what? What of it? Why should he not do or say weird things or look strange or disgusting? Why should the shit not run down his legs? Why should those he loved not lift and bend and feed and wipe him, when he would gladly do the same for them? He'd been afraid to be lessened by the lifting and bending and feeding and wiping, and was still afraid of that, and yet, at the same time, now saw that there could still be many— many drops of goodness, is how it came to him—many drops of happy—of good fellowship—ahead, and those drops of fellowship were not—had never been—his to withheld. Withhold. (248–49)

In the end, the story—like so many of Saunders's best pieces—asserts the inherent value and dignity of the individual. But it also demonstrates that it takes a great shock to the system for the individual to be able to let go of inherited ideas of how one should act. Complete disorientation, up to and including coming face-to-face with death, is necessary before re-orientation is possible.

Saunders, like the Catholic writers who came before him and those who follow after, believes in the power of literature to change both readers and writers. In an interview with Michael Murphy, director of the Hank Center for the Catholic Heritage at Loyola Chicago, Saunders connected his understanding of the function of art to sacramental practice, stating,

> I've had the idea that the sacred or the sacramental is the ritual reminding of yourself that the habitual is not correct. So you go in once a week and you have your bell rung by just a slight moment where the curtain drops and you go, "Oh yeah, I'm going to die, there are forces that this pea brain can't grasp." Then you return to your regular life just with a little resonance of that. That's why we do it. Because it's easy enough to skate along in this delusional relative state. I think especially in a materialist culture like ours we're encouraged to do that. The system would like us to. But to take yourself out of that habitual state through a religious practice or through art is just a way of saying—most of my life I'm insane. Most of my life I'm deluded. And so is everyone else. And we go along playing. Then maybe for a few days at the end of your life the light comes on. Or when someone that you love dies the light comes on. And it goes back off. But sacramental means reminding ourselves that this state of mind is off.

Throughout each of the chapters of this book, we have seen just this practice at work. These stories flip on the lights so that we can catch glimpses of reality, even for the briefest of moments. They serve as reminders that the conventional narratives proffered by society are inadequate and incomplete, and sometimes these reminders can be enough to help reorient a life.

Epilogue

Phil Klay, Kirstin Valdez Quade, and the State of Contemporary Catholic Literature

While I do not find questions about the viability or ongoing existence of the Catholic novel to be particularly compelling[1] (the Catholic novel—like the novel in general—will continue to exist in one form or another, even as critics and readers continue to forecast its death), I am interested in the ways the Catholic novel continues to evolve and change to reflect the contemporary moment. The authors I have discussed thus far were all born before Vatican II, and so have, to various degrees, been formed by the ritual and dogma of the preconciliar Church. While Tim Gautreaux, Alice McDermott, and George Saunders are still publishing, there is a younger generation of Catholic authors, all born after Vatican II, who are creating vibrant vital stories that carry on the conversation of what faith looks and feels like in the twenty-first century. I close this study of American Catholic fiction by looking at two of the most exciting voices in this cohort: Phil Klay and Kirstin Valdez Quade. Both Klay and Quade write powerful stories that are structured so as to affect the way their readers see and understand the world. Both, in very different ways, explicitly explore the role of faith in shaping one's worldview. And both use moments of violence as a key aspect of their fictional aesthetic. In Klay's fiction, violence is tied directly to the experiences of war and its aftermath; Quade connects the violence to systemic breakdowns in the social fabric, but also to the experience of faith itself, and she explores whether moments of violence really lead to the kinds of transformation we have come to expect from other Catholic stories.

"We Don't Suffer Alone": Phil Klay's War Stories

Phil Klay was born in 1983 in Westchester, New York, and grew up Catholic. He attended Regis High School in New York City, which is run by the Jesuits. As he told Nick Ripatrazone, for *Image*, at Regis, "I was introduced to the study of theology and to writers like Flannery O'Connor, Graham Greene, Evelyn Waugh, François Mauriac, Walker Percy, and Shūsaku Endō. I had phenomenal teachers who modeled a particular type of intellectual engagement with the world"; he went on to explain that this formation "certainly influenced" aspects of his fiction. In a more recent interview, he returned to the significance of this Catholic formation in his high school years:

> When I was in high school, I was part of a group called Chi-Rho, in which we read religiously inflected literature and worked at a hospice run by a group of nuns. Part of the ethos of Chi-Rho is that there ought to be a direct connection between the literature we were reading and the work we were doing in the world, that it ought not be just an aesthetic or intellectual enterprise. In that sense, I've always felt that literature isn't some abstract realm removed from one's place in the world, but directly related to it. ("Point of War")

In both form and content, his fiction reinforces this connection between literature and one's actions in the real world.

Klay's first story collection, *Redeployment*, which won the 2014 National Book Award, displays his Jesuit training in a number of ways. The stories in the collection grew out of his time as a member of the US Marine Corps, where he served in Iraq from 2007 to 2008 as a public affairs officer, and they reflect the violence and turbulence of war, while at the same time being shot through with an underlying religious sensibility that draws attention to the ways that life-or-death moments point individuals toward questions of faith. This is not to say that Klay tries to draw some facile correlation between the trauma of war and an embrace of religion. On the contrary, as he notes in an essay for the *American Scholar*, "the most intense horrors of the world do not always lead to faith. There are plenty of atheists in foxholes, and some of them are atheists because of what they experienced in foxholes. . . . War leads less to faith than it does to a moment of choosing." Klay's fiction often builds to these moments of choice, either on or off the page.

This pattern is found throughout his first novel, *Missionaries*, which is—among other things—a profound meditation on the far-ranging impacts of globalized, depersonalized war. The novel is intensely violent; it features characters carrying out, suffering, and reporting on horrific violence. One of Klay's central concerns is to demonstrate both how pervasive this violence actually is, and how invisible it is to much of the Western world. It asks the American reader to reflect on our culpability for participating in a system that leads to this kind of devastation while completely ignoring it. It also connects this kind of suffering back to that of Jesus; when asked what makes his writing particularly Catholic, he responded that a defining feature is that "It suspects that if you don't have a bloody, beaten body dying in agony at the center of your symbolic system, you're not playing the game right" (Burton). In his work, there is no shortage of suffering bodies, and he works, subtly but insistently, to connect this kind of suffering back to the underlying Catholic conception of reality.

For our purposes, though, it is best to look closely at one of the most moving stories from *Redeployment*, "Prayer in the Furnace," which is a story about how individuals respond to violence, both that they themselves have perpetuated and that they have suffered. It is also a story about the steps we can take, in a broken world, to possibly be made whole again. The story is narrated in the first-person voice of a priest who is serving as an army chaplain in Iraq. It opens with a Marine named Rodriguez encountering the chaplain shortly after the twelfth member of their battalion has been killed. Rodriguez is struggling with his grief over the death of his friend, but he is also clearly troubled by the overall actions of his squad. He tells the priest that they have been deliberating provoking Iraqi insurgents in an attempt to drive up the number of firefights in which they engage. He also intimates that they have been firing upon civilians as well. He tells the priest, "'If you killed somebody . . . that means you're going to hell. . . . If other people did it, too, when you're out there, and you don't stop them. Do you go to hell, too?'" (139 [*sic*]). The priest senses that the "it" here refers to more than the kind of combat covered by the standard rules of engagement, but Rodriguez does not elaborate on what he means. It is evident, though, that he wants the chaplain to do something about what has been going on. He closes the conversation by saying, "'I'm not confessing shit. I ain't sorry for shit. You can tell anybody you want'" (140).

The priest does try to raise the issue through the chain of command, but no one is particularly interested in looking into whether Marines have been committing war crimes. As the story moves along, the priest recognizes that something is clearly wrong with Charlie Co., but there does not seem to be any way to address this. Rodriguez tells him, "'I used to think you could help. . . . But you're a priest, what can you do? You gotta keep your hands clean'" (152). The priest responds with a relatively vacuous retort: "'No one's hands are clean except Christ's. . . . And I don't know what any of us can do except pray He gives us the strength to do what we must'" (152). But he recognizes the emptiness of his own response, noting, "I wasn't sure I believed the words I was saying to him or if there were any words I'd believe in. What did words matter in Ramadi?" (152).

The story does push back against this idea that words are entirely meaningless and ineffective, though. Throughout his narrative, the priest makes reference to countless writers, from Augustine and Aquinas, to St. Paul and John of the Cross, to Georges Bernanos and Wilfred Owen. He finds a level of comfort and insight from the words of these writers; they help guide him, and he relies upon their wisdom. He also finds a great deal of comfort in a letter written by his mentor, "Father Connelly, an elderly Jesuit who'd taught me Latin in high school" (it is Father Connelly who references Bernanos) (155). In this letter, Father Connelly reminds the narrator that "sin is a lonely thing" and that the kind of isolation that it brings cuts off the soul, "shielding it from love, from joy, from communion with fellow men and with God" (156). He advises the narrator, "Your job, it seems, would be to find a crack through which some sort of communication can be made, one soul to another"[2] (156). The narrator uses this insight to help craft the sermon that in some ways serves as the climax of the story.

Earlier in the story, he describes a memorial service for a fallen Marine where he reads from 2 Timothy: "I have fought the good fight. I have finished the race. I have kept the faith" (131). He admits that he uses this passage "to set an appropriate tone" (131). He knows it is not a particularly consoling message, but he does not want to unsettle anyone (which, given the situation, is appropriate). But in this latter sermon, he does want to challenge them, so he goes into detail about the suffering of the innocent, both outside of war and within it. As he speaks, he notes "confusion on the faces of the Marines in the audience. That was good" (157). Although earlier in the narrative he doubted the authenticity and efficacy of his words, here he is using them to try and connect, to break through the isolation he knows they are all experiencing. One way to do this is by drawing attention to the ways in which suffering unites people, both to each other and to Christ.[3]

As he tells the Marines, "'*All* of us suffer. We can either feel isolated, and alone, and lash out at others, or we can realize we're part of a community. A church . . . [and] being Christian means we can never look at another human being and say, "He is not my brother"'" (159, emphasis in original). Although the sermon is powerful, Klay does not attempt to make us believe that it alone is going to immediately change hearts and minds. Although the priest ends the sermon feeling "flushed, triumphant," he also notes the "sermon hadn't gone over well. A number of Marines didn't come up for Communion" (160). If his hope is that the Church can help unite isolated individuals in their suffering, then the refusal of this Communion is both literal and symbolic. There are clearly limits on the efficacy of words, no matter how well crafted.

The effects of the war linger long after the Marines return home. The priest notes the high number of postdischarge deaths, crimes, drug use, abuse, and suicide among the members of Charlie Company. They have all been scarred by the violence they have suffered and that they have carried out. The story ends as it begins, with Rodriguez coming to the priest shortly after the death of a comrade, this time to suicide. Here again, Klay shows the limits of language to make things right. There is no solution to violence and trauma. Even the rituals of prayer and the sacrament of confession can only do so much. But there is something to be said for empathetic listening and simply being present for another isolated, hurting individual. The narrator closes the story by telling Rodriguez, "'In this world, He only promises we don't suffer alone'" (167). Rodriguez doesn't seem particularly comforted by this; he spits on the ground and offers a seemingly sarcastic "'Great'" in response. Klay does not end the story with an overt display of grace, or hint that anyone's experience of violence and suffering will lead to a profound conversion.

But this is not Klay's message. He does not want to use violence as a redemptive or purifying experience. In his work, he emphasizes the ways in which war breaks individuals and communities, while at the same time maintaining the possibility that faith in Christ's own experience of suffering really does mean that no one needs to suffer alone. This is something that the title of the story "Prayer in the Furnace" helps make clear. The title is an allusion to the story of Shadrach, Meshach, and Abednego, from Daniel 3, in which the three Hebrew men are thrown into a fiery furnace by the Babylonian king Nebuchadnezzar for refusing to worship a golden idol. But God is present with them in the furnace—"I see four men unbound and unhurt, walking in the fire, and the fourth looks like a son of God" (Daniel 3:92)—and they do not burn.

In Klay's story, the narrator, while praying the Divine Office, reads from this chapter of the book of Daniel, which leads him to offer his own prayer: "I stopped reading and tried to pray with my own words. I asked God to protect the battalion from further harm. I knew He would not. I asked Him to bring abuses to light. I knew He would not. I asked Him, finally, for grace" (147). But this moment of prayer does not seem to lead to comfort or consolation: "When I turned back to the Divine Office,

I read the words with empty discouragement" (147). Ultimately, though, the central insight from this chapter of Daniel becomes the central insight of the story—that the son of God is present with us in moments of suffering. In day-to-day life, whether in the midst of war or not, God does not (generally speaking) keep the fire from burning us; the narrator accepts that God will not protect the battalion from harm. Christ will not keep us from suffering, but he will accompany us in our suffering.

Klay begins his masterful essay "Tales of War and Redemption" by talking about how when he was a child he used to read a comic book titled *The Big Book of Martyrs*. He notes that the dramatic violence of these stories made a significant impact on his youthful imagination, but that he could not help but notice how God "was always protecting his martyrs before their deaths, but (to my eyes) in what seemed like the laziest, most halfhearted way imaginable." God initially saves them from death or defilement, but since these are stories of martyrs, they all still eventually die in brutal ways. But Klay goes on to note that when he revisits these stories of martyrdom as an adult, through the perspective of his own experiences in Iraq, they strike a different chord. He writes,

> To anyone with any kind of experience in war, a story of God saving the good would feel less like a comfort and more like an indictment. Any soldier can tell you that no amount of prayer provides security for the defenseless in a war zone. The good die. The bad die. The combatants die, and the children die. The old men and the women and the fathers and mothers and sisters and daughters and sons die. Sometimes, often, they die horribly. When we return home, a new knowledge follows with us, the viscerally felt knowledge that men are cruel, that history is bloody and awful, and that the earth is a place where, no matter where you live, whether it's New York or Fallujah, Chicago or Baghdad, we are regularly failing to protect our most vulnerable, our poor, and our desperate.
>
> We recoil at religious platitudes intended to get around this truth or to make it less bitter. So we can appreciate the way stories of martyrdom unrelentingly focus on suffering, refusing to suggest that faith might spare us from horror. . . . But that leaves us with the other piece of the story: the insistence on the miraculous in the midst of the suffering, the tales of pain as a means of inspiring us and drawing us closer to God, complete with dramatic miracles to underline the point.

God will not alleviate all suffering or protect from all harm, but God will be present with us, just as we should be present for each other. This is the Catholicism that is threaded throughout Klay's works, one that demands we be more than silent bystanders in the face of suffering. In *Redeployment* and *Missionaries*, Klay repeatedly depicts moments of violence, terror, sorrow, and suffering, as well as the occasional glimpse of hope or redemption. There is no easy connection between the presence of violence and the presence of grace, but his work does gesture toward God's presence and asks the reader to seek out this presence in unlooked-for places.

And it is, ultimately, in the impact that these stories potentially have on the reader that we can connect his work back to the tradition of Catholic literature I have been exploring throughout this book. Klay, like the Catholic writers who came before him, believes in literature's power to affect the reader. He views his work as a way "to confront the reader" with "issues of moral, aesthetic or spiritual concern," which in turn leads the reader to respond. This experience is often destabilizing. As he notes, when we encounter a challenging work of art, "We're left adrift before a vision of the world that compels us morally, politically, aesthetically and spiritually, that doesn't lend itself to abstract truths or cheap pity, that expands our conception of the world in the way that only art can because it is too vivid and concrete to fit into the old categories. And then we, the readers, decide what to do about it" ("False Witnesses"). Klay does not supply his readers with easy answers, but time and again he does present us with the kinds of startling figures that challenge us to engage with the themes of his work in our lives outside of the pages of the text.

"Epiphany after Epiphany": Suffering and Holiness in Kirstin Valdez Quade's Fiction

Kirstin Valdez Quade also writes destabilizing stories in which the presence of grace can be found amid systemic, structural violence. Her first book, the short-story collection *Night at the Fiestas* (2015), won awards from the National Book Critics Circle and the American Academy of Arts and Letters, as well as a "5 Under 35" award from the National Book Foundation. Her first novel, *The Five Wounds* (2021), also received rave reviews, including starred reviews from *Kirkus* and *Publishers Weekly*. Valerie Sayers, writing in *Commonweal*, described the novel as "a Catholic telenovela of a book," in which "even the most extreme Catholic ritual, iconography, and vocabulary . . . become natural, even inevitable, elements" (56).

Quade, who is currently an assistant professor of creative writing at Princeton University, was born in 1980 in Albuquerque and grew up in the American Southwest, and most of her work is set amid this Catholic Hispanic culture. As she told Mary Kenagy Mitchell, for *Image*, "We spent much of my childhood moving. We lived in trailers and out of our van and in tents, all over the Southwest. I went to something like thirteen schools before high school. But New Mexico really was home. That was where my grandparents lived, where we returned to, and where my early childhood had been; it was where I felt a sense of belonging." This sense of place, and of searching for belonging, is a central theme in both of her books.

Another theme that unites her works is her exploration of Catholicism, both as a cultural signifier and as a belief system, which Quade links to her childhood experiences. As she told Jane Ciabattari, "As a child, I was an enthusiastic mass attendee, and I remain attached to Catholic ritual: the liturgy, the processions, the reenactments. I'm really interested in public demonstrations of faith." Her Catholic identity is not something she left behind as a child, though. It remains a central aspect of her work and her own sense of self: "Catholicism is central to my sense of identity as a New Mexican and a member of my family—it feels integral to New Mexico itself. I can't think of Santa Fe without thinking about going to mass with my grandmother. Later, we lived in Salt Lake City for several years, and there I really felt my difference in not being a Mormon in a predominantly Mormon community. As so often happens, different aspects of your identity stand out more vividly in different contexts. It was in Salt Lake City that we were Catholic, and that became a central part of my identity" (Mitchell).

While not all of her stories feature overtly Catholic characters and themes, a large number of them do. For instance, a story like "Christina the Astonishing (1150–1224)" is a retelling of a Catholic saint's life; "Ordinary Sins" is, in part, a story about the isolating life of the priesthood; "The Five Wounds" is a short story about individuals taking part in the Catholic rituals of Holy Week; the title itself comes from the five wounds of Christ's crucifixion, and the novel that grew out of the short story is structured around Liturgical time—the three sections are titled "Semana Santa" (Holy Week), "Ordinary Time," and "Lent." Like the other Catholic writers discussed here, Quade is not particularly interested in trying to impart some form of Catholic catechesis, but Catholicism does provide a structure and through line for her work. The Catholicism we encounter in her stories is recognizable, but at the same time her fiction explores elements of the faith that are often glossed over. We would expect encounters with saints to be edifying; we might expect that an individual who embraces the rituals of the *penitentes* might be transformed by them. But her work gets at something deeper, unexpected, and equally transformative—and like so many of the writers discussed throughout this book, one tool she uses to bring about this transformation is literary violence.

The "Terrible, Lonely Holiness" of Christina the Astonishing

The first story of Quade's that I recall reading is "Christina the Aston-ishing (1150–1224)," which appeared in the July 24, 2017, issue of the *New Yorker*. This story caught my attention in part because it is so immediately apparent as being a Catholic story—meaning it features Catholic characters (churchgoing individuals, nuns, and priests) and Catholic themes (sacra-mentality, sanctity, the nature of belief, and of course, disturbing moments of violence). The story is structured like a medieval saint's life narrative, with section titles like "How harshly she suffered for those souls detained in purgatory, but remained unharmed in body." But unlike a typical re-counting of a saint's life, Quade's story is not hagiography; while we do see Christina's power—she rises from the dead, she flies, she makes accurate prophecies, she demonstrates unnatural power—the depiction of sanctity, rather than inspiring devotion, is confounding.[4] Outsiders can tell stories about Christina's power, her holiness, and her wisdom, but for those who know her intimately, who spend their days with her, the experience is quite different. Life with Christina is hard and unpleasant, particularly for those closest to the saint herself. Quade is indicating that firsthand exposure to the mystery and power of God is not inherently reassuring or comforting.

The story opens with the death of Christina. Her sister, our narrator Mara, is mourning her loss. Initially, Mara claims that death brings a form of clarity, a new sort of understanding that eluded her in life (a theme we have seen borne out in other Catholic stories). She states, "Even this morn-ing, on the way to the church, I couldn't help noticing that the world was suddenly clean and raw, filled with new color and new light, everything unbearably radiant. I loved Christina, I did! I see this now. She was dif-ficult, yes, unknowable, but I loved her. Generosity floods me, as clear and calm as well water—and gratitude, too, to God, who has let me weep for her." But when Christina rises from the dead and flies up into the rafters, the narrator must admit that this "clarity" was a lie—an attempt to make herself feel better about her own conflicted feelings for her sister. It is, after all, easier to refashion a narrative when the object of the story we are telling ourselves is dead. Here, Quade is showing us how the insights gained from suffering and loss, which feature so prominently in many of our stories, are often, in reality, inauthentic.

Throughout the story we get no real indication of why God has cho-sen Christina to be miraculously raised from death. In her first life, Chris-tina was, at best, unpleasant to be around. After her resurrection, she is worse: "After Christina's resurrection, she spends her days perched in the branches of a yew on the road to town. She shrieks at people as they pass, accusing them of their sins, which, she says, she can smell on them, can see spread across their faces like fungus." She cannot stand the presence of others, their corrupt flesh and human desires, or even the presence of her own body; she cuts away her own flesh and attempts to drown herself. Her peers attempt to make sense of all of this, and to fit it within their preestablished religious framework: "Later, they will say that my sister suffered for the souls in Purgatory. They will say she mortified her flesh and starved her body so that, one by one, the waiting souls might be released like bubbles into Heaven."

Mara, though, retains her doubts. The resurrected Christina does, after all, continue to make her sisters' lives miserable: "Christina upturns the clothes box and shreds our shifts and kirtles. 'Go naked like the harlots you are!' she screams." When their third sister, Gertrude, becomes pregnant before marriage, Christina intervenes to prevent her marriage to the baby's father, and then, in the one "miracle" we see her perform, she uses her powers to cause Gertrude to have a miscarriage. After tormenting her sisters, Christina goes off into the world to counsel the powerful, and she leaves her sisters behind. Gertrude mourns her lost baby and lover; Mara, who once desired to join a convent, finds, "My prayers won't cohere; the words slip from my mind, and God, who once was everything, has vanished." Even the nuns who eventually care for the aging Christina find her to be a heavy burden.

The lasting image of Christina's sanctity is Mara's claim that "Ordinary people no longer come near us, because they fear what Christina knows and what she might accuse them of. They fear her terrible, lonely holiness." In "Christina the Astonishing," both the saint and those close to her suffer; the power of God, manifest in this young woman, is undeniable, but it is also inscrutable. In Quade's vision, divine power is connected to moments of violence, including Christina's self-harm and suicidal actions, and her infliction of a miscarriage on her sister, but the violence does not serve as an indication of the divine will (there is no reason to believe that this kind of suffering is what God desires for Christina or her family), and it does not lead to insight (for characters or for readers). Rather, it serves to demonstrate that God's ways are not our ways, and that the power and mystery of God are beyond comprehension. Quade's work shows that attempts to limit this mystery, to frame it within the confines of familiar hagiography, are misguided.

Violence and Insight in *The Five Wounds*

The Five Wounds, like "Christina the Astonishing," illustrates how the familiar narratives we spin around sanctity—around moments of conversion, or violent epiphanies leading to holiness or transformation—are limited. It makes sense to end this study of American Catholic fiction with this short story and novel because in these two incarnations Quade both uses the arc we have become so familiar with, where violence leads to insight and change, and also completely undermines it. The short-story version foregrounds the experiences of Amadeo Padilla, a thirty-three-year-old unemployed alcoholic, who is living with (and sponging off) his mother, Yolanda. As the story opens he is preparing to play the role of Christ in a local reenactment of the Passion, and his focus on this ritual is disrupted by the unexpected appearance of his fifteen-year-old daughter, Angel, who is pregnant. She has had a fight with her mother and has come to stay with Yolanda. The story is a powerful exploration of Amadeo's failures, as a parent and as a son, and it uses the Crucifixion as a way to unite Amadeo's frailties with the moments of the Passion, and ultimately with Christ's suffering and death.

As Amadeo prepares for the ritual, he hears about a man who, when inhabiting the role of Christ many years earlier, was literally nailed to the cross, and once Amadeo is up on the cross himself, he asks for the nails as well. It is an overly dramatic gesture, one he chooses in part to impress his community. The story ends with the nails going into his palms, and Amadeo coming to the realization that his performance does not really connect his suffering to Christ's; rather, he comes to see that the actual suffering he has been blind to is that of his daughter: "It's Angel who has been forsaken. All at once he sees her. He is surprised by the naked fear on her face. . . . And she feels not only fear—Amadeo sees that now—but pain, complete and physical. Nothing he can do will change this, and soon it won't be just her suffering, but the baby, too" (*Night* 85).

As in so many of the stories we have looked at throughout this volume, his moment of clarity and insight comes on the heels of violence, and while we cannot know how, exactly, this revelation will change Amadeo, we are left with the impression that his epiphanic moment will change his life—that he will be able to come down and be a changed man, a better father and a better son. The structure of the story uses the rituals and forms of Hispanic Catholicism to unite Amadeo's journey with the commemoration of the Passion—he goes through a journey of suffering and purgation, only to come to a place of grace at the end. If Quade had left the story there, it would still have served as a fitting coda for this study.

But, compellingly, Quade saw fit to revisit and reimagine the arc of this story. Instead, the short story, in slightly altered form, serves as the opening chapter of the novel of the same name, and the novel explodes the idea that this moment of violence will provide lasting insight or change for Amadeo. In the novel, when Amadeo is nailed to the cross he no longer comes to the moment of clarity about Angel's suffering. Instead, Quade draws our attention to the differences between how Amadeo had envisioned this moment and the actual reality of it: "He imagined the pain spreading through him like silent fire, unbearable in the most pleasurable of ways, like the burn of muscles pushed to their limits. He imagined the holy expansiveness that would swell in him until he was, finally, good" (*Wounds* 38). In other words, he had imagined that getting literally nailed to the cross would transform him and bring him grace and insight; he had imagined it would result in the kind of epiphany that closed the short story.

But here, it leads only to physical suffering: "The pain is so immediate, so stunningly distilled, that Amadeo's entire consciousness shrinks around it" (38). There is no room for insight here, just pain, and a "confused searing clamor" (38). And immediately after this moment, Quade shifts the scene to the emergency room, where Angel is ashamed of, and angry at, her father. While Amadeo had been dreaming of transcendence, Angel is focused on the practical implications of Amadeo's choices; she points out that with his injured hands he will not even be able to help care for his newborn grandson: "'How're you going to hold the baby? Or didn't you even think of that?'" (42). This is where the chapter ends; not with the moment of spiritual insight that closes the short story, but with a much more practical complication that arises from Amadeo's choices.

This is one of the great joys of this novel. As noted, Quade structures the book around the Church calendar and uses the Crucifixion as a uniting motif, but she repeatedly grounds the plot itself in the gritty, everyday realities of working-class life. She shows how systemic inequalities lead to limited options for individuals; she does not make excuses for her characters, but she does demonstrate how their opportunities are impacted by their environment.[5] Everyone in this novel suffers; everyone makes poor choices. Amadeo, in particular, cannot stop screwing up. He vows to stop drinking, but instead he gets in drunken arguments with his sister and drives around while intoxicated; he vows to start his own business repairing cracked windshields, but instead he just uses the people around him to try to get it off the ground, and even once he's given the opportunity to actually do the work, he botches the job and runs away (in a novel filled with a number of almost unbearable moments, this scene might be the most excruciating to read). He is not a good caretaker for his dying mother, his overburdened daughter, or his infant grandson. But Quade does show him trying, again and again, even as he keeps failing. And this perseverance ultimately allows for him to change.

In Quade's reimagining of this story in novel form, grace is present, but it is not something that comes from a shocking moment of life-changing violence;[6] instead, the novel traces out moment after moment of trauma, and they slowly build toward a meaningful and lasting transformation. As Quade told Michael Welch, "I think in life too, real character change rarely happens from a single epiphany. Sometimes we need epiphany after epiphany, as well as a lot of steady work to change."

The novel builds to a similar insight as the one found in the climax of the short story. Amadeo, while praying on Ash Wednesday with the other members of his community, acknowledges that he "once believed there was a single, big thing he could do to make up for his failings. He missed the point. The procession isn't about punishment or shame. It is about the need to take on the pain of loved ones. To take on that pain, first you have to see it. And see how you inflict it" (404). While this recognition is more or less the same insight that he came to while on the cross in the short story, here it feels both more earned, and more permanent. In the short story, it is something he comes to alone, in a flash. In the novel, it is significant that he is joined by his community; he is not suffering alone. He is moved by their stories of grappling with addiction, and even though he is not particularly close to these other men, he is united with them as part of the suffering, broken body of Christ. It is as a member of this community that he is able to recognize his own brokenness, and his need for grace to aid him in putting in the work to actually be a better man. And in this moment, it feels possible that this knowledge will stay with him, and will actually last.

Coda

Both Klay and Quade focus their fictions on suffering and violence, and while these stories hold out hope that grace can be present amid this suffering, they do not hide from the reality that in many cases this violence can be overwhelming. Flannery O'Connor spoke of her "prophetic function of recalling people to known but ignored truths" (*Conversations* 89); by focusing their fictions on the suffering of often marginalized communities, Klay and Quade do something similar. Their stories are not polemics, but they do demand the reader pay attention to the often ignored or overlooked far-ranging effects of the violence of war, and the legacy of systemic oppression. As both Amadeo in *The Five Wounds* and the chaplain in "Prayer in the Furnace" come to realize, we are called to pay attention to the suffering of others and to do what we can to alleviate it. Engaging with these stories reminds the reader of this known but ignored truth, and calls for, in Ricoeur's formulation, "a reader who responds" ("Between" 395). For both Klay and Quade, this kind of response entails a spiritual dimension. As Klay states, "If we want to reshape the world, or reform institutions, or simply live well in a world full of dehumanizing forces, we can't think of ourselves and others simply in terms of ethical or psychological struggles, but must consider spiritual ones as well" ("Point of War"). By foregrounding this spiritual aspect in their fiction, they help shape the readerly response.

Of course, reading a story is not necessarily going to lead one to put into practice the precepts of charity, or lead one to look beyond a purely secular understanding of existence and develop a relationship with God. But encountering a literary text can be one important step on the journey, and to be a Catholic (writer or reader) is to believe in the power of language to change one's life. As George Saunders reminds us,

> I think it's important to be respectful of how mysterious the whole deal is: a person being moved by a story another person made up. It's weird but it happens and it can really change people's lives. I think fiction at its best can serve as a moment of induced bafflement that calls into question our usual relation to things and reminds us that our minds, as nice as they are, aren't necessarily up to the task of living, and shouldn't get cocky. (Treisman)

Throughout this study we have seen a number of ways that Catholic writers use some form of O'Connor's "large and startling figures" to "induce bafflement"—to disorient, confuse, and ultimately reorient characters and readers alike. We have also seen that it takes more than an epiphanic moment to change one's life. We continually need to be nudged, reminded. And then we need to do the work to change.

Acknowledgments

Over the course of this book I have been discussing the various ways that authors structure their texts so as to affect their readers and lead them to new insights. But of course, just as an author can impact his or her readers, each author, and each text, is shaped by a combination of factors as well. This project has been many years in the making, and it would not be possible to list all of the people who have contributed—directly or indirectly—to shaping it (and/or shaping me, as I worked on it), but it is important to acknowledge at least some of the most formative influences.

First I want to express my gratitude to the various teachers and mentors who, over the years, contributed to my understanding of the Catholic Literary Tradition, and who modeled the life of scholarship and teaching for me. Since this project had its origins in my dissertation, I am particularly grateful to the members of my dissertation committee—Fr. Mark Bosco, Peter Shillingsburg, and Farrell O'Gorman—whose thoughtful critiques and comments helped to clarify and improve the earliest incarnations of this work. I am especially thankful for Fr. Bosco, who chaired the committee; his work on the Catholic Imagination first drew me to Loyola University Chicago, and this project would not exist without his support and mentorship over the years. At Loyola I also want to acknowledge Michael Murphy, director of the Hank Center for the Catholic Intellectual Heritage. I am also grateful to the faculty at Boston University, particularly Jack Matthews, who helped me realize I did not want to be a Renaissance scholar, and whose historically oriented approach to southern literature worked its way into a few chapters here. There are also a number of professors at Notre Dame, in a variety of disciplines, who were instrumental in laying the groundwork for this project, and who shaped my approach to studying literature. Particular thanks are due to Fr. Charles Gordon, who first introduced me to the study of the Catholic novel; to Michael Baxter, who pointed me toward the ethical demands of both Catholicism and literature; to Jesse Lander, who helped mentor me through the grad school application process; and especially to Tom Werge, who first introduced me to the study of the religious imagination, and who, as the director of my honors thesis on violence in the work of Flannery O'Connor, walked with me on the first hesitant steps of what would eventually evolve, more than twenty years later, into this book.

I also want to thank all of the people at Fordham University Press who have helped shepherd this project to completion in such a professional manner, particularly Fredric Nachbaur and Angela Alaimo O'Donnell. In addition, I am grateful to the two peer reviewers whose thoughtful and detailed feedback helped me to refine and clarify the themes of the manuscript.

Earlier versions of two chapters in this book first appeared in journal form—much of the J. F. Powers chapter first appeared in *American Catholic Studies* 129.3 (2018), and parts of the Alice McDermott chapter first appeared in *Religion and the Arts* 20 (2016)—and I am grateful to both of these journals for allowing me to include this material here, in modified form. I also wish to express my thanks to the peer reviewers who provided helpful feedback on earlier drafts of these two essays.

I would never have been able to complete this book without the friends and family members who have supported me by providing emergency (or regular) childcare, by reading and commenting on working drafts of chapters, or by giving emotional support and/or a nonacademic social outlet. In this last regard, particular thanks are due to Jon Rosemeyer, Dan Baig, and Will McGrath, as well as Mike Shiel and Mark Rastetter. I am not sure I would have made it through the last stages of the revision process without the regular support and feedback of Cynthia Wallace, who has been a true model of rigorous and faith-filled scholarship. My father, Patrick, bought me my first copies of many of the books discussed in this study, and has provided me with a wonderful model of how to be both a scholar and a dad; my mother, Suzanne, gave me my first example of how to be a full-time parent while simultaneously pursuing academic success, and has always known when to check in and when to send brownies. Thank you also to Peter and Teresa Beyer, who have welcomed me and made me feel at home since the first time we met. I am also grateful for the love and support of my siblings, Mary, David, and Stephen, and Julie, Megan, Jessie, Darryl, Allison, and Carlos.

And, finally, we reach the point in the acknowledgments where words are inadequate to express the depth of my gratitude and love. To my boys, Owen, Timothy, and Henry, who always remind me of the real meaning of things, and whose imagination and creativity are a continual inspiration. And to my wife, Lauren, who is still my best reader, and who has supported me in this project from before the beginning. Thank you for joining me on this adventure; I look forward to many more.

Notes

Introduction. "Surprise Me": Going inside the "Black Box" of Catholic Fiction

1. There are two concepts here worth clarifying before going any further: what qualifies as Catholic literature, and what is meant by a secular age. There are any number of ways to go about setting parameters for what counts as "Catholic literature," and the large number of studies of Catholic literature demonstrate a proliferation of effective approaches one can take. Anita Gandolfo's *Testing the Faith: The New Catholic Fiction in America* (1992) and Theodore Fraser's *The Modern Catholic Novel in Europe* (1994) both provide helpful analyses of the influence of Vatican II on the form of the Catholic novel. Ross Labrie's *The Catholic Imagination in American Literature* (1997) provides a useful overview of the development of American Catholic literature, and Paul Giles's *American Catholic Arts and Fictions* (1992) is the most comprehensive treatment of American Catholic literature in all its myriad forms. More recently, John C. Waldmeir's *Cathedrals of Bone: The Role of the Body in Contemporary Catholic Literature* (2009), and Nick Ripatrazone's *The Fine Delight* (2013) and *Longing for an Absent God* (2020), all map the contours of postconciliar Catholic fiction in compelling ways. For my purposes, I choose to define the essential aspect of Catholic literature as being works of art that are the product of an incarnational and sacramental religious worldview. The Catholic sacramental view of reality indicates that the world, and everything in it, can lead one to experience grace, or to have an experience of the divine. Central to this belief is the idea that literature itself is, in a sense, sacramental. Catholicism, by maintaining a belief in real presences, keeps open a space for the sacramental power of language.

My description of contemporary society as being "a secular age" is informed by Charles Taylor's magisterial work of the same name. In Taylor's definition, the secularity of our current age "consists, among other things, of a move from a society where belief in God is unchallenged and indeed, unproblematic, to one in which it is understood to be one option among others, and frequently not the easiest to embrace" (3). He goes on to clarify the endpoint of his work: "the change I want to define and trace is one which takes us from a society in which it was virtually impossible not to believe in God, to one in which faith, even for the staunchest believer, is one human possibility among others" (3), and where "the eclipse of all goals beyond human flourishing becomes conceivable" (19). The following chapters illuminate the various strategies used by Catholic authors to make a transcendent worldview, or goals beyond human flourishing, seem viable and meaningful, particularly for an audience that does not already subscribe to such a worldview.

2. My understanding of how contemporary Catholic literature "does something to the reader" relies on the interplay between textual object and the reader's construction of meaning in reaction to what is present in the text. Paul Ricoeur's account of the reading experience is a helpful way to approach this concept. For Ricoeur, the experience of reading is about the productive dialectic generated by the encounter between the differing worldviews of author/text and reader: "only when the world of the text is confronted with the world of the reader . . . does the literary work acquire a meaning in the full sense of the term, at the intersection of the world projected by the text and the life-world of the reader" (*Time 2* 160). Ricoeur emphasizes that the strategies employed by an author have real and demonstrable effects on the reader: "the reader is, finally, the prey and the victim of the strategy worked out by the implied author, and is so to the very extent this strategy is more deeply concealed" ("Between" 398). He remarks especially upon the reader of modern fiction, who is forced to navigate a variety of "disorient[ing]," "provok[ing]," and even "dangerous" narrative techniques (394–95). Ricoeur claims, "The moment when literature attains its highest degree of efficacy is perhaps the moment when it places its readers in the position of finding a solution for which they themselves must find the appropriate questions, those that constitute the aesthetic and moral problem posed by the work" (407). In the chapters that follow, I attempt to illuminate the solutions found in the texts that I study, as well as reconstruct the questions that the authors and readers must pose in order to make coherent sense of the work of art.

3. To be clear, I am not describing a conversion to a Catholic worldview, but rather a conversion in one's mindset, a revolution in thinking, an awakening to something new.

4. In a separate interview, he connects this belief in the power of stories to his Catholic upbringing: "I loved growing up Catholic. There was something so powerful about the way they respected metaphor, and all of the symbols, and the incense and so on. They expected you to understand that there are truths that are not overt, but implied, and that the best way to imply that kind of truth is through metaphor and ritual. I think that once you get immersed in that kind of beauty, and really feel it, even once, you will always be looking for that. Which is maybe where art comes in later" (*Conversations* 110–11).

5. My understanding of a kairotic moment as a divinely initiated experience that allows for personal (or universal) transformation is indebted to theologian Paul Tillich. Tillich explains that, "in Christian usage . . . [kairos] is a state of things in the world which makes the appearance of something divine possible. There are always those two aspects—the conditions themselves and the intervention of something beyond time and space, coming into time and space" (126).

6. Indeed, one of the challenges in writing this book was deciding which authors to include. For instance, one could write about similar themes in the French (Mauriac, Bernanos) or British (Greene, Waugh, Spark) Catholic traditions. I decided to focus solely on American writers, both because this is the tradition I understand best, and because I wanted to be able to trace out the ways the various writers drew inspiration from each other and developed their work in response to what others had done. In my estimation, O'Connor, Percy, and Powers best represent the American Catholic tradition in their given time period, but outside of these three, it would be possible to choose an entirely different set of American writers whose work could profitably be read through this lens (in addition to Wolff, Dubus, and Hansen), including, say, Cormac McCarthy, Annie Dillard, and Toni Morrison. All write stories focused on violence, mortality, and suffering, and yet still point the reader toward some hope of transcendence. In the end, though, I found that Gautreaux, McDermott, and Saunders best represented the disparate approaches to Catholic storytelling that I wanted to focus on, and I liked tracing out the connections between these three writers and those who came before them, and Klay and Quade, who come after.

7. In a perhaps too-tidy tying together of these three authors, Ron Hansen quotes this passage from Wolff on Dubus in his own essay collection, *Hotly in Pursuit of the Real: Notes toward a Memoir* (2020).

8. It is worth noting that there is a significant death in the novel; Mariette's beloved older sister, Mother Céline, dies of cancer, and her bodily suffering is depicted in graphic detail. And there are also moments of violence, including one particularly harrowing scene in which Mariette is assaulted in her cell, and it is left unresolved whether the assault is demonic in nature or if it is carried out by unknown human assailants. The novel also contains scenes where characters practice mortifications of the flesh, including one sister wrapping rose thorns around her ribcage and Mariette wrapping barbed wire around her thigh.

1 / The "Blasting Annihilating Light" of Flannery O'Connor's Art

1. I have found the following books to contain the most illuminating explorations of violence in O'Connor's work: Frederick Asals, *Flannery O'Connor: The Imagination of Extremity* (1982); John Desmond, *Risen Sons: Flannery O'Connor's Vision of History* (1987); Robert Brinkmeyer, *The Art and Vision of Flannery O'Connor* (1989); Susan Srigley, *Flannery O'Connor's Sacramental Imagination* (2004), particularly chapter 3: "The Violence of Love"; and John Sykes, *Flannery O'Connor, Walker Percy, and the Aesthetics of Revelation* (2007).

2. For an excellent discussion on O'Connor's conception of audience, see L. Lamar Nisly's *Wingless Chickens, Bayou Catholics, and Pilgrim Wayfarers: Constructions of Audience and Tone in O'Connor, Gautreaux, and Percy* (2011).

3. O'Connor made these remarks in a lecture at Georgia State College for Women, 1/7/60; the quote is published in Kathleen Feeley, *Flannery O'Connor*, 45.

4. These adjectives call to mind Saul's blinding on the road to Damascus, which initiated his conversion (Acts 9:3–9).

5. The grandmother surely does consider the bare-chested Misfit to be "common," and her attempt to elevate his class status is merely an act of self-serving flattery. This absurd attempt reveals the depth of her commitment to a class-based view of society; she is initially unable to recognize, even at this crucial juncture, the emptiness of this worldview.

6. It is of note that the crime he is convicted of is patricide; society locks him away for killing his father, or destroying his lineage. In this he personifies the fears of the reactionary South: he goes beyond disrespecting his family to actually killing the patriarch. The Misfit maintains his innocence, but regardless of whether he killed his father, his imprisonment has turned him into the sort of person that society fears: a violent force that disrupts the stability of the social order.

7. This reading of the ending is in line with the interpretation that O'Connor offered for what will eventually happen to the Misfit: "the old lady's gesture, like the mustard-seed, will grow to be a great crow-filled tree in the Misfit's heart, and will be enough of a pain to him there to turn him into the prophet he was meant to become" (*Mystery* 113).

8. For more on the influence of the war on Hazel, and the overall structure of the novel, see Stacey Peebles's "He's Hunting Something: Hazel Motes as Ex-Soldier" (2011).

9. By murdering Solace, Hazel destroys his inauthentic double, a man who has mirrored his every act without believing that these actions have any inherent meaning, yet the removal of this inauthentic representation of Hazel's worldview does not clarify Hazel's own identity or sense of self. Solace, in other words, is not Hazel's Other, but rather just a manifestation of himself that he cannot overcome through external violence. This is why Hazel ultimately needs to direct his violence inward, against the inauthenticity inside of himself.

10. Throughout her career, O'Connor uses the automobile as a symbol for the particularly American sense of self-satisfied autonomy, the unlimited freedom to go wherever, and do whatever, one wants. See Brian Ragen's *A Wreck on the Road to Damascus* (1989) for an insightful analysis of the importance of Hazel's automobile, specifically its connection to Emersonian ideal of freedom (5); see also Mark Schiebe's "Car Trouble: Hazel Motes and the Fifties Counterculture" for a more discursive discussion of the role of the automobile in O'Connor's fiction.

11. The ambiguity embedded in the text itself has led to one of the more animated critical debates in O'Connor studies. Among those critics who analyze the Christian themes in O'Connor, Susan Srigley offers the most eloquent, and extreme, condemnation of Hazel's actions: "Hazel Motes's violence is the outward expression of his rejection of God: he kills his conscience and blinds himself to spiritual reality" (92). She contends that Hazel's conversion lacks any real spiritual insight, and that his self-violence isolates him and prevents him from joining into the community that is a requisite aspect of true Christianity: "With his willful self-blinding at the end of the story Hazel Motes follows his closed vision to its logical conclusion, and while he thus imitates Asa Hawks in order to see what Hawks claims to see, Motes does so without any spiritual perception. His final observation of the sky before he blinds himself . . . is dimmed and blank, still suggesting a depth upon depth. . . . He is unable to see beyond his own small universe" (65). Debra Cumberland agrees, writing that since "there is not a single moment of human connection, genuine kindness, or . . . expression of love" in the novel (7), *Wise Blood* can only qualify as a Christian novel "because it portrays a Christian vision of hell—the path to it, the state of it" (19).

Frederick Asals stakes out a middle ground on Hazel's fate; he writes that *Wise Blood* reveals a "Manichean" vision of life (58), and describes Hazel's ultimate fate as "a thoroughgoing rejection not only of a secularized age but of life taken in through the senses at all—life in a world of matter. . . . By the end of *Wise Blood* the chasm between inner and outer, spirit and matter, is absurdly and terrifyingly absolute" (56). John Sykes counters the critique of the novel as being entirely Manichean by claiming that once Hazel "sees the error of his ways, it is not to a corrected preaching that he gives himself, but to mortification of the flesh. The implication is that the path to his salvation lies in silent action. It is as though language itself has failed him, or at least that it has taken him as far toward God as it is able to go" (48–49). John Desmond offers a similar interpretation, and defense, of Hazel's self-mortifying actions, stating that although "this chosen purgation might be seen as an attempt at self-redemption . . . it is not like the self-redemption he preaches in his Church Without Christ, since he punishes his body now in order to witness explicitly to the integrity of his conscience" (*Risen* 61). Ralph Wood, too, defends Hazel's penitential acts, stating they "are not self-justifying sacrifices meant to earn Motes's salvation; they are deeds of radical penance offered in gratitude for the salvation that has already been won for him" by Christ's death and resurrection (*Haunted* 169). The lack of consensus here, despite all of these critics attempting to understand O'Connor's work on her own, explicitly Christian terms, speaks to the fundamental ambiguity O'Connor has woven into the story. She wants the reader to be unsettled, and to ask these kinds of questions; she wants us to become like Mrs. Flood.

12. In this sense, he is much like Hansen's Mariette, another character whose bodily suffering served as a (confounding) sign both for her contemporaries and for the reader.

13. The word "habit" is a significant one for O'Connor, reflected in the title of her collection of letters, *The Habit of Being*. As Sally Fitzgerald explains in the introduction to these letters, for O'Connor, drawing on Maritain, habit did not mean "mere mechanical routine, but . . . an attitude or quality of mind" that shapes an individual's conception of the world (*Habit* xvii).

2 / Disorientation and Reorientation in J. F. Powers's Fiction

1. Over the course of his career, Powers produced three short-story collections, *Prince of Darkness and Other Stories* (1947), *The Presence of Grace* (1956), and *Look How the Fish Live* (1975), and two novels (which came out twenty-six years apart); the first, *Morte D'Urban* (1962), won the National Book Award, and the second, *Wheat That Springeth Green* (1988), was nominated for it. To once again compare him to O'Connor, both writers produced a similar body of work—*The Stories of J. F. Powers* contains thirty stories; O'Connor's *The Complete Stories* contains thirty-one, and both writers published only two novels each. Of course, O'Connor's life was cut short by lupus, whereas Powers was simply a less productive writer, particularly in the latter stages of his career.

2. If personal experience is of any use here, I studied contemporary American fiction with a focus on Catholic writers, in both undergraduate and graduate school at Catholic universities, and was never once required to read a Powers story, let alone either of his novels.

3. Powers was born in Jacksonville, Illinois, in 1917, and grew up in one of the few Catholic families in a predominantly Protestant town. He took classes at Northwestern University but left before earning his degree, and then worked a variety of jobs, including insurance salesman, chauffeur, and bookseller, while working on his

writing. He sold his first story in 1943, and while he had moderate success placing his work (some of his first stories appeared in the *Catholic Worker*; later, he published many in the *New Yorker*), as his collected letters make clear, he continually struggled to balance the challenge of being a full-time writer and providing for his family (he married the writer Betty Wahl in 1946, and they eventually had five children). He continually moved the family back and forth between Ireland, where the cost of living was cheaper, and various teaching jobs in the United States, including short stints at the University of Michigan and Smith College; they eventually settled in Collegeville, Minnesota, where he was Regents' Professor of English at St. John's University from 1975 until his retirement in 1993; he passed away in 1999.

4. For more on Father Hugo, and both the development and significance of the retreat, see Jack Lee Downey's *The Bread of the Strong: Lacouturisme and the Folly of the Cross, 1910–1985* (New York: Fordham UP, 2015).

5. In a sense, this is a similar dynamic to what O'Connor does with Mrs. Flood in *Wise Blood*, where the reader identifies with the perspective of a seemingly rational character, only for the story to reveal the shortcomings of this rational framework. In Powers's work, though, this kind of insight does not require being exposed to Hazel's extreme penitential acts; sometimes even just a disappointing letter will serve as the wakeup call (at least for the reader, if not for the character).

6. Or at least not explicitly. There are a number of places in the story that, to a contemporary reader, raise flags. Powers describes Fr. Burner "molesting [a younger priest] with his eyes" (180), and later we see Burner wishing that he had "brought along one of the eighth-grade boys" on his trip to the hamburger stand. The most alarming imagery appears in a confessional scene late in the story, when a "miserable boy coming into puberty" enters the confessional. Powers leans heavily into phallic imagery and wordplay here: Fr. Burner is depicted as "stroking strongly in Latin" and "finishing first"; the boy is left "breathless . . . an ear of corn shucked clean." At the end of the scene, Burner is explicitly likened to a predator: "A big spider drowsy in his web, drugged with heat and sins" (200).

7. Ricoeur links this movement to the role of criticism itself. In *The Symbolism of Evil* he writes, "If we can no longer live the great symbolisms of the sacred in accordance with the original belief in them, we can, we modern men, aim at a second naiveté in and through criticism. In short, it is by *interpreting* that we can *hear* again" (351). For a helpful overview of Ricoeur's understanding of the first and second naiveté, see chapter 3 of Mark Wallace's *The Second Naiveté: Barth, Ricoeur, and the New Yale Theology* (1995).

8. It is worth noting that Hagopian claims that it is only Urban, not Powers, who views the order as mediocre. For instance, Hagopian writes that Fr. Wilfred is in fact "a dedicated, hard-working priest whose pretenses at omniscience and optimism are largely deliberate tactics for getting an impossible job done" and that the provincial of the Order is a "humble man who seeks to use only humble means to lead his flock to salvation" (124), but there is little textual evidence to back up these descriptions, even if we account for the bias inherent in Urban's perspective.

3 / Walker Percy and the End of the Modern World

1. I would argue that Muriel Spark is the first Catholic writer who can rightly be discussed as a postmodernist, since *The Comforters* (1957), which deals with

postmodern questions of authenticity and representation, predates *The Moviegoer* (1961).

2. Percy, while not embracing Derridean deconstruction, was deeply interested in the "linguistic turn" in literary studies; his study of linguistics, which appears in both his nonfiction and fiction (particularly *The Second Coming* [1980]), engages with poststructuralism on its own terms.

3. Percy's work, in its depiction of a world where things have fallen apart, clearly shares many thematic concerns with the modernists as well, but unlike the many modernists who looked to the past for answers, such as Yeats and his turn toward Celtic history or Eliot and his "fragments . . . shored against my ruins," Percy rejects such a nostalgic move.

4. Percy's nonfiction provides more overt examples of these tendencies, but while he may explain both his critique of society and his understanding of possible solutions more clearly in *The Message in the Bottle* (1975) and *Lost in the Cosmos* (1983) than in his novels, his fiction and his nonfiction both manifest the same worldview. The primary difference is that in his fiction, Percy is interested in depicting the problem and possible solutions, not explaining them. This approach invites the reader into the process of discovering the solutions to these problems for him- or herself.

5. His insistence that race and class are unrelated to what "has gone badly wrong here" is a problematic claim, worth further discussion. For more on Percy and race, see Akins's "'A Failure of Love': Racism and Original Sin in Walker Percy's *Love in the Ruins*" and O'Gorman's "Walker Percy, the Catholic Church and Southern Race Relations (ca. 1947–1970)."

6. For a thorough examination of Percy's influences, see Luschei, chapter 2: "Some Light from the Existentialists," Desmond's Introduction to *Walker Percy's Search for Community*, and Wilson's *Walker Percy, Fyodor Dostoevsky, and the Search for Influence*.

7. O'Connor recommended Guardini's *The Lord* (1954) to both Sally Fitzgerald and Betty Hester, calling it "very fine" and "his masterpiece," and stating that "there is nothing like it anywhere, certainly not in this country" (*Habit* 74, 99). She also reviewed six of his books for *The Bulletin*, her local diocesan paper, which is twice the number she reviewed for any other writer.

8. In this sense, his protagonists are often similar to Powers's; in both cases, the individuals unthinkingly subscribe to society's expectations and internalize a set of values without reflecting on whether or not they should. A key difference is that, for the most part, Percy's plots are overtly about characters coming to question and reject these narratives, whereas in Powers's stories the characters often never come to an awareness that these values are not worth pursuing; that work is done by the reader alone. For both authors, though, the overall fictional project seems to be similar—awakening the reader to the ways that they, too, are like Guardini's "mass men."

9. The selections are, in order, from pages 50, 101, 108–9, and 105.

10. For instances in which Percy cites Guardini's influence, see *More Conversations with Walker Percy* (74 and 118) and *Signposts in a Strange Land* (208).

11. Lancelot Lamar is an exception; he is a Percy protagonist who certainly has too much faith in his own intellect and abilities, although he, too, finally surrenders his autonomy, perhaps unwittingly, to unexamined narratives, as discussed below.

12. While Percy's novels do usually include a priest or a nun whose actions are held up as exemplary, these individuals are always marginalized figures within the institutional Catholic Church. Val Vaught is working alone in an isolated and forgotten school in *The Last Gentleman*; Fr. Smith locks himself up in a fire tower where no one can reach him in *The Thanatos Syndrome*; Percival is not even an active priest for most of *Lancelot*. They are hardly representative of the hierarchical aspects of Catholicism.

13. This is not to say that movies cannot probe existential questions, but Percy is sure to point out that the movies that Binx goes to see substitute empty answers to these questions: "The movies are onto the search, but they screw it up. The search always ends in despair. They like to show a fellow coming to himself in a strange place—but what does he do? He takes up with the local librarian, sets about proving to the local children what a nice fellow he is, and settles down with a vengeance. In two weeks' time he is so sunk in everydayness that he might just as well be dead" (*Moviegoer* 13).

14. Farrell O'Gorman uses Kierkegaard's terminology to differentiate the modes of belief at work in the novel, including commitment to "a complacent 'aesthetic' life devoted to pleasure-seeking—the life of the consumer," a religious orientation, and "a third possibility: that of the ethical life, the principles of which are derived solely from human reason and tradition rather than divine revelation" (*Crossroads* 177). O'Gorman notes that although this ethical orientation is appealing to Percy, he repeatedly shows it to be ultimately insufficient, "characterized by a secret self-absorption and despair" (177). Alongside these three modes of living, Percy also positions, and critiques, what Amy Hungerford describes as the widespread postwar "faith in faith—a version of religious thinking that minimizes the specificity of religious doctrine in service to usually nationalistic goals of civic connection" (3). Binx is continually fascinated, and mystified, by his countrymen's professions of faith, particularly evident in the radio program *This I Believe* (*Moviegoer* 94–96), which evince belief without context or substance. For Percy, as for O'Connor, true belief requires specificity and cost.

15. Lewis Lawson traces this motif in Percy's work back to Percy's reading of Tolstoy's *War and Peace*. Lawson notes the similarity between this particular scene in *The Moviegoer* and the language that Percy uses to describe Prince Andrei's injury in his "Man on a Train" essay, where Percy writes, "Prince Andrei transcended everydayness and came to himself for the first time when he lay wounded on the field of Borodino" (*Message* 99). Lawson notes that Percy did not see Prince Andrei's injury as leading to "permanent relief from alienation" (412); in Percy's own work, these violent moments are often the precursors to the kinds of radical reorientation that do provide such permanent relief.

16. See, in particular, John Barth's "The Literature of Exhaustion," where he describes how the contemporary writer needs to navigate "the used-upness of certain forms or the felt exhaustion of certain possibilities" (64).

17. See Susan V. Donaldson's "Tradition in Amber: Walker Percy's *Lancelot* as Southern Metafiction" for a fuller treatment of the postmodern aspects of this novel.

18. Robert Brinkmeyer notes that Lancelot's "original sin" is a form of pride; his adherence to "the myth of the autonomous self" leads him to disregard "the rights and even the lives of other people (since all value is located within the autonomous self)" ("Dynamics" 161).

19. Percy indicates that he had this conception of evil in mind when writing this scene: "When he [Lancelot] gets to the heart of evil, what he thinks is evil, he finds nothing—which is incidentally, orthodox Thomist doctrine, you know. Thomas Aquinas defines evil as the absence of essence" (*Conversations* 155).

20. The phrase "off the dead center" is the exact phrase used by Kate in *The Moviegoer* as justification for her suicide attempt (181).

21. See Sykes, chapter 7, for more on the stoic roots of Lance's new world order.

22. See, for instance, Simone Vauthier's "Story, Story-Teller and Listener: Notes on *Lancelot*" for a particularly nuanced account of the dynamic encounter between Lance and Percival.

23. This is the form of Catholicism that appears in Val Vaught's work with the Tyree children in *The Last Gentleman* or Fr. Smith's work with the old and dying in *The Thanatos Syndrome*.

4 / Tim Gautreaux and a Postconciliar Approach to Violence

1. The only critic to study the three authors together is L. Lamar Nisly, whose excellent study *Wingless Chickens, Bayou Catholics, and Pilgrim Wayfarers: Constructions of Audience and Tone in O'Connor, Gautreaux, and Percy* (2011) explores the different imagined audiences for these three authors, and the ways their varying regional experiences of Catholicism influenced their work. Much of what I write here builds on elements of Nisly's work on Gautreaux.

2. In this, his work calls to mind Dubus's "A Father's Story," as discussed in the Introduction.

3. For more on the connections between ethics and literature, see Wayne C. Booth's *The Company We Keep: An Ethics of Fiction* (1988) and Martha Nussbaum's *Love's Knowledge: Essays on Philosophy and Literature* (1990). Marshall Gregory provides a helpful overview of contemporary ethical criticism in "Redefining Ethical Criticism" (2011).

4. In this sense, his work is more thematically in line with the work of J. F. Powers. Gautreaux never discusses Powers's work, though, most likely for the reasons covered in the beginning of chapter 2.

5. Nisly sees the difference between Gautreaux and his southern Catholic predecessors as a question of audience. He argues that O'Connor and Percy saw their readers as hostile or indifferent to their Catholic message, but Gautreaux views his as "companions," and as such he "feels no need to make a case for Catholic beliefs and values or the importance of community because they have become ingrained in him and, he assumes, in his audience" (Nisly, *Wingless* 136). I think this is too simplistic an account of both Gautreaux's imagined audience and his fictional aims, and that his work does challenge his readers to engage with a Catholic worldview, but that the specific nature of this Catholicism, with its emphasis on practical action over transcendent signification, is where the principal difference between his work and that of O'Connor and Percy resides.

6. The story first appeared in the *Atlantic Monthly* in June 1991 and was republished as the first story in his first collection, *Same Place, Same Things* (1996).

7. She, like many of the characters in Percy's *Lancelot*, is seduced by the Hollywood idealization of what life should be like.

8. Julie Kane, in her entry on Gautreaux in *Twenty-First-Century American Novelists*, notes a number of similarities between this story and O'Connor's work, including "the 1930s Southern rural setting, the attractive traveling 'mystery man,' the sudden turn toward violence, and the hope of grace and transcendence." All of these O'Connor-esque elements are present, but they take on a very different valence in Gautreaux's story. The traveling "mystery man" in Gautreaux's story, unlike Manley Pointer or Mr. Shiftlet, is the victim, not the purveyor, of violence, and this act of violence is not particularly redemptive for any of the actors involved in the drama.

9. Ed Piacentino reads Gautreaux's story in this way, as being about a "self-absorbed and standoffish" man whose failure to help Ada indicates that "the prospect of meaningful connections with others in the future seems unlikely" (116–17). I think that readers might be inclined to interpret the story in this way in large part because O'Connor's fiction teaches us to read it this way—within her fiction, the protagonists almost always have an unacknowledged fault, upon which the (violent) action of the story hinges. I am arguing that Gautreaux is conscious of this pattern and deliberately inverts it, in order to draw attention to human decency and morality, not the lack thereof.

10. For more on Ricoeur and the reader, see pages 64–65.

11. In particular, Nisly's essay on *The Missing* draws on the US Catholic Bishops' Pastoral Letter, *The Challenge of Peace: God's Promise and Our Response*, to persuasively demonstrate how the themes of the novel reflect specific aspects of Catholic social teaching.

12. Gautreaux revisits this theme later in the novel when Byron and Randolph debate whether the assassination of the kaiser would have been a moral act even though, as Randolph says, "'It's wrong, By. It's a sin'" (183).

13. Bauer draws a connection between Randolph's journey down to the mill and Marlowe's journey in *Heart of Darkness* (152).

14. In an interview with Margaret Bauer, Gautreaux articulated his position on how using violence alters the individual: "It just happens that everybody that gets involved in the business of shooting people with rifles winds up damaged and changed" (*Conversations* 138).

15. Even Sam's backstory in World War I reiterates the condemnation of war and violence found in *The Clearing*. Although Sam misses out on active duty, his experience of its after-effects changes him: "He looked out and saw half a million soldiers going at each other in a freezing rain, their bodies shredded by artillery, their faces torn off, their knees disintegrated into snowy red pulp, their lungs boiled out by poison gas, and all of this for four years, spread out as far and wide as the continent itself" (11). Sam's exposure to the chaotic violence of the war contributes to his pacifist stance: "After his experience in the war, he wanted nothing further to do with guns" (37).

5 / Belief and Ambiguity in the Fiction of Alice McDermott

1. Since Elie first made these comments in 2012, McDermott has been a keynote speaker at the first three biennial Catholic Imagination conferences (held at USC in 2015, Fordham in 2017, and Loyola Chicago in 2019), and she is now widely praised as a writer whose work "reveal[s] how literary faith looks in a secular age" (Ripatrazone, *Longing* 179). She is acknowledged to be, in Gregory Wolfe's words, one of the "contemporary writers [who] take[s] on the fundamental question of belief versus

unbelief" (*First Things*, 2013). In part, this shift in critical attention may be attributed to the success of her most recent novels—*Someone* (2013) and *The Ninth Hour* (2017)—as well as the growth in the larger conversation about the state of contemporary Catholic fiction.

2. For a full exploration of the uncanny in McDermott's early novels, see Patricia Coughlan, "Paper Ghosts: Reading the Uncanny in Alice McDermott."

3. In her essay collection *What about the Baby: Some Thoughts on the Art of Fiction* (2021), McDermott relates an anecdote about a friend asking about her novel in progress: "'Is someone going to die in this one, too? All of your novels are about someone dying.'" To which McDermott responds, "She was right—it's perfectly true" (81).

4. McDermott told Charlie Reilly that this was the guiding principle for her narrative technique; the entire novel functions as Theresa's attempt to "stop time. This is how she takes a stand against those songs about the deaths of children. This is how she banishes the world in which children die. She writes this story" (Reilly 565).

5. In addition to the significance of this dynamic in *Child of My Heart*, discussed above, the theme is also foregrounded in many of her other novels, including the way the community remembers and relives the violent showdown between the young hoods and the suburban fathers in *That Night* (1987), the various characters' attempts to make sense of May's death in *At Weddings and Wakes* (1992), the ways the Keane family members react to the death of Jacob in the Vietnam War in *After This* (2006), and the central role of Jim's suicide at the start of *The Ninth Hour* (2017). It is also a central thematic concern in *Someone* (2013), discussed below.

6. It is significant that this passage, like the narrator's meditation on "the end," draws attention not to actions but to feelings; one might expect the passage to read "nothing you've *done*" not "nothing you've *felt*," but McDermott's focus is on subjectivity, because how one feels about life and the world—whether this be despair, anger, or love—drives both one's beliefs and one's actions. What Maeve is claiming in her despair is that her interior disposition, which is the motivating factor for everything else in her life and defines who she is as an individual, is essentially meaningless.

7. Paul Contino's "Gleams of Everlasting Life in Alice McDermott's *Someone*" is particularly insightful on the various thematic "echoes, rhymes of images and phrases" that formally tie the novel together (507).

8. Falling, too, functions in both literal and metaphorical ways in *Someone*; it is a literal plot element—Pegeen falls to her death; Marie's husband falls out of his airplane; Marie falls and is caught by her health-care aide in the last chronological moment in the book—and through these continual references McDermott is also invoking a metaphorical sense of the Fall.

9. The inability to distinguish between imagination and reality calls to mind the similar passage in *Charming Billy* (discussed above), but whereas in that novel the blurring of the lines between the two is indicative of the arbitrary nature of faith, here it points toward the persistent underlying mystery of existence.

10. This theme is echoed in a scene where Tom reflects on Gabe's time in the psychiatric facility. Tom is frustrated by the psychiatrists' attempts to define Gabe by his sexual orientation, "'to reduce everything to a couple of easy words about sex'" (227). Tom sees humanity as being much richer and more complex than this: "'Who can know the heart of a man?'" (227). This idea, that one's humanity is not reducible to biological determinism, is reinforced by the entire structure of the novel.

11. As McDermott told one interviewer, as she worked on *The Ninth Hour* she thought to herself, "I've always balked a little at being labeled a Catholic novelist . . . but there were times when I thought about this one, 'You want a Catholic novel? I'll give you a Catholic novel!'" (Leavy).

12. See chapter 1, pages 28–32, for much more on this dynamic.

13. Mary Gordon singles out this technique as one of the novel's few flaws, noting that "for the literal-minded among us it seems unlikely that a third party could provide the intimate details that so enrich the novel, or be so familiar with the other characters' inner lives." For the reasons discussed above, with regard to *Charming Billy*, I think Gordon's critique is misguided. When questioned about the narrative technique of *The Ninth Hour*, McDermott described her process as "a way to convey the certainty, the vividness, with which the faithful regard things unseen (which includes the past), while at the same time acknowledging the somewhat patchwork and uncertain way in which such faith is achieved—the whole through-a-glass-darkly part of belief. The novel is built on the collective narrators' own experiences, on the stories they've been told, phrases they have heard, anecdote, speculation, even a bit of research, but none of these elements can completely account for the vividness and the certainty of the story's linear narrative—a narrative that must, in some ways, be taken as 'accurate' on faith alone" (Domestico).

14. Margaret Hallissy notes the novel's "unprecedented emphasis on the damaged, distorted, mutilated, suffering body" (94).

15. Maureen Corrigan likens the journey, which she describes as "one of the most mesmerizing sections of the novel," to the "infamous Nighttown chapter in James Joyce's *Ulysses*"; Hallissy likens it to the part of the *Odyssey* where "Odysseus visits the underworld" (96).

6 / "Life Is Rough and Death Is Coming": George Saunders and the Catholic Literary Tradition

1. The quote comes from O'Connor's essay "The Fiction and Writer and His Country," (*Mystery* 27); Saunders quotes from it frequently (see *Conversations with George Saunders*, 67, 95, 117, 151, 201).

2. W. Brett Wiley highlights the importance of confession in the story "Offloading for Mrs. Schwartz," noting that the narrator repeatedly seeks out absolution through penitential acts and various "attempt(s) at confession, albeit through a non-religious source, as he seeks forgiveness for his perceived moral failure" (405).

3. In addition to the surprising way Saunders depicts the afterlife, another way the novel is destabilizing for the reader is the form of the novel itself. It is structured as a collagelike combination of monologues from characters in the book and historical passages, some of which are real and some of which Saunders has invented (and it is never clear to the reader which passages are which). Even the layout of the text on the page looks more like a screenplay than a traditional novel. All of these techniques contribute to the disorienting effect of stepping into the "black box" of this work.

4. Zadie Smith, upon finishing the novel, told Saunders, "Something in me was changed by *Lincoln in the Bardo*, and the great sublime/grotesque risk of your ghosts was a part of it. Are you writing fiction with the intention of creating some change inside a person?" (Saunders, *Conversations* 175). Over the course of that interview, and many others, it is clear that his answer is yes.

5. It is worth noting that Whitehouse views this shift toward a horizontal axis as a negative development. His *Vertical Man: The Human Being in the Catholic Novels of Graham Greene, Sigrid Undset, and Georges Bernanos* (1999) concludes with a particularly bleak view of the state of contemporary Catholic fiction. In his analysis, the main impact of Vatican II has been to disorient the Catholic believer, replacing a properly oriented hierarchical relationship between humanity and God with an understanding of "Man as a social unit with no significant personhood, a conditioned operant existing in a horizontal continuum where all is relative, contingent and ultimately value free" (207). Saunders (and, presumably, the other authors discussed in the latter half of this book) would disagree with this negative assessment.

6. Cummings imagines himself "h[olding] court on the porch in a white Whitmanesque suit while Mom hovered behind him getting everything wrong about his work and proffering inane snacks to his manifold admirers" (185). Readers familiar with O'Connor's own complex relationship with her mother, Regina, will surely see an echo of that dynamic here.

7. Morse's worry about being mistaken as a pervert further aligns—and contrasts—his character with Mr. Paradise.

8. In an interesting (and perhaps meaningless) parallel, this somewhat odd choice of an adjective to describe Morse's body is the exact same one that Dubus uses to describe the body of the young man who is the victim of the hit-and-run in "A Father's Story": "He was long; that is the word that came to me, not tall" (*Selected* 470). "The Falls," like "A Father's Story," asks the reader to consider what we owe to strangers, what we owe to our families, and what the cost of true, selfless love looks like.

9. For more on Percy's conception of the diagnostic novel, see chapter 3.

10. As well as Wolff's "Bullet in the Brain," as discussed in the Introduction.

11. There is a side plot about how the narrator's parents have been murdered but do not realize they are dead (an idea that becomes a central theme in *Lincoln in the Bardo*).

12. One way Saunders demonstrates the effect of the brain tumor on Eber's thought processes is by occasionally inserting the wrong word into his stream of consciousness (for instance: "Let me do it cling. Clean. Cleanly" [226–27] and "What a victory he was wresting. From the jaws of the feet . . . from the jaws of defeat" [230]).

13. This dynamic, where one individual is contemplating suicide only to be saved when a second individual falls into freezing cold water and needs to be rescued, calls to mind another classic work of Catholic art: Frank Capra's *It's a Wonderful Life*.

14. For more on this facet of his writing, see Clare Hayes-Brady's "Horning In: Language, Subordination and Freedom in the Short Fiction of George Saunders" and Adam Kelly's "Language between Lyricism and Corporatism: George Saunders's New Sincerity"; both can be found in Coleman and Ellerhoff's *George Saunders: Critical Essays* (2017).

Epilogue. Phil Klay, Kirstin Valdez Quade, and the State of Contemporary Catholic Literature

1. For a few years, in the early 2010s, there was a robust debate about whether Catholic literature was in decline. Important pieces in the discussion include: Robert Fay's "Where Have All the Catholic Writers Gone?" (*The Millions*, 2011), Paul Elie's "Has Fiction Lost Its Faith?" (*New York Times Sunday Book Review*, 2012), Gregory

164 / NOTES TO PAGES 136-45

Wolfe's "Whispers of Faith in a Postmodern World" (*Wall Street Journal*, 2013), Randy Boyagoda's "Faith in Fiction" (*First Things*, 2013), Nick Ripatrazone's "Counter and Strange: Contemporary Catholic Literature" (*The Millions*, 2013), Dana Gioia's "The Catholic Writer Today" (*First Things*, 2013), and Wolfe's "The Catholic Writer, Then and Now" (*Image*, 2014). One productive result of these discussions has been the Biennial Catholic Imagination Conference (held at the University of Southern California in 2015, Fordham University in 2017, Loyola University Chicago in 2019, and [after a COVID-related delay] the University of Dallas in 2022), which has provided a venue both to discuss the contours of the Catholic Imagination and to showcase the work of a variety of contemporary Catholic writers—including both Phil Klay and Kirstin Valdez Quade.

2. This calls to mind the passage from Guardini's *The End of the Modern World*, about one lonely soul crying out to another, which I discuss in chapter 3. Both Klay and Percy depict isolated individuals, though the immediate cause of the brokenness of Klay's characters is usually more easily attributable to their circumstances.

3. This is one of the themes of Hansen's *Mariette in Ecstasy*, discussed in the Introduction.

4. In this, she mirrors the protagonist of *Mariette in Ecstasy*. It is worth noting, though, that Mariette acts more or less as we might expect a holy person to act—with love and care and gentleness—and the "Elusive. Other. Upsetting" aspects of her nature, which I discussed in the Introduction, are tied to the supernatural signs and torments she experiences. Christina, on the other hand, does not map neatly onto our expectations of holiness.

5. In an interview with Michael Welch, Quade links the trials of the Padilla family to the legacy of colonialism and cultural oppression: "Our family histories are a part of broader cultural histories, and broader cultural histories make their way into our families. There is this really painful history of conquest and reconquest that started with the Spanish arrival in the region of New Mexico. And over the centuries since, there have been economic conquests and the borders have shifted; there's been so much change and so much pain there, and that history is still alive today. It's palpable. And these discussions are happening today about how we revisit these narratives of our history, and how we come to terms with that legacy of violence and possession. So I think there's no way for that kind of pain both suffered and inflicted to not make its way into the family."

6. It is worth noting that in the novel, there is still one traumatic moment that does lead directly to the final insight and permanent change for Amadeo. While driving drunk, with the baby in the car, Amadeo gets into an accident. Because he was intoxicated, he had not properly secured the car seat, and the entire carrier goes flying out the window; in a somewhat miraculous turn of events, it lands right side up, and the baby is unharmed. The knowledge that he could have killed his grandson is what finally leads him to stop drinking. It is his experience of what Alcoholics Anonymous call "hitting bottom," and while it makes sense that such a moment would lead him to reform his life, I think the novel would be more effective without this scene. Quade already subverted the connection between trauma and insight with her revisions to the crucifixion scene, and this moment somewhat undercuts the effectiveness of that change.

WORKS CITED

Akins, Adrienne V. "'A Failure of Love': Racism and Original Sin in Walker
    Percy's *Love in the Ruins.*" *Southern Quarterly* 47:1 (Fall 2009): 65–73.
Asals, Frederick. *Flannery O'Connor: The Imagination of Extremity.* Athens:
    University of Georgia Press, 1982.
Barth, John. "The Literature of Exhaustion." In *The Friday Book: Essays and
    Other Nonfictions.* New York: G. P. Putnam's, 1984. 62–76.
Bauer, Margaret Donovan. *Understanding Tim Gautreaux.* Columbia:
    University of South Carolina Press, 2010.
Benson, Robert. "Purgatory in the Midwest: The White Martyrdom of Urban
    Roche." In *Place in American Fiction: Excursions and Explorations,* ed.
    H. L. Weatherby and George Core. Columbia: University of Missouri Press,
    2004. 183–99.
Booth, Wayne. *The Company We Keep: An Ethics of Fiction.* Berkeley:
    University of California Press, 1988.
Bottum, Joseph. "The Greatest Catholic Writer of the 20th Century." *First
    Things,* 7 Sept. 2006.
Boyagoda, Randy. "Faith in Fiction." *First Things,* Aug. 2013.
Brinkmeyer, Robert. *The Art and Vision of Flannery O'Connor.* Baton Rouge:
    LSU Press, 1989.
———. "*Lancelot* and the Dynamics of the Intersubjective Community." In
    Walker Percy: Novelist and Philosopher, ed. Jan Nordby Gretlund and
    Karl-Heinz Westarp. Jackson: UP of Mississippi, 1991. 155–66.
Burton, Tara Isabella. "Toward a Christian Aesthetics: Novel-Writing in an
    Age of COVID." *Breaking Ground,* 15 July 2020.
Ciabattari, Jane. "Kirstin Valdez Quade on Literary Community and
    Intergenerational Narratives." *Literary Hub,* 27 April 2021.

Ciuba, Gary. *Walker Percy's Books of Revelations*. Athens: University of Georgia Press, 1991.

Coleman, Phillip, and Stephen Gronert Ellerhoff, eds. *George Saunders: Critical Essays*. Cham, Switzerland: Palgrave Macmillan, 2017.

Contino, Paul. "Gleams of Everlasting Life in Alice McDermott's *Someone*." *Christianity and Literature* 63.4 (2014): 503–11.

———. "This Writer's Life: Irony & Faith in the Work of Tobias Wolff." *Commonweal*, 17 Oct. 2005.

Corrigan, Maureen. "Salvation and Self-Sacrifice; The Irish-Catholic Women in Alice McDermott's Novels Feel the Pull of Martyrdom." *Wall Street Journal*, 15 Sept. 2017.

Coughlan, Patricia. "Paper Ghosts: Reading the Uncanny in Alice McDermott." *Eire-Ireland* 47 (2012): 123–46.

Cumberland, Debra. "Flannery O'Connor and the Question of the Christian Novel." In Han 3–24.

Desmond, John. *Risen Sons: Flannery O'Connor's Vision of History*. Athens: University of Georgia Press, 1987.

———. *Walker Percy's Search for Community*. Athens: University of Georgia Press, 2004.

Dolan, Jay P. *In Search of an American Catholicism: A History of Religion and Culture in Tension*. New York: Oxford UP, 2002.

Domestico, Anthony. "Where the Mystery Lies: An Interview with Alice McDermott." *Commonweal*, 15 Dec. 2017.

Donaldson, Susan V. "Tradition in Amber: Walker Percy's *Lancelot* as Southern Metafiction." In *Walker Percy: Novelist and Philosopher*, ed. Jan Nordby Gretlund and Karl-Heinz Westarp. Jackson: UP of Mississippi, 1991. 65–73.

Donoghue, Denis. "Introduction." In *The Stories of J. F. Powers*. New York: New York Review of Books, 2000. vii–xii.

Downey, Jack Lee. *The Bread of the Strong: Lacouturisme and the Folly of the Cross, 1910–1985*. New York: Fordham UP, 2015.

Dubus, Andre. *Selected Stories*. New York: Vintage, 1996.

Eagleton, Terry. "Awakening from Modernity." *Times Literary Supplement*, 20 Feb. 1987.

Edmondson, Hank. *Return to Good and Evil: Flannery O'Connor's Response to Nihilism*. Lanham, MD: Lexington Books, 2002.

Elie, Paul. "Bartleby on the Prairie: The Unspent Life of J. F. Powers," *Harper's Magazine* (Sept. 2013): 83–88.

———. "Criticism, Not Committee Work." *Everything That Rises* [blog], 1 March 2014.

———. "Has Fiction Lost Its Faith?" *New York Times Sunday Book Review*, 23 Dec. 2012: BR1.

Ellsberg, Robert. "Introduction." In *All the Way to Heaven: The Selected Letters of Dorothy Day*, ed. Robert Ellsberg. Milwaukee, WI: Marquette UP, 2010.

Evangelii Gaudium. Pope Francis. 24 Nov. 2013. http://www.vatican.va/archive.

Farnsworth, Elizabeth. "Interview: Alice McDermott." *PBS Newshour*, 20 Nov. 1998.

Fay, Robert. "Where Have All the Catholic Writers Gone?" *The Millions*, 28 Nov. 2011.

Feeley, Kathleen. *Flannery O'Connor: Voice of the Peacock*. New York: Fordham UP, 1982.

Felski, Rita. *The Limits of Critique*. Chicago: University of Chicago Press, 2015.

Fraser, Theodore. *The Modern Catholic Novel in Europe*. New York: Twayne, 1994.

Gandolfo, Anita. *Testing the Faith: The New Catholic Fiction in America*. New York: Greenwood, 1992.

Gaudium et Spes: Pastoral Constitution on the Church in the Modern World. Vatican II. 7 Dec. 1965. http://www.vatican.va/archive.

Gautreaux, Tim. *The Clearing*. New York: Knopf, 2003.

———. *Conversations with Tim Gautreaux*, ed. L. Lamar Nisly. Literary Conversations. Jackson: UP of Mississippi, 2012.

———. "Idols." *The New Yorker*, 22 June 2009, 70–79.

———. *The Missing*. New York: Knopf, 2009.

———. *The Next Step in the Dance*. New York: Picador, 1998.

———. *Same Place, Same Things*. New York: St. Martin's, 1996.

Giles, Paul. *American Catholic Arts and Fictions: Culture, Ideology, Aesthetics*. Cambridge: Cambridge UP, 1992.

Gioia, Dana. "The Catholic Writer Today." *First Things*, Dec. 2013.

Gordon, Mary. "In Alice McDermott's Novel, A Cloistered Life Blows Open." *New York Times*, 2 Oct. 2017.

Grantham, Dewey W. *The South in Modern America: A Region at Odds*. New York: HarperCollins, 1994.

Gregory, Marshall W. "Redefining Ethical Criticism: The Old vs. the New." *JLTonline*, 24 Jan. 2011.

Guardini, Romano. *The End of the Modern World*. Wilmington, DE: ISI Books, 1998.

———. *The Lord*. Chicago: Henry Regnery, 1954.

Gussow, Mel. "J.F. Powers, 81, Dies; Wrote about Priests." *The New York Times* 17 June 1999.

Hagopian, John. *J. F. Powers*. New York: Twayne, 1968.

Hallissy, Margaret. *Understanding Alice McDermott*. Columbia: University of South Carolina Press, 2020.

Han, John J., ed. *Wise Blood: A Reconsideration*. New York: Rodopi, 2011.

Hansen, Ron. *Hotly in Pursuit of the Real: Notes toward a Memoir*. Eugene, OR: Slant, 2020.

———. *Mariette in Ecstasy*. New York: HarperPerennial, 1991.

Harvey, David. *The Condition of Postmodernity: An Enquiry into the Origins of Cultural Change*. Malden, MA: Blackwell, 1990.

Hayes-Brady, Clare. "Horning In: Language, Subordination and Freedom in the Short Fiction of George Saunders." In Coleman and Ellerhoff 23–39.

Howard, H. Wendell. "J. F. Powers's *Morte D'Urban*." *Logos: A Journal of Catholic Thought and Culture* 19.2 (2016): 81–99.

Hungerford, Amy. *Postmodern Belief: American Literature and Religion since 1960*. Princeton, NJ: Princeton UP, 2010.

Kakutani, Michiko. "A Teenager's Summer of Puzzling Relationships." *New York Times*, 18 Nov. 2002.

Kane, Julie. "Tim Gautreaux, 1947–." In *Twenty-First-Century American Novelists*, ed. Lisa Abney and Suzanne Disheroon-Green. *Dictionary of Literary Biography* 292. Detroit: Gale, 2004. 119–25.

Kelly, Adam. "Language Between Lyricism and Corporatism: George Saunders's New Sincerity." In Coleman and Ellerhoff 41–58.

Kilcourse, George. *Flannery O'Connor's Religious Imagination: A World with Everything off Balance*. New York: Paulist, 2001.

Klay, Phil. "False Witnesses: On Writing about War." *The Point Magazine*, 26 April 2022.

———. *Missionaries*. New York: Penguin, 2020.

———. "The Point of War Literature: Myles Werntz Interviews Phil Klay about His Novel *Missionaries*." *Plough*, 31 May 2021.

———. *Redeployment*. New York: Penguin, 2014.

———. "Tales of War and Redemption." *American Scholar*, 4 Dec. 2017.

Krieg, Robert A. *Romano Guardini: A Precursor of Vatican II*. Notre Dame, IN: University of Notre Dame Press, 1997.

Labrie, Ross. *The Catholic Imagination in American Literature*. Columbia: University of Missouri Press, 1997.

Lake, Christina Bieber. "The Violence of Technique and the Technique of Violence." In *Flannery O'Connor in the Age of Terrorism: Essays on Violence and Grace*, ed. Avis Hewitt and Robert Donahoo. Knoxville: University of Tennessee Press, 2010. 25–39.

Lawson, Lewis A. "From Tolstoy to Dostoyevsky in *The Moviegoer*." *Mississippi Quarterly* 56.3 (2003): 411–19.

Leavy, Adrienne. "'I Love the Gifts of the Church and Am Constantly Dismayed by Its Failings.' Interview with Alice McDermott." *Irish Times*, 19 Oct. 2017.

Luschei, Martin. *The Sovereign Wayfarer: Walker Percy's Diagnosis of the Malaise*. Baton Rouge: LSU Press, 1972.

Lynch, William. *Christ and Apollo: The Dimensions of the Literary Imagination*. Wilmington, DE: ISI Books, 2004.

Malloy, Kristin. "The Catholic and Creativity: J. F. Powers (An Interview with J. F. Powers)." In *J. F. Powers*, ed. Fallon Evans. St. Louis: B. Herder, 1968.

Martin, James. *Jesus: A Pilgrimage*. New York: HarperCollins, 2014.

McClure, John. *Partial Faiths: Postsecular Fiction in the Age of Pynchon and Morrison*. Athens: University of Georgia Press, 2007.

McDermott, Alice. *After This*. New York: Farrar, Straus & Giroux, 2006.

———. *At Weddings and Wakes*. New York: Farrar, Straus & Giroux, 1992.

———. *Charming Billy*. New York: Farrar, Straus & Giroux, 1998.

———. *Child of My Heart*. New York: Farrar, Straus & Giroux, 2002.

———. "The Lunatic in the Pew: Confessions of a Natural-Born Catholic." *Boston College Magazine*, Summer 2003.

———. *The Ninth Hour*. New York: Farrar, Straus & Giroux, 2017.

———. "Redeemed from Death? The Faith of a Catholic Novelist." *Commonweal*, 3 May 2013, 14–16.

———. *Someone*. New York: Farrar, Straus & Giroux, 2013.

———. *That Night*. New York: Farrar, Straus & Giroux, 1987.

———. *What about the Baby? Some Thoughts on the Art of Fiction*. New York: Farrar, Straus & Giroux, 2021.

Merton, Thomas. *The Hidden Ground of Love: Letters*, ed. William H. Shannon. New York: Farrar, Straus & Giroux, 2011.

———. "J. F. Powers—*Morte D'Urban*: Two Celebrations." *The Literary Essays of Thomas Merton*, ed. Br. Patrick Hart. New York: New Directions, 1981. 147–51.

———. *A Search for Solitude: The Journals of Thomas Merton*. Volume 3: *1952–1960*, ed. Lawrence S. Cunningham. San Francisco: HarperCollins, 1996.

Meyers, Jeffery. "His Bleak Materials: J. F. Powers at 100." *Commonweal*, 7 July 2017.

Mitchell, Mary Kenagy. "A Conversation with Kirstin Valdez Quade." *Image* 103 (2020).

Nisly, L. Lamar. "Presbyterian Pennsylvanians at a Louisiana Sawmill, or Just How Catholic Is Gautreaux's *The Clearing*?" *U.S. Catholic Historian* 23.3 (2005): 109–19.

———. "Tim Gautreaux's *The Missing*: Journeys of Vengeance or Belonging." *Religion and the Arts* 15 (2011): 193–209.

———. *Wingless Chickens, Bayou Catholics, and Pilgrim Wayfarers: Constructions of Audience and Tone in O'Connor, Gautreaux, and Percy*. Macon, GA: Mercer UP, 2011.

Nussbaum, Martha. *Love's Knowledge: Essays on Philosophy and Literature*. New York: Oxford UP, 1990.

O'Brien, Joseph. "Restoring Faith in Fiction: A Visit with Walker Percy and Paul Elie." *Dappled Things*, Dec. 2013.

O'Connor, Flannery. *Conversations with Flannery O'Connor*, ed. Rosemary Magee. Jackson: UP of Mississippi, 1987.

———. *Flannery O'Connor: Collected Works*. New York: Library of America. 1988.

———. *Flannery O'Connor: The Habit of Being*, ed. Sally Fitzgerald. New York: Farrar, Straus & Giroux, 1979.

———. *Mystery and Manners*. New York: Farrar, Straus & Giroux, 1969.

———. *The Presence of Grace and Other Book Reviews.* Athens: University of Georgia Press, 1983.

O'Gorman, Farrell. *Peculiar Crossroads: Flannery O'Connor, Walker Percy, and the Catholic Vision in Postwar Southern Fiction.* Baton Rouge: LSU Press, 2004.

———. "Walker Percy, the Catholic Church and Southern Race Relations (ca. 1947–1970)." *Mississippi Quarterly: The Journal of Southern Cultures* 54:1 (Winter 1999/2000): 67–88.

Pacem in Terris. Pope John XXIII. 11 April 1963. http://www.vatican.va /archive.

Peebles, Stacey. "He's Hunting Something: Hazel Motes as Ex-Soldier." In Han 371–88.

Percy, Walker. *Conversations with Walker Percy,* ed. Lewis A. Lawson and Victor A. Kramer. Literary Conversations. Jackson: UP of Mississippi, 1985.

———. *Lancelot.* New York: Farrar, Straus & Giroux, 1977.

———. *The Last Gentleman.* New York: Farrar, Straus & Giroux, 1966.

———. *Lost in the Cosmos: The Last Self-Help Book.* New York: Farrar, Straus & Giroux, 1983.

———. *Love in the Ruins.* New York: Farrar, Straus & Giroux, 1971.

———. *The Message in the Bottle.* New York: Farrar, Straus & Giroux, 1975.

———. *More Conversations with Walker Percy,* ed. Lewis A. Lawson and Victor A. Kramer. Literary Conversations. Jackson: UP of Mississippi, 1993.

———. *The Moviegoer.* New York: Farrar, Straus & Giroux, 1961.

———. *The Second Coming.* New York: Farrar, Straus & Giroux, 1980.

———. *Signposts in a Strange Land,* ed. Patrick Samway. New York: Farrar, Straus & Giroux, 1991.

———. *The Thanatos Syndrome.* New York: Farrar, Straus & Giroux, 1987.

Piacentino, Ed. "Second Chances: Patterns of Failure and Redemption in Tim Gautreaux's *Same Places, Same Things.*" *Southern Literary Journal* 28.1 (2005): 115–33.

Powers, J. F. *Morte D'Urban.* New York: New York Review of Books, 2000.

———. *The Stories of J. F. Powers.* New York: New York Review of Books, 2000.

Powers, Katherine A., ed. *Suitable Accommodations: An Autobiographical Story of Family Life: The Letters of J. F. Powers, 1942–1963.* New York: Farrar, Straus & Giroux, 2013.

Prickett, Sam. "Consciousness Is Not Correct: A Conversation with George Saunders." *Weld: Birmingham's Newspaper,* 14 Feb. 2017.

Quade, Kirstin Valdez. "Christina the Astonishing (1150–1224)." *The New Yorker,* 24 July 2017.

———. *The Five Wounds.* New York: Norton, 2021.

———. *Night at the Fiestas.* New York: Norton, 2015.

Quinlan, Kieran. *Walker Percy: The Last Catholic Novelist.* Baton Rouge: LSU Press, 1996.

Ragen, Brian. *A Wreck on the Road to Damascus: Innocence, Guilt, and Conversion in Flannery O'Connor.* Chicago: Loyola UP, 1989.

Reichardt, Mary. "Introduction." *Between Human and Divine: The Catholic Vision in Contemporary Literature*, ed. Mary Reichardt. Washington, DC: Catholic University of America Press, 2010. 1–14.

———, ed. *Catholic Women Writers: A Bio-Bibliographical Sourcebook.* Westport, CT: Greenwood, 2001.

Reilly, Charlie. "An Interview with Alice McDermott." *Contemporary Literature* 46.4 (2005): 557–78.

Ricoeur, Paul. "Between the Text and Its Readers." In *A Ricoeur Reader: Reflection and Imagination*, ed. Mario Valdes. Toronto: University of Toronto Press, 1991. 390–424.

———. *The Symbolism of Evil.* Boston: Beacon, 1967.

———. *Time and Narrative. Volume 2.* Chicago: University of Chicago Press, 1985.

Ripatrazone, Nick. "A Conversation with Phil Klay." *Image* 87 (Winter 2015).

———. "Counter and Strange: Contemporary Catholic Literature." *The Millions*, 16 April 2013.

———. *The Fine Delight: Postconciliar Catholic Literature.* Eugene, OR: Cascade, 2013.

———. *Longing for an Absent God: Faith and Doubt in Great American Fiction.* Minneapolis: Fortress, 2020.

Saunders, George. *CivilWarLand in Bad Decline.* New York: Riverhead, 1996.

———. *Conversations with George Saunders*, ed. Michael O'Connell. Literary Conversations. Jackson: UP of Mississippi, 2022.

———. "Hank Center Presents / A Public Voices Series: George Saunders." Interview by Michael P. Murphy. *YouTube.* Uploaded by the Hank Center for the Catholic Intellectual Heritage, 10 May 2018.

———. "Hypocrites." *The New Yorker,* June 9 and 16, 2008.

———. *In Persuasion Nation.* New York: Riverhead, 2006.

———. *Lincoln in the Bardo.* New York: Random House, 2017.

———. *Pastoralia.* New York: Riverhead, 2000.

———. *A Swim in a Pond in the Rain: In Which Four Russians Give a Master Class on Writing, Reading, and Life.* New York: Random House, 2021.

———. *Tenth of December.* New York: Random House, 2013.

Sayers, Valerie. "Hope for Suffering Souls." *Commonweal,* May 2021, 56–58.

Schiebe, Mark. "Car Trouble: Hazel Motes and the Fifties Counterculture." In Han 405–24.

Sessions, W. A. "The Ambiguity of Vocation: Or, What Flannery Meant by 'Malgre Lui.'" In Han 231–54.

Spadaro, Antonio. "A Big Heart Open to God: An Interview with Pope Francis," *America,* 20 Sept. 2013.

Spark, Muriel. *The Comforters.* Philadelphia: Lippincott, 1957.

Srigley, Susan. *Flannery O'Connor's Sacramental Imagination.* Notre Dame, IN: University of Notre Dame Press, 2004.

Sykes, John D., Jr. *Flannery O'Connor, Walker Percy, and the Aesthetic of Revelation.* Columbia: University of Missouri Press, 2007.

Tartt, Donna. "The Glory of J. F. Powers." *Harper's Magazine*, July 2000.

Taylor, Charles. *A Secular Age*. Cambridge, MA: Harvard UP, 2007.

Tillich, Paul. *Ultimate Concern: Tillich in Dialogue*, ed. D. Mackenzie Brown. New York: Harper & Row, 1965.

Tolson, Jay. *Pilgrim in the Ruins: A Life of Walker Percy*. New York: Simon and Schuster, 1992.

Tracy, David. *The Analogical Imagination: Christian Theology and the Culture of Pluralism*. New York: Crossroad, 1981.

Treisman, Deborah. "George Saunders on the Induced Bafflement of Fiction." *The New Yorker*, 12 Aug. 2019.

Vauthier, Simone. "Story, Story-Teller, and Listener: Notes on *Lancelot*." In *Critical Essays on Walker Percy*, ed. J. Donald Crowley and Sue Mitchell Crowley. Boston: GK Hall, 1989. 184–99.

Waldmeir, John. *Cathedrals of Bone: The Role of the Body in Contemporary Catholic Literature*. New York: Fordham UP, 2009.

Wallace, Mark. *The Second Naiveté: Barth, Ricoeur, and the New Yale Theology*. Macon, GA: Mercer UP, 1995.

Welch, Michael. "The Possibility of Change and Movement in *The Five Wounds*." *Chicago Review of Books*, 8 April 2021.

Whitehouse, J. C. *Vertical Man: The Human Being in the Catholic Novels of Graham Greene, Sigrid Undset, and Georges Bernanos*. London: Saint Austin, 1999.

Wiley, W. Brett. "Invocation as Self-Change: George Saunders's Use of Prayer." *Religion and the Arts* 24 (2020): 399–414.

Wilson, Jessica Hooten. *Walker Percy, Fyodor Dostoevsky, and the Search for Influence*. Columbus: Ohio State UP, 2017.

Wolfe, Gregory. "The Catholic Writer, Then and Now." *Image* 79 (2014).

———. "Cultural Anorexia: Doubting the Decline of Faith in Fiction." *First Things*, 23 Dec. 2013.

———. "Whispers of Faith in a Postmodern World." *Wall Street Journal*, 10 Jan 2013.

Wolff, Tobias. "Introduction." In Andre Dubus, *Broken Vessels*. Boston: David R. Godine, 1991. xi–xix.

———. *The Night in Question*. New York: Knopf, 1996.

Wood, Ralph. *Flannery O'Connor and the Christ Haunted South*. Grand Rapids: Eerdmans, 2004.

———. "The Scandalous Baptism of Harry Ashfield." In *Inside the Church of Flannery O'Connor: Sacrament, Sacramental, and the Sacred in Her Fiction*, ed. Joanne Halleran McMullen and Jon Parrish Peede. Macon, GA: Mercer UP, 2007. 189–204.

Index

Michael O'Connell is a writer, editor, and teacher whose scholarship focuses primarily on the intersections of religion and contemporary literature. He is the editor of *Conversations with George Saunders* (2022).

Studies in the Catholic Imagination: The Flannery O'Connor Trust Series

Angela Alaimo O'Donnell, *Radical Ambivalence: Race in Flannery O'Connor*
Martyn Sampson, *Between Form and Faith: Graham Greene and the Catholic Novel*

Ingram Content Group UK Ltd.
Milton Keynes UK
UKHW011958130723
425097UK00006B/201